15.95

LIBRARY PLANNING AND DECISION-MAKING SYSTEMS

The MIT Press
Cambridge, Massachusetts and London, England

LIBRARY PLANNING AND DECISION-MAKING SYSTEMS

Morris Hamburg
Richard C. Clelland
Michael R. W. Bommer
Leonard E. Ramist
Ronald M. Whitfield

Copyright © 1974 by
The University of Pennsylvania

Copyright is claimed until February 1, 1979. Thereafter, all portions of this work, covered by the copyright, will be in the public domain. This work was developed under a grant from the U.S. Office of Education, Department of Health, Education, and Welfare. However, the content does not necessarily reflect the position or policy of that agency, and no official endorsement of this work should be inferred.

All rights reserved. No part of this book may be reproduced in any form or by any means, electronic or mechanical, including photocopying, recording, or by any information storage and retrieval system, without permission in writing from the publisher.

This book was set in Baskerville
printed on Mohawk Neotext Offset
and bound in G.S.B. S/535/1 "Space Blue"
by The Colonial Press Inc.
in the United States of America.

Library of Congress Cataloging in Publication Data

Main entry under title:

Library planning and decision-making systems.

  Bibliography: p.
  1. Library administration. I. Hamburg, Morris, 1922–
Z678.L486   025.1   73-16422
ISBN 0-262-08065-6

CONTENTS

Figures	xi
Tables	xiii
Preface	xv

1
INTRODUCTION AND SUMMARY — 1

2
LIBRARY OBJECTIVES AND OVERALL PERFORMANCE MEASURES — 9

Introduction	9
Library Objectives	10
Development of Performance Measures	13
Analysis and Synthesis of Objectives	13
Alternative Performance Measures	18
Measuring Exposure	20
Matching Exposure and Costs	24
Illustrative Computation of Overall Annual Performance Measures	26
Population Served	27
Exposure Hours	28
Costs	30
The Imputed Value of an Exposure Hour	33
Library Standards	37
Conclusion	39

3
A FRAMEWORK FOR LIBRARY DECISION MAKING — 41

Introduction	41
Aspects of a Rational Management System	41
The Process of Planning and Decision Making	43
Objectives and Performance Measures	46
Program Structure	46
Constraints	46
Alternative Programs and Their Indicators	46
Determination of Feasible Program Packages	47
Evaluation of Feasible Program Packages	47

Multiyear Program and Financial Plan 47
Budgeting 47
Program Structure Design 47
Population 49
Documents 57
Functions 59
Organization 66
Example of a Public Library Program Structure 67
Example of a University Library Program Structure 70
Program Evaluation 71
Conclusion 74

4
LIBRARY MODELS AND EMPIRICAL FINDINGS 76
Introduction 76
Provision of Building Area 77
Centralization versus Decentralization 77
Branch Location 81
Hours 84
Seating and Space Utilization 84
Maintenance 84
Selection of Documents 85
Choice of Book Subject Matter and Year 85
Number of Copies 90
Theoretical Foundation of Journal Selection 94
Journal Selection 101
Selection Effort 107
Acquisition of Documents 107
Processing of Documents 108
Processing Work Flow 108
Binding of Serials 108
Classification and Cataloging of Documents 109
Indexing 109
Original versus Temporary Cataloging 111
Dewey and Library of Congress (LC) Correlation 112
Cataloging at the Library of Congress 112

Catalog Use	113
Control of Location and Use of Documents	113
Selection of Materials for Compact Storage	113
Storage of Library Materials	118
Loan Period	121
In-Library Use	122
Security Guards	122
Return of Circulated Library Materials	122
Summary	123
Facilitation of Use of Documents	124
Photoduplication	124
Microfiche	124
Maintenance and Weeding of Documents	125
Book Relabeling	125
Book Weeding	125
Journal Weeding	126
Summary	133
Aids for Location of Documents in Other Libraries	133
Facilitation of Access to Other Libraries	134
Interlibrary Borrowing Decision Rules	134
Retrieval Systems	135
Networks	135
Personal Assistance	136
Publications, Advertisements, and Exhibits	138
Library Initiative Communication	138
Planning and Administration	139
Library Legislation	139
Library/User/Funder Analysis	139
Participative Decision Making	140
Data Processing	141
Projecting Library Growth	141
Overall University Library Resource Allocation	142
Overall Public Library Resource Allocation	143
Conclusion	150

5 DEVELOPMENT OF A MANAGEMENT INFORMATION SYSTEM FOR LIBRARIES — 151

- Introduction — 151
- Characteristics of an Information System — 152
- Specific Content of the Information Input — 152
- Selectivity of the Data — 153
- Time Lags — 154
- Accuracy — 154
- Reliability — 155
- Generality — 155
- Flexibility — 155
- Library Information System Structures — 156
- Benefit and Cost Criteria for Management Information System Elements — 165
- Evaluation of Data Elements — 167
- General — 167
- Data for Library Performance Measures — 170
- Number of Document Exposures — 172
- Other Data Requirements — 178
- Item-Use-Day — 178
- Document Exposure Time — 179
- Data for Program Indicators — 182
- Financial Data System — 187
- Introduction — 187
- Funds Received — 187
- General Accounting for Expenditures — 188
- Cost Accounting and Program Budgeting — 189
- External Financial Data — 191
- Conclusion — 191

6 HIGHER-LEVEL LIBRARY DECISION MAKING — 197

- Library Systems — 198
- National Level — 199
- National Libraries — 199

Congress	200
Office of Education	200
State Level	203
Future Library Trends	208
Appendix I—University Library Subject Categories and Areas	213
Appendix II—Document Subject Matter Categories	219
Appendix III—Public Library Program Structure	227
Appendix IV—University Library Program Structure	237
Selected Bibliography	243
Index	269

FIGURES

2.1	Benefits of library activity	14
2.2	Effects of libraries, formal educational institutions, and other institutions on societal objectives	15
2.3	Average item-use-days or average exposure time per circulation as a function of circulation loan period	22
3.1	Elements of a library management system	42
3.2	Library PPBS process	45
4.1	Accumulated number of relevant articles as a function of the common logarithm of the accumulated number of journals, when journals are arranged in descending order of productivity	95
4.2	The Bradford distribution relating x, a given fraction of the most productive journals, and $F(x)$, the fraction of all useful references included in these journals	97
4.3	The suggested Groos refinement of Bradford's law	98
4.4	Cumulative number of relevant articles as a function of the logarithm of the cumulative number of journals, when journals are arranged in descending order of productivity	99
4.5	Exponential law of obsolescence	102
4.6	Semilog plot of the exponential law of obsolescence	128
5.1	Hayes-Becker library information system	157
5.2	Alternative library information system design	157
5.3	Relationship between library performance and program output	182

TABLES

2.1	Calculation of E, the Number of Exposure Hours in the 1970 Fiscal Year, to Documents from The Free Library	29
2.2	Current per Unit Costs of New Library Materials	31
2.3	Calculation of Total Costs C	34
2.4	Use of Data from The Free Library of Philadelphia to Transform Three 1968 Data Elements Published by the Office of Education into 1969–1970 Estimates of E, C, and N	35
2.5	Ratio Performance Measure and Imputed Exposure Value by Population Size	36
3.1	Public Library Age Categories	51
3.2	Public Library Educational Level Categories	53
3.3	Library Functions	60
4.1	Burton and Kebler Findings of Literature Half-Lives	127
5.1	Crosswalk between Seventeen Functions and Hayes-Becker Subsystems	158
5.2	Crosswalk between Hayes-Becker Subsystems and Appropriate Function Numbers	158
5.3	Selected Cost Measures by Library Function	192

PREFACE

In recent years the problems of managing libraries have been multiplying at a frenetic rate. The operations of libraries have become increasingly complex, involving in many cases mechanization, centralization, and computerization of library services. There has been rapid growth in the size and scope of collections, in the variety of services offered, and in the expectations of users. A concomitant expansion has taken place in the development of cooperative arrangements among libraries. These increasing complexities of library organizational arrangements and expansions in activities and services make it extremely important that libraries utilize comprehensive frameworks for planning and decision making concerning their operations and resources.

It is in the spirit of making a contribution to the development of such frameworks that this book has been written. The research project which produced this book concentrated on the problem of the design and development of statistical information systems that would provide quantitative information for effective management of university and large public libraries. Since there is an inseparable need not only for improved library statistical data systems but also for the above-mentioned frameworks for rational planning and decision making, we have devoted considerable effort to the development of analytical models that might assist library administrators in making decisions that would maximize the flow of benefits imparted to the communities the library serves. Some of the results of this model-building effort are reported in these pages.

This book has been written primarily for those concerned with the problems of management of university and large public libraries. Some of the methods discussed in this text fall within the discipline known as management science (or operations research). There is a large communications gap between librarians, who use English to make themselves understood, and management scientists, who routinely use mathematics as a language. We have tried to communicate clearly to those concerned with library management, and, except in parts of Chapter 4, we have managed to keep the presentation on a verbal rather than a mathematical level. This book should also be of interest to systems analysts, statisticians, management scientists (operations researchers), and all those with an interest in the use of quantitative methods for management of complex organizations. We hope too this book may assist in motivating library administrators to involve quantitatively oriented people in working on the problems of library management.

The research reported in this book was carried out at The Wharton School of the University of Pennsylvania. Professor Morris Hamburg was director of the project, and Professor Richard C. Clelland assisted in the research. Dr. Michael R. W. Bommer, Leonard E. Ramist, and Ronald M. Whitfield served as research associates on the project. Each of these research associates worked on a doctoral dissertation that received financial support from the project. These dissertations are "An Economic Model for the Effective Management of a University Library" by Michael R. W. Bommer (completed in 1971), "A Model to Aid Large Public Libraries in Allocating Operating Funds to Programs" by Leonard E. Ramist, and "The Allocation of Funds at the State Level for Library Service" by Ronald M. Whitfield. At the time of this writing, the latter two dissertations are still in process.

The authors of this report express grateful appreciation to Emerson Greenaway and Keith Doms, successive directors of The Free Library of Philadelphia, J. Warren Haas, formerly director of libraries, and Bernard J. Ford, assistant director of libraries at the University of Pennsylvania, for their generous assistance and for providing access to their library staffs and facilities in the course of our research.

We also received assistance from advisory committees for public and university libraries, government officials, library directors and librarians at a variety of administrative levels, officials of library associations, research workers, and others. The list of persons who rendered this aid is so long that no attempt is made here to give individual citations. However, our sincere appreciation is expressed to all of them.

We are deeply indebted to the many research assistants who worked on this study, and to Helen Anthony and Louise Ternay for their cheerful, and excellent assistance in secretarial and typing work. We express grateful appreciation to Estelle Taylor for her fine services as an administrative assistant and secretary. Especial gratitude is extended to Sylvia Balis for her loyal and superb secretarial and typing assistance, not only in this book but in every phase of the work of the research project.

Lastly, we gratefully acknowledge the support of this research by the U.S. Office of Education, Department of Health, Education, and Welfare under grant number OEG-0-8-080802-4687(095).

Morris Hamburg
The Wharton School
University of Pennsylvania

1

INTRODUCTION AND SUMMARY

This book is the result of a research project to design and develop a model for a library statistical information system (or synonymously "management information system") for university libraries and large public libraries. The purpose of the model is to provide an information system that constitutes a comprehensive and flexible framework for library administrators for rational planning and decision making concerning library operations and resources.

Why is such a book needed?

In answering this question, let us consider libraries as social institutions. Libraries, as well as all other public and social institutions, compete for society's limited resources. In the private sector of the economy of the United States, the market system determines the allocation of resources among the producers of goods and services. That is, by and large, those things are produced that consumers desire. However, there are many goods and services that are not produced by the private sector and, therefore, are provided by the public sector, at the federal, state, or municipal level. Examples of such public goods and services are those provided by water supply, law enforcement, public education, and judicial systems. It is a fair generalization to characterize the services provided by libraries as falling mainly within the area of education, and hence as being primarily public or social in nature. In the intensifying competition for financial support, libraries as well as other social institutions are being increasingly called upon to provide relevant information for the evaluation of their effectiveness, the extent of their use, and the costs of providing their services. In the past, libraries have been accustomed to detailed accounting for their costs, since fiscal accountability has always been required and has been recognized as essential. However, libraries, again as well as other social institutions, have not been acclimated to the problem of measuring their performance in ways that would provide meaningful evaluations of the effectiveness of this performance. Stated somewhat differently, libraries have been reasonably well attuned to the requirement of measuring their inputs or needs but far less accustomed to the corresponding requirement of measuring their outputs. More generally, library accounting systems are oriented primarily to accounting for funds received and spent, rather than to supplying meaningful information for managerial purposes.

In addition to reacting to external pressures, the library community, at the levels of both public and university libraries, has recently been increasingly engaged in a process of rigorous self-examination. One aspect of this examination has been a recognition of the importance of management information and analysis to improve the effectiveness of planning, decision making, and control and to obtain the best allocation of the library's scarce resources for serving library users. Several projects are under way in library professional organizations, governmental agencies, and other public agencies which relate to various facets of the general problem of the provision of improved information systems for the library field. Appropriate remedial actions for even the currently perceived problems would require many large-scale research studies and massive long-range coordinative efforts among governmental agencies, library professional organizations, library systems, and individual libraries.

The overall management problems of university and large public libraries have increased tremendously in recent years. In both types of libraries the nature of user demand and expectations has changed considerably. Many trends in higher education and in the changing population composition of urban areas have had profound impacts on university libraries and large public libraries, respectively. Library organizational arrangements have become increasingly complex as libraries have strained to meet their intensifying problems. There have been great expansions in the development of cooperative arrangements among libraries, centralization of library services, mechanization, computerization, sizes of collections, and in the scope and variety of services offered by libraries.

Logical and systematic frameworks are needed to cope with the aforementioned problems and developments, to coordinate what is known about the organizational environment, and to deal with the economic problem of allocating and controlling limited resources in such a way as to produce maximum benefits. A rational management system provides the required framework. The main elements of such a system are a process for planning and decision making, quantitative information, and analytical tools for analyzing and using this information. This book concerns itself with all of these essential elements of a rational management system.

The study on which this book is based was carried out by a research group of faculty members and graduate students at The Wharton School of the University of Pennsylvania. The research concentrated on the development of a system to provide the required statistical information for effective management of libraries and for decision making about libraries. The problem was delimited by focusing this effort on university libraries and large public libraries. Intensive studies were carried out at the University of Pennsylvania Libraries and The Free Library of Philadelphia, as examples of university libraries and large public libraries, respectively. However, in recognition of the fact that there are differences in objectives, organizational structure, collections, and so forth among libraries of a given type, such as large university libraries, we have attempted to develop an extremely flexible information system to accommodate these differences. Yet, despite the aforementioned differences, libraries of a given type have many common characteristics and functions and, therefore, have similar key information requirements.

We have used a management science approach in this study. Our analysis began by inquiring into the objectives of the library. Then we studied library planning and decision making as means of achieving library objectives. We pursued two levels of model construction, operating from the principle that the basic purpose of a statistical information system is to carry relevant information to decision makers. The first level of model construction was the design of a model of the library management planning and decision process. The second level of model construction was the design and development of the information system to assist in obtaining the best results from this planning and decision-making process. In this connection we have attempted to specify the types of data required to describe the functioning of the library, its outputs in terms of services to users, and the required inputs in terms of resources. From appropriate analyses of the measures of performance obtained, library administrators can decide on actions required to increase the flow of benefits to users per unit cost or to decrease costs for a given level of benefits.

The statistical information systems we have proposed for large public libraries and university libraries possess both similarities and differences. The systems are similar in that they are both developed by analyzing objectives, and subsequently by specifying the types of data required to describe the functioning of the library, its services to users, and the inputs required to accomplish these services. The differences in the information systems between these two types of libraries are in terms of the nature of the data required. Since the specific objectives, the populations served, and the documents offered in these two types of libraries differ, there naturally are differences in the types of data that characterize these and other factors.

In analyzing recorded objectives of public and university libraries, we found that these objectives were not sufficiently explicit to be of direct assistance to management in planning and decision making for libraries. This sort of finding occurs in management science analyses of virtually every large-scale organization or system. Hence, further analysis was required to develop an objective which was both explicit and measurable in order that library performance may be evaluated in terms of the degree of objective attainment. We moved back from ultimate benefits and focused on the sine qua non of library activity, the most important aspect of all public and university library objectives: *exposure of individuals to documents of recorded human experience.* Under the assumption that the basic objective of libraries is to maximize exposure to documents (direct or indirect, in the library or outside the library, in the short run and in the long run), we proposed several measures of library performance based upon document exposure. These are exposure counts, item-use-days, and exposure time. When any one of these measures of exposure is related to the costs or inputs, output per unit input measures of performance are derived. We have defined and specified how to calculate such performance measures, and we have discussed their conceptual advantages and disadvantages and the comparative difficulties in their estimation. These performance measures, which are based on the relationship between exposure benefits and costs, are particularly appropriate for libraries that have a significant active or promotional component of library service. On the other hand, in certain types of special libraries and certain university libraries, the users are primarily sophisticated specialists who are seeking specific materials or information. Such libraries tend to emphasize reaction to users and may attribute very little importance to promotion of library use. In such cases, narrower performance measures such as proportion of user demands satisfied and document retrieval time may adequately reflect library performance and may be preferable to measures of document exposure.

In our analysis of what a library tries to accomplish (its objectives), and our proposed library performance measures to evaluate how well the library is achieving these objectives, we considered the area of library standards. We concluded that existing library standards tend to be neither objectives nor performance measures but rather are either descriptive rules for "proper" management or are quantitative rules for "minimum" inputs of materials, personnel, and physical facilities. They represent a static concept pointed toward the evaluation of library resource inputs but do not focus on the outputs of library service. It was found that these descriptive rules are useful in increasing library receipts, resulting therefore in an increase of library inputs of materials, personnel, and physical facilities, in turn resulting in greater document exposure. However, the standards fail to provide a basis for meaningful evaluations of library performance. We have attempted to develop an information system that emphasizes the dynamic concepts of relating the outputs of library service to users to the inputs required to deliver these benefits.

The search for a suitable framework for a statistical information system for libraries is a difficult one. In the private profit-making sector of society, the objective of profit making is quite clearly defined. Therefore, a natural framework exists for a management information system in terms of the data required for the profit and loss statement of a company. The balance sheet in terms of assets and liabilities is a similarly useful organizational structure for a component of the data system. On the other hand, no similar natural framework exists for public libraries and university libraries. They do not have a profit-making function, and their services are not transmitted in a marketplace of monetary transactions. However, the problem of every library is to allocate and control scarce resources, and to manage and control library activities, so as to maximize benefits imparted to society. The Planning-Programming-Budgeting-System (PPBS) represents one of the most logical and useful planning and decision-making systems to achieve this end. The basic elements of PPBS for a library or for any organization are specification of objectives, derivation of performance measures to evaluate achievement of these objectives, specification of a program structure oriented toward achievement of stated objectives, specification of input and output indicators for programs in the program structure, determination of relationships between performance measures and input and output indicators, and development of a multiyear plan.

The statistical information system that we are proposing has been designed to support planning, decision making, and evaluation in a program budgeting context. However, we have attempted to design a flexible information system that does not necessarily depend upon the employment of PPBS or any other particular managerial planning and budgeting structure. For this purpose we found it useful to classify all library activity into seventeen functions. These functions are a combination of services offered to users and operations performed which are necessary for internal library use. Virtually every activity a library performs can be classified under one of these functions. Furthermore, it is possible to identify and isolate the inputs and outputs of each function. Consequently, the functional breakdown that we present in Chapter 3 provides a convenient framework for a management system and thus for a management information system. This particular arrangement of library activities is certainly not unique. Other combinations of functions are possible and indeed may be preferable for specific purposes.

It is clear that even with an ideal flow of information, unless there are rational structures for using the data for decision purposes, the information system cannot fulfill its purposes. In the course of our current research, we have become convinced of the need for analytical decision models in the library area for improved allocations of resources to programs in order to accomplish goals and objectives.

Managerial decision making has become much more complex and difficult in both the private and public sectors as the American economic, political, and social structures, and the corresponding business, governmental, and social organizational units have grown larger and more complicated. Logical apparatuses and frameworks are needed to bring an objective systematic approach to planning and decision making in keeping with the objectives of these organizations. To answer this need, analytical decision models are being increasingly utilized. A model is simply a representation of some aspects of the real world and is often mathematical in nature. Such models change complex management problems, which may seem too chaotic or too uncertain to handle, except by intuition, to rational structures that can be analyzed by quantitative, objective methods. The past can be described, and predictions can be made of changes that would take place in the real-world situations represented by the models. The overall purpose of such models is to seek out the best combinations of factors under the control of the decision maker to improve performance of the organization and to make its goals more achievable.

We have summarized some of the most important library quantitative models and have presented them according to their application to appropriate library decisions and functions. Also we have reported on some of our own work on analytical decision models for allocations of funds in university and large public libraries. A combination of improved management information systems for libraries and the aforementioned decision models could bring about a more systematic approach to decision making in and concerning libraries. These systems and models are clearly not intended to replace managerial intuition and experience. Rather, they represent attempts to provide the basic information and alternatives to which managerial judgment may be applied.

Another essential component of an information system for library managerial planning, decision making, and control is information about library operations and services, the relationships between the library and its users, and the populations to be served. Clearly there are so many activities and items that might potentially be reported that the danger exists of swamping managers with data that are not particularly useful for management decisions. Hence, a major effort in designing an information system is to evaluate the usefulness for decision making and the effort required to collect data elements for inclusion in the system. As an indication of appropriate directions for the development of an improved information system for library-planning and decision-making purposes, we have specified data elements and their subdivisions that are relevant to each of the library functions presented in Chapter 3. In addition we have formulated a number of input and output indicators for each function and have presented criteria for evaluating the benefits and costs associated with collecting these data.

It may be noted that this study does not deal with the technology required for the processing of the flow of statistical information. However, the system guidelines which we have proposed are adaptable to any level of computerized operations. The specific ways in which libraries collect and store information will doubtless continue to differ widely in the future.

It is also important to note that the general nature of this statistical information system is flexible and is not pinned to any specific state of the art in any area of library activities. For example, as noted earlier, this is a dynamic period for the application of computer technology to libraries, and there are strong tendencies toward increased cooperation among libraries and centralization of library functions. However, the nature of program budgeting as a management communication and coordination system and the general functional breakdown of library activities such as previously outlined do not depend on any particular state of these trends or tendencies. We believe that our efforts represent an initial but necessary step toward structuring the important considerations of the decision-making and planning process and the associated statistical information system for university and large public libraries. The management process and hence the supporting statistical information system should not be fixed entities but, rather, must be in a continual state of development.

In Chapter 2, library objectives and overall performance measures are examined. A major emphasis in this analysis is to define library objectives in an operationally meaningful manner in order that the degree of attainment of these objectives may be measured by performance indicators. In Chapter 3, a framework for library planning and decision making is presented. Program structures along dimensions of population, documents, functions, and organization are discussed. Essentially, this chapter specifies how a library may incorporate systematic analysis into its management activities by providing a rational organization for planning and decision making. In Chapter 4, a summary is given of library quantitative models classified according to their application to library decisions and functions. The recurrent theme in this chapter is that data are useless unless they are suitably organized to assist a manager in making decisions. Decision models organize data by relating them to decision alternatives. Hence, decision models are useful in providing criteria for which data are needed for decision making and for specifying how these data are to be used. Furthermore, they provide the managerial tools for making predictions and evaluations of library programs. In Chapter 5, information systems for the support of library planning and decision making are discussed. The characteristics and structures of such systems, data requirements for library performance measures and program indicators, and benefit-cost criteria for information system elements are specified. Finally, in Chapter 6, we look beyond the level of individual libraries to library systems and state and national levels to examine some of the factors involved in the development of effective management information systems for higher-level library decision making.

2

LIBRARY OBJECTIVES AND OVERALL PERFORMANCE MEASURES

Introduction

A logical starting point in the development of a managerial system is specification of what the organization is attempting to achieve. In order for managers and administrators to evaluate alternative courses of action in planning and decision making, the following are needed:
1. Statements of objectives should be explicit, unambiguous, and operationally meaningful.
2. Suitable measures must be developed for evaluating the degree to which objectives are obtained.

In most organizations, including libraries, these statements tend to be quite vague, providing little or no guidance to the planner or decision maker. Hence, it is generally impossible to determine degree of success in pursuit of the objectives. Also, the objectives usually are in conflict. Objectives calling for different aspects of better service are in conflict among themselves for scarce funds and against objectives calling for lower costs. Organizational units following conflicting objectives tend to act in competition with each other rather than in cooperation toward a common purpose.

Of course, any attempts to define library objectives and to measure performance and the benefits and costs of alternative courses of action concerning library services encounter a host of theoretical and practical difficulties. Furthermore, the pressures for the making of such determinations are on the increase. Doubtlessly, it is true that all public or social institutions, and their component parts, are currently competing for limited funds, and in this context, are under increasing pressure not only to specify their needs or required "inputs" but to indicate in some meaningful and measurable way what their "outputs" are. It is in the spirit of attempting to suggest some aids in this difficult task that this research was conducted.

In this chapter, we review recorded objectives of public and university libraries. We analyze these objectives for the purpose of removing ambiguity. After these objectives are transformed into explicit statements of purpose, we propose measures for ascertaining how well the library is performing. We discuss the advantages and disadvantages of these measures and illustrate their computation. Finally, we review library standards and distinguish them from objectives and performance measures.

Library Objectives

There is a great variety of written statements identifying both public library and university library objectives. For public libraries, these statements relate to both formal and informal education. Under formal education, the emphasis is upon the supplementation, enrichment, and further development of educational programs of schools and colleges. Under informal education, the objectives emphasize the library materials, the process of communicating with the user, or the end result of library use.

Recorded objectives that relate specifically to library materials emphasize variety in subject matter, point of view, and media; the meeting of research needs; good organization of materials to make them easily and temptingly available; and good distribution of materials. Examples of objectives referring to the process of communicating with the user are encouraging reading of socially significant materials; interpreting materials; expressing ideas; providing information; and entering into the educational, civic, and cultural activities of community groups. Finally, many recorded objectives relate to the end result of library use: individual self-development; increase of reading enjoyment and ability; human understanding; better family and community members; aid in daily occupations; consumer and health education; creative use of leisure time; culture; creative and spiritual capacities; and new and extended individual and group activities.

Although the objective and ultimate benefits of a university library are quite similar to those of a public library, there are some distinctive differences. First, the population of potential users of a university library is relatively more homogeneous and operates at higher intellectual and reading levels than the public at large. Indeed, the public library has such a heterogeneous population of potential users that it includes university students and faculty, as well as, for example, the disadvantaged groups.

Second, whereas the public library responds to the societal objectives of the entire community, the university library is an integral part of a small subset of that community, namely, the university. Hence, the university library's objective must relate to those of the parent university.

The objectives of a university are generally stated in terms of the functions it performs in the areas of instruction, research, and community service. Since the university library is supportive of university programs, objectives for the university library should be in terms of the needs and requirements of the personnel involved in the teaching and research efforts of the university concerned.

A statement adopted by the ACRL Board of Directors represents a basis for a workable objective. It reads:

The primary purpose of any library is *to serve the reading, reference and research needs of its users.* All authorized users of college and research libraries have a right to expect library services up-to-date and commensurate with their needs, provided by competent librarians and founded on adequate collections which are easily available in suitable quarters. (ACRL News, "Statement of Service to Library Users," 1966.)

As was true for the analogous statements of objectives for public libraries, this type of statement is not sufficiently explicit to be of direct assistance to management in the planning and decision-making process. Such statements do not yield a criterion for evaluating alternative policies. They are not helpful in determining how well the library is performing and how proposed plans and alternative decisions may affect the performance. There are problems in measuring these objectives and in associating them with library programs.

For instance, is the use of public libraries for formal education programs an indication that the public library is doing well or that the school and college libraries are doing poorly? Considering that there are usually many different kinds and levels of schools in a public library's area with a great variety of degree programs, courses, reading assignments, and individualized paper writing, how can we measure how well the library is aiding formal education?

Is the provision of library materials an end of library service or a means to an end? If we measure the extent and variety of library materials, are we measuring the attainment of an objective (an output) or are we measuring an allocation of funds (an input)? Does the fact that the more a library spends on staff for personal communication, the less it has left over for library materials mean that the personal communication and library material provision objectives are in conflict? Should there be a specific objective for minimizing costs? If an individual has difficulty in finding what he wants, how can we tell whether there is a need for more extensive library materials or whether the need is for better organization of the existing library materials? Is a good distribution system one that waits for the individual to take the initiative? Under what circumstances does a long loan policy provide better distribution than an in-library loan policy?

How can we measure communication by the library to members of the library's population of potential users? Should we count the number of personal contacts? Should contacts be treated equally? How can we distinguish a successful contact from an unsuccessful one? Are persons obtaining the information they are seeking? What are they doing with this information? Could they get it elsewhere?

How do we measure individual self-development? How do we know that a library user develops himself more than one who engages in other activities? Can we find out how an individual relates to others and how he functions in his community, and, if so, can we distinguish a good family and community member from a bad one? If we could discern specific changes in reading ability, in education of the disadvantaged, in culture, or in creative and spiritual capacities, how much of these changes could we relate to the effect of libraries, as opposed to other social institutions?

There is an implication that the greater the extent, variety, and quality of activities, the better the library is doing. Perhaps, one way of increasing the extent and variety of one's activities is to stay out of the library. If improvement in the quality of activity is the significant library effect, how can we possibly measure that? How much of the GNP is attributable to the existence of libraries? There are similar measurement problems inherent in stated objectives of university libraries. There are no guidelines to determine how well the library is serving the reading, reference, and research needs of its users.

Even if we could measure the stated objectives, we would have great difficulty in using these measures as criteria for evaluating library programs. This difficulty is due to both the interrelatedness of the objectives and the conflict between them.

As an example of the interrelatedness of objectives, let us look at the provision of a single book on sensory-awareness techniques. To one person, the book may satisfy a need for a psychology course in a college. To another, reading the book may be a significant personal growth experience. To another, the volume may represent an introduction into the world of encounter groups and openness in relationships, significantly affecting his individual and group activities. To yet another, it may be relaxing, leisure-time reading. Alternatively, the book may affect one person in all of these ways.

The problem created by this interdependence of objectives for measures of performance is primarily one of allocation. For example, suppose a new library program were introduced, and we wished to measure the performance of this program in terms of the statements of objectives. Assume the new program resulted in increased library usage. In view of the interdependence of the objectives, how much achievement of each of the objectives was brought about by the new program? Although some programs affect certain objectives more than others, if one book may significantly affect attainment of almost all of the stated library objectives, then a program to provide many books and perhaps other library services would have a decidedly multidimensional effect. The allocation difficulties are manifest.

The conflict between objectives also poses problems of quantitative measurement. For example, there is conflict between objectives such as provision of library materials and personal communication to potential users. The conflict is present because investment in library materials competes with investment in library staff for the library's scarce funds. Hence, a library program that attempts to maximize the degree of attainment of one of these objectives would be at the expense of failing to maximize the level of attainment of the other. Another conflict is created by the implied objective of providing library services at the lowest possible cost, thereby keeping investment in both library materials and staff as low as possible.

Development of Performance Measures

Analysis and Synthesis of Objectives

Further analysis of the statements of objectives is necessary to make them explicit and measurable. In this manner, we develop the potential for measuring library performance in terms of the degree of objective attainment.

In the prior section, we have indicated the difficulties inherent in allocating library use among many interrelated objectives and in operating with conflicting objectives. We could eliminate the need to allocate library use, and we could remove conflict by recognizing a higher-level, more general objective that encompasses all the objectives. By measuring this objective in the best possible manner, we would then have a yardstick to determine how well the library is serving society (or the university) and to choose between alternative programs.

In an initial attempt to specify and measure a more general objective, let us trace the benefits of library use. Satisfaction of the reading, reference, and research needs of individuals in the university community and fulfillment of each of the stated objectives of the public library involve bringing together potential users and documents of recorded human experience. Figure 2.1 indicates that library activity produces the intangibles of educational endeavors: knowledge, ability, creativity, motivation, and confidence. The ultimate benefits of this investment in intangibles include progress toward the fulfillment of *all* societal objectives, involving every aspect of human endeavor. The real outputs of library service are the stimulated student or teacher, the scientific discovery, the informed voter, the successful businessman, and so on.

As shown in Figure 2.2, the highest level, most general library objective is to enhance major societal objectives in areas such as science; politics and law; production, marketing, labor, and finance; transportation; public safety; physical and mental health; recreation; and cultural and spiritual inspiration. These benefits are in the interface between library users and society. They occur when members of the public or university community apply what they have obtained from the library for the betterment of society. The library contributes to all societal objectives, but it is only one of several institutions that contribute to any single objective of society. In developing a performance measure, ideally it would be desirable to measure

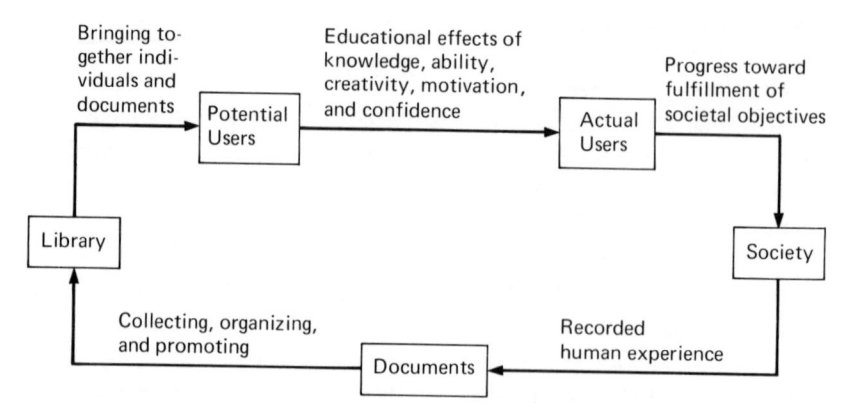

Figure 2.1. Benefits of library activity.

15 Development of Performance Measures

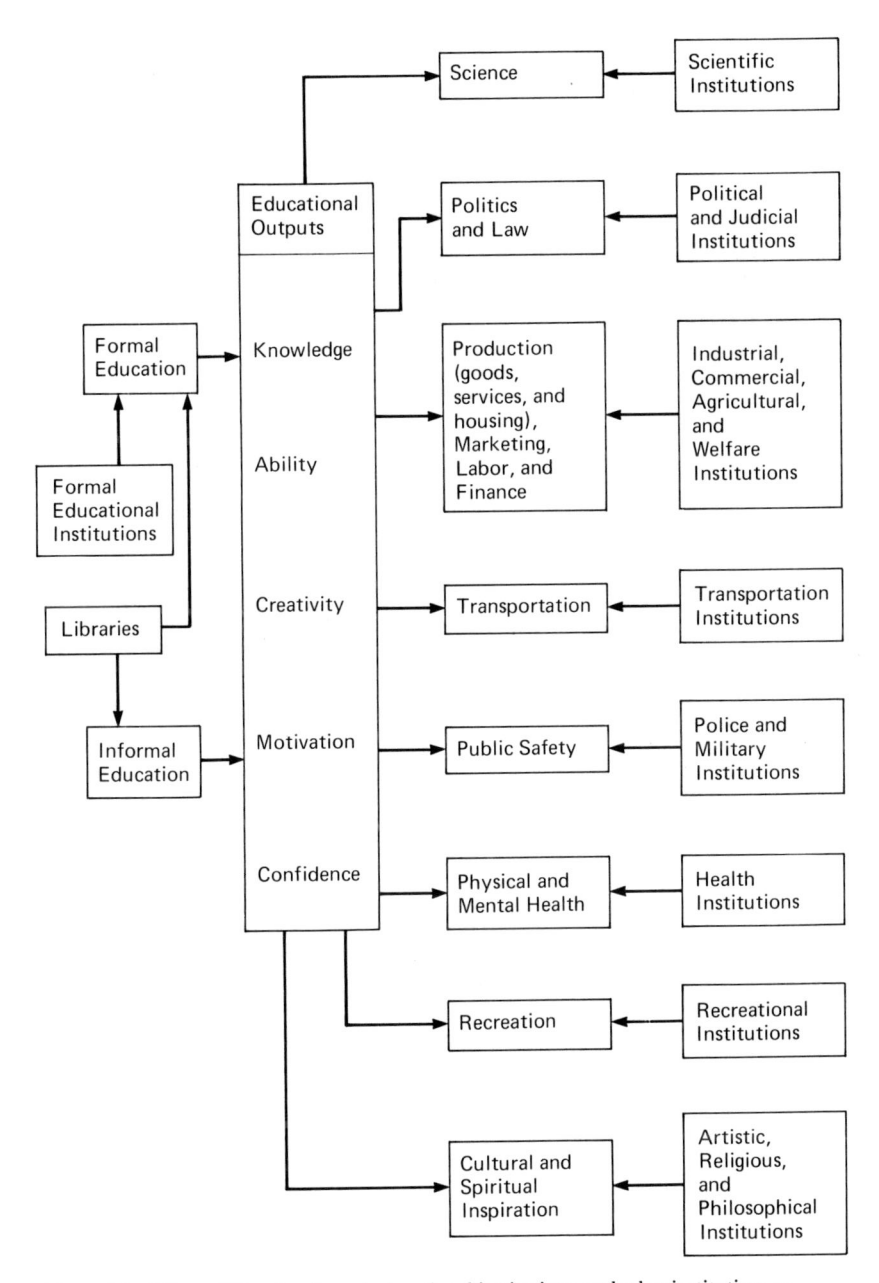

Figure 2.2. Effects of libraries, formal educational institutions, and other institutions on societal objectives.

the library effect on societal objectives. However, it is an insurmountable task to isolate library effects from those of other institutions.

It is necessary to step back in order to measure these ultimate benefits in somewhat of a less direct but perhaps more feasible manner. Rather than attempt to analyze the interface between library users and society, a more reasonable approach is to focus on the interface between the library and its population of potential users. A possibility is to measure the library educational effects on knowledge, ability, creativity, motivation, and confidence. Nevertheless, here too it is difficult to isolate library effects from effects of formal educational institutions, the family, peers, and the community. Also, since a library use is particularly individualized, educational measurement in libraries would be much more difficult than in formal educational institutions.

Taking one more small step back from ultimate benefits, we focus upon the *sine qua non* of library activity, the most important aspect of all public and university library objectives: *exposure of individuals to documents of recorded human experience*. Figure 2.1 illustrates how this exposure is two steps removed from the ultimate library effect on societal objectives. "Document" is used throughout this book to include all library material regardless of form, except for indexes or catalogs, which are used primarily to locate and identify documents.

Exposure can occur either directly or indirectly, in the library or outside the library, in the short run or in the long run. Direct exposure occurs when it would appear to a reasonable third party that the individual in question is applying at least one of his senses—seeing, hearing, or touching (tasting and smelling seem inappropriate at our present levels of communication)—to a document. For example, if he is sitting with a book open in front of him, there is direct exposure. Other examples are observing a picture, watching a film, listening to a recording, and touching Braille.

Direct exposure is the result of certain library transactions, some of which are typically recorded and others are not. An individual may take a document from its storage location or charge it out from a reserve room in order to use it in the library. He may charge it out from general circulation or make photocopies in order to use it either in the library or outside. Finally, he may obtain a document by means of interlibrary loan.

Indirect exposure occurs when a library employee communicates to an individual as a substitute for direct exposure. Examples are the answering of an informational request, either in person or by telephone, and a storytelling session for children.

Not all library activity is designed to bring about immediate exposure. Some activity may be described as investment in future exposure, similar to business investment in capital expenditures, goodwill, and prepaid expenses. Some examples are purchasing and processing documents that are to be used sometime in the future and promoting the use of the library, which may result in converting nonusers to users.

A number of serviceable concepts of library objectives involving the idea of exposures can be constructed. One useful conceptualization of library objectives is to maximize document exposure (direct or indirect, in the library or outside the library, in the short run or in the long run) per dollar of input expenditures (cost) used to obtain these exposures. Alternatively, if an imputed dollar value of exposures is derived, then another useful way of viewing library objectives is to maximize the difference between this value of exposures and the cost of obtaining the exposures. An illustration of the computation of these types of performance measures is presented at a later point in this chapter. Included in that illustration is a discussion of how we constructed measurements of document exposure time for The Free Library of Philadelphia.

It may be argued that these statements of library objectives, as encompassing as they are, do not cover all library benefits. In particular, it may be argued that the facilities provided by libraries are used, and are intended by the library to be used, in endeavors other than exposure to documents obtained through the library. For example, a university library may be used for study or reading of one's own materials, for socializing, and for classes. Also, a public library may be used as a general community meeting place for functions unrelated to document exposure.

However, we propose measures of performance based solely on document exposure. The exclusion of the tangential benefits that result from the existence of library facilities is partly a matter of expediency. Also, this exclusion is partly based on the notion that when the library is performing these additional services, it is not acting in its capacity as a library, which is to serve the social function of bringing together individuals and recorded experience.

Although the performance measure of document exposure is not a perfect measure, it includes the substantial portion of benefits due to library activity. If a library director feels that efficient maximization of document exposure is a conceptualization of his library's objectives that is too limited, he may allocate part of the costs of facilities for activities which yield benefits lying outside the realm of the stated performance measure. The allocation may be accomplished by sampling users to determine the extent of use of library facilities for purposes unrelated to exposure to documents obtained through the library. The remaining cost of facilities then may be associated solely with document exposure.

There are other possible variants of measures of performance based on document exposure. For example, the manager of a library may choose to state his objective in terms of maximizing the number of users of the library. For this purpose, a user may be defined as anyone whose usage of the library falls above some minimum level of document exposure. Of course, alternative measures may be used by management at any particular time. Hence, for example, in the private sector, management might use the ratios of profit-to-capital, profit-to-sales, and the dollar value of net profit as measures of the overall performance of a firm. Similarly, it might use measures such as ratios of current assets to current liabilities and inventories to sales for evaluation of particular aspects of a company's operations. Clearly, certain measures are more valid or useful for some purposes than others.

Alternative Performance Measures

Library activity consists of two rather distinct aspects:
1. A passive or reactive aspect of satisfying demands by users for library materials and information
2. An active aspect of promoting library materials to create demands and to influence them

The reactive aspect may consist of almost all activity for certain types of libraries where users are highly educated individuals who are motivated toward library use and know what they want, for instance, medical or legal libraries. Many of these libraries may function much more like an information center than a library. Although the active aspect is of very little importance in professional libraries, and of only somewhat more importance in college and university libraries, it is quite significant in public libraries (particularly in disadvantaged areas), as evidenced by its emphasis in the recorded public library objectives presented earlier.

The concept of document exposure includes both aspects. If a library creates demands that otherwise would not exist, document exposure increases. If a library improves its ability to react to and satisfy demands by users, document exposure increases. Satisfactions result immediately in exposure, and satisfied users tend to return for future exposure.

Document exposure also reflects the opposite picture of the reactive aspect. Unsatisfied demand is lost, and disappointed users often do not return. One may think that document exposure is not an adequate measure for the user who frustratedly pores through many irrelevant documents before he finds what he is after. However, if a user meets with frustration often, he will tend to search elsewhere or not at all, with a long-run resultant decrease in document exposure.

If almost all of the users of a library look for very specific materials or information, then the library most likely emphasizes reaction to users and attributes very little importance to promotion of library use. For these libraries, there are two performance measures that adequately reflect overall library performance and may be preferable to document exposure because of their simplicity:

1. The proportion of user demands satisfied, used by Morse (1968) and Buckland, Hindle, Mackenzie, and Woodburn (1970)
2. The average time it takes to get the document or information to the user, used by Orr, Pings, Pizer, and Olson (1968) and Orr, Pings, Pizer, Olson, and Spencer (1968).

For the types of libraries referred to earlier which emphasize reaction to users, as for example, many types of special libraries that function mainly as information centers, it may even be argued that *minimizing exposure time* is the essential goal. For example, in an engineering corporation's special library, where engineers may go primarily to look up very specific items of information, the library should aim at enabling its clients to find correct answers as quickly as possible. Clearly, appropriate performance measures should be devised in view of the particular types of libraries under consideration. Furthermore, as noted earlier, especially for public libraries, and to a large extent also for college and university libraries, the goals of library activity encompass an active aspect as well as a reactive one.

With respect to the proportion of user demands satisfied, the concepts of "demand" and "satisfaction" are not easy to measure. Except for closed access reserve, an unsatisfied demand usually escapes contact with the library. This measure requires recurrent questionnaires to ascertain demands and whether or not they are satisfied. Also, it is not clear whether a demand is satisfied if an individual uses an alternative document to the one originally requested. Buckland, Hindle, Mackenzie, and Woodburn (1970) use two demand satisfaction rates: one for demands for a single title that are immediately satisfied and another for demands satisfied that are not necessarily for a single title. Morse (1968) avoids questionnaires by developing a model to infer demand or unsatisfied demand from circulation. In Chapter 4, we discuss a model we have developed to estimate demand from university course enrollments and research activity.

Document retrieval time may be obtained by means of a document delivery test, in which a sample of documents is taken from citations of articles relevant to the user population. The library is requested to supply each of the documents in the sample. The library is rated with respect to the time it takes the user to obtain the documents. Time is dependent on which of several states of availability the documents are in. The test has several good points, including the fact that it is not biased by users' perceptions of the library. It is based on the concept that a library exists to transmit documents to users as fast as possible. In this respect, it yields more information than the demand satisfaction rate because it signifies not only whether demands are satisfied but how long it takes the library to satisfy the demands.

The Institute for the Advancement of Medical Communication also suggests a second measure: an inventory of library services. It has developed a checklist of possible library services and an inventory guide to obtain the information from the head librarian. A measure is obtained by weighting the services in such a way as to allocate a total of 1000 points among them. This measure may be made to reflect document exposure by assigning weights on the basis of the effect that the service has on document exposure.

Some other measures also have been suggested, including circulation, attendance, and registrants per capita. Finally, occasional mathematical formulae have been proposed, although usually without adequate empirical or theoretical justification.

Measuring Exposure

For libraries in which the active library aspect of promoting materials is important, we propose document exposure measures. We suggest now three methods for measuring document exposure: exposure counts, item-use-days, and exposure time.

The first method is to count each circulation (and each renewal), each direct in-library use, each interlibrary loan, and each indirect exposure as one unit of exposure. All exposures may be added together, or separate counts may be kept for each exposure type. This method is easily accomplished for recorded exposures, such as circulations, interlibrary loans, and certain types of indirect exposures. For unrecorded exposures of in-library use and for some indirect exposures, these counts are more difficult. However, sampling methods may be used to estimate the number of direct and indirect in-library exposures per attendance. In this manner, attendance estimates may be converted into estimates of direct and indirect in-library exposures.

There are some disadvantages to this method of counting exposures. If separate counts are kept by exposure type, there is a multidimensional measure of output of library activity. Especially for the construction of library models, and for many evaluation purposes, this situation is awkward. For instance, it does not lead to an output per unit input nor to an output less input measure. Also, a separate measure for each exposure type would be difficult to construct because of the necessity of allocating inputs among exposure types.

If, on the other hand, we add all exposures together, we may be adding essentially dissimilar things. For instance, five charges from a reserve desk of a particular book, each charge having a time limit of one hour, results in five exposures. If the same book is circulated for four weeks, and even if it is used for much more than five hours, there is still only one exposure. A fast informational request is also one exposure. In addition, browsing exposures to ten different documents in an hour are not necessarily more beneficial than an hour of in-depth exposure to one document. One problem with a performance measure based on counting exposures and aggregating them is that a library could improve its performance merely by making its loan period very short. Whereas use for a particular period of time could have been accomplished with one circulation, the library could necessitate several renewals, that is, several exposures, for use during the same period of time.

An alternative method for obtaining a single measure of output, without merely adding exposures, has been suggested by Meier (1961). It entails counting "item-use-days." This measure differs from that of counting exposures because a long circulation involving exposure during X different days is counted as X item-use-days rather than as one exposure.

This method has the advantage of using a common unit of measurement across exposure types. Aggregation is accomplished by estimates of item-use-days. In this way, it overcomes some of the difficulties inherent in the exposure count measure. Only one additional estimate, the average number of days of use per circulation or interlibrary loan, is needed for the calculation of this more refined measure. No additional estimation is necessary for direct or indirect in-library use. Each of these exposures involves only one day and is counted as one item-use-day.

The estimate of the average number of days of use per circulation may be obtained by questioning the user, upon return, about the number of days he or anyone else had spent with a circulated document. If two or more persons use a circulated document on a given day, an equivalent number of item-use-days is assigned to that day and document. By questioning users of similar libraries that differ in loan period, a curve of the type indicated in Figure 2.3 could be obtained.

Some of the arbitrary qualities inherent in the exposure count measure are present also in the item-use-day measure. For example, five exposures of one hour each by an individual to a document on five different days are not necessarily better than a single five-hour exposure on one day. In the former case there are five item-use-days, compared to only one in the latter case. Also, browsing exposures to ten different documents in an hour result in ten item-use-days, whereas an hour of in-depth exposure to one document results in only one item-use-day.

A third measure, which eliminates the difficulties of the other two and creates some new ones, focuses upon the amount of time an individual is exposed to a document. The common units for aggregation are estimates of exposure time. For recorded exposures, such as circulations and informational requests, there is a need to estimate the average amount of time for

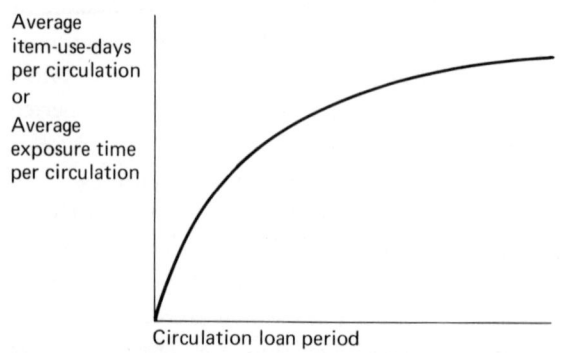

Figure 2.3. Average item-use-days or average exposure time per circulation as a function of circulation loan period.

each exposure type. This estimate may be obtained in a similar manner to that of item-use-days, by questioning users, upon the return of a circulated document, about time spent with it. Although individual recall may not be very accurate, from research carried out thus far, the aggregate estimated average time per circulation appears quite reliable. A curve similar to that for item-use-days would be expected. Estimates of document exposure time for informational requests may be made by library staff members.

For in-library exposure time, there is no need to count exposures. An estimate of the average time an individual spends in the library could be obtained by monitoring arrivals and departures. The other necessary element is to estimate the percentage of the time that users are in the library during which they are in direct exposure to library materials or receive indirect document exposure from the library staff, as opposed to searching for library materials, talking with others, using bathroom facilities, and so on. The estimates probably are quite stable over time for each library.

Skeptics concerning the desirability of an objective of maximizing any of the foregoing three exposure measures may put forth the hypothetical case of a library increasing exposure by promoting "worthless" literature and pornographic materials. This case highlights two implied assumptions for using these measures:

1. Exposure of an individual in the library population to any document obtained through the library does enhance his self-development, and, through this means of informal or formal education, yields a benefit to society.
2. The amount of societal benefit does not vary greatly from one individual-document exposure to another.

The first assumption is that the acquisition process considers only documents that have social value, or—all documents have social value of some kind. The promotion of worthless literature to increase exposure violates the first assumption.

If a library does not wish to evaluate exposure for different types of individuals and types of documents, it may be willing to accept the second assumption. Otherwise, a library may apply different weights to different exposures, in terms of population and document subsets, in order to attribute different social values to them. This possibility is discussed in Chapter 3.

An important reservation about the use of a performance measure to maximize document exposure arises when one considers the predicament of public libraries today. There is an increasing demand for library services of all types which involve or lead to document exposure. At the same time, there is a great financial bind. The financial prognosis for the near future is not encouraging. Childers (1971) concludes that the public library should stop trying to satisfy everybody for everything. An alternative is for the library to provide a narrow range of services not easily obtained elsewhere. For instance, for most documents, the library could act as a Sears catalog-type distribution center. Other services may be limited to information on daily living, school work space and materials, presentation of new media items, and exploration of issues currently important to the community. The logical target population primarily would be the poor.

Some use of the public library is made by persons whose needs otherwise could be met by other libraries. Other use is made of documents by users who, in the absence of the public library, would be ready, willing, and financially able to purchase the documents. For the remaining use, the existence of the public library is essential. The need could not otherwise be satisfied conveniently or the motivation for use could not occur.

Perhaps, the value to society of merely shifting document exposure to the public library from other libraries or from individual purchases is relatively small compared to document exposure that would be otherwise lost. Here again the difference of value may be expressed in a performance measure by applying different weights to different exposures, in terms of population and document subsets. The weights may be specified to reflect the subjective probability that the exposure would be lost without the existence of the public library. Population and document subsets and weights are discussed in Chapter 3.

Matching Exposure and Costs

An essential part of any performance measure is a periodic matching of the outputs (benefits) and inputs (costs) of an organization. A basic corporate accounting practice is the periodic matching, usually annually, of revenue and expense to determine net profit or loss.

Nevertheless, in libraries, as well as in most nonprofit organizations, the only periodic matching is of cash receipts and disbursements. Usually, there is neither an attempt to measure library output nor to estimate the true costs of library operations. Therefore, it is impossible to match outputs and costs in order to evaluate library performance.

As indicated earlier, possible measures of the outputs of library activity include exposures, item-use-days, or exposure time. Library performance evaluation can be accomplished only by matching with the exposures occurring in any period of time the costs of facilities, equipment, resources, staff, and contracted services necessary to produce this exposure. Proper timing is a major problem because costs in a given year are not necessarily designed to produce exposure in that year. Present exposure often is a result of past expenditures, and present costs are often designed, in part if not completely, to produce future exposure. This fact is self-evident for all outlays that are acknowledged to be capital expenditures. However, it is also true that purchase and processing expenditures for library materials (documents) are designed to produce exposure in future years, in addition to the years of the initial expenditure. Even staff expenditures for certain library promotion programs may be investments in future exposure.

Corporate accounting practice recognizes that it is necessary for evaluation purposes to resolve timing problems inherent in all businesses. Libraries have analogous problems. Although separate records are generally kept for cash flows, the accrual basis of accounting is widely accepted. Revenue, the dollar measure of output of business operations, is recognized in the period in which goods are sold or services performed, and expenses are recorded for appropriate time periods, irrespective of actual collection or payment in cash. In this manner, revenues and expenses are recognized in the year to which they relate, and the annual matching of revenues and expenses results in a more meaningful income determination.

An essential part of the accrual method is adjustment for prepayments. Payments that ordinarily influence revenue in more than one accounting period are first charged to asset accounts, such as Merchandise Inventory, Unexpired Insurance, Land, Building, and Equipment. At the end of each accounting period, an appropriate part of these assets is charged to current expense. For relatively short-term prepayments, these charges are the result of a determination, usually by inventory, of the difference between (1) the sum of the beginning asset book value and current charges to the asset account and (2) the asset value at the end of the period. For relatively long-term prepayments, these charges are accomplished by a depreciation procedure over the estimated useful life of the asset.

In library accounting, because there is generally no periodic matching of output and input, and no attempt to measure true costs for particular time periods, depreciation and prepayment methods are usually considered inappropriate. However, it is essential for the evaluation of library performance to allocate capital expenditures and prepayments of all types over time in order to match them with resulting exposure. This allocation may be accomplished by depreciation.

There are several methods of depreciation commonly employed in corporate practice. The simplest is straight-line depreciation, in which an equal amount of the cost less salvage value is allocated to each of the N estimated years of useful life. In illustrating how this method may be applied to libraries, Brutcher, Gessford, and Rixford (1964) use hypothetical useful life estimates of 40 years for buildings, 20 years for periodicals, 10 years for books, and 5 years for most equipment.

Straight-line depreciation may be used if the asset is assumed to be associated with the same amount of exposure in each of the T years of useful life. However, document use has been found to decrease exponentially over time. This principle is discussed in Chapter 4. In order to reflect it, relatively high cost allocations may be made in initial years, decreasing exponentially each year. A common method used to accomplish this result is the declining-balance method, in which a constant rate of depreciation is applied to a declining balance. If r is the fraction of the remaining balance depreciated each year, then depreciation of the principal P in the tth year is $rP(1 - r)^{t-1}$.

The opposite result may be sought if, for example, a university library invests in documents that it is anticipated will be used by members of a planned but as yet nonexistent department. In this case, for purposes of constructing performance measures, the depreciation on the investment may be deferred until the department is formed and the document exposures take place.

Illustrative Computation of Overall Annual Performance Measures

The concepts of exposure and the accrual method of matching expenditures with their output may be used to construct performance measures. Generally, there are two standard types of performance measures: a ratio of benefits to costs and the difference between benefits and costs. The ratio performance measure is used particularly to evaluate most governmental operations when it is difficult to attribute a monetary value to benefits. For libraries, it would be exposure (counts, item-use-days, or hours) per dollar.

The difference measure is analogous to profit in the private sector. It may be used for libraries if we can impute a monetary value for each unit of exposure. Then, the performance measure would be the difference between the imputed monetary value to society of exposure and the costs used to produce the exposure. This measure may be more meaningful in per capita form.

Let us illustrate the computation of overall annual ratio and difference performance measures for The Free Library of Philadelphia for its fiscal year July 1, 1969, to June 30, 1970. In this case, we define benefits in terms of exposure hours during the fiscal year and costs in terms of all expenditures that produce the exposure hours included in the benefits. We also define

E = the number of exposure hours in the fiscal year by individuals to library documents obtained from The Free Library.

V = the imputed monetary value to society of one exposure hour.

C = total costs in the fiscal year including current expenditures designed to produce current exposure and allocated past expenditures.

N = the population of potential users.

The library benefits may be described in terms of E, exposure hours; E/N, exposure hours per capita; VE, the imputed value of exposure hours; or VE/N, the imputed value per capita. The ratio measure that relates exposures to cost is E/C, exposure hours per dollar. The difference measure is $VE - C$, which, in per capita form, is $(VE - C)/N = V(E/N) - C/N$.

Population Served

Although The Free Library performs district services for libraries in counties surrounding Philadelphia and performs resource services in certain subject areas for the state, we will define E and C solely with respect to services performed primarily for residents of the city of Philadelphia. Therefore, N is an estimate of the number of potential users of these services. The Bureau of the Census advance report of 1970 population characteristics indicates that the total population of the city of Philadelphia is 1,948,609, including approximately 126,816 children under the age of four. Let us exclude these children on the grounds that most of them are too young to be considered potential users, thereby reducing the population to 1,821,793.

Most of the document exposure produced by The Free Library by means of services for Philadelphia residents are utilized by these residents. However, the library also permits nonresidents to utilize these services. In addition to residents, let us include in the population of potential users an estimate of the number of nonresident users in the fiscal year.

There were 565,576 persons registered during the year. A random sample of 16,455 registrants indicated that 9.7 percent of the registrants are nonresidents. Therefore, $(.097)(565,576) = 54,861$ persons are estimated to be registered nonresidents. A random sample of nonresidents entering the library shows that 72.4 percent are registered; for each 10,000 registered nonresidents, there are an estimated additional $(.276)(10,000)/.724 = 3812$ nonresidents who are not registered. Therefore, in addition to the 54,861 registered nonresidents, there are an estimated $(54,861)(.3812) = 20,913$ nonresident users who are not registered. Adding these $54,861 + 20,913 = 75,774$ nonresidents to the 1,821,793 resident potential users, we get $N = 1,897,567$.

Exposure Hours

The total number of exposure hours E consists of both circulation and in-library use. There was an annual circulation of 5,259,543. A random sample survey of 308 persons returning 951 items of library materials indicated that the average amount of time spent by the borrower or anyone else with a circulated document is 2.25 hours (90 percent confidence interval of from 1.86 hours to 2.64). Therefore, there were an estimated $(5,259,543)(2.25) = 11,833,972$ exposure hours via circulation.

In order to ascertain the number of in-library exposure hours, the first step is to estimate annual library attendance. Three library units—Central, Northeast Regional, and Mercantile—compile attendance records by means of turnstile counts: the annual total was 1,556,568.

The attendance at the other 46 library units (44 branches and 2 bookmobiles) was estimated by dividing circulation by the average number of circulations per visit. We sampled five library units, in May 1971, which were chosen at random from each of five groups created by a cluster analysis with respect to circulation, bookstock, size of building, and educational level of the surrounding population. The total number of persons entering these branches during the sampling activity was 767, and there were 699 circulations, yielding $699/767 = .911$ circulation per visit.

An analysis of several years of monthly attendance and circulation records at Central, Northeast Regional, and Mercantile yielded monthly indices of the number of circulations per visit. The monthly index for May is, by coincidence, .911. The May number of circulations per visit is 91.1 percent of the annual average. Therefore, the best estimate of circulations per visit for the 46 library units without attendance counts is May sample circulations per visit/May index $= .911/.911 = 1.00$. At these units, the

Computation of Overall Annual Performance Measures

annual circulation was 3,831,867. The estimate of attendance is number of circulations/circulations per visit = 3,831,867/1.00 = 3,831,867. Adding this figure to the attendance of the three units having turnstile counts yields an annual Free Library attendance of 1,556,568 + 3,831,867 = 5,388,435. Some of these persons stayed only for a few minutes and others stayed for hours. Based on an analysis of questionnaires on which time was recorded, we estimate that the average stay was 25.5 minutes (standard error of .77 of a minute), or .425 of an hour. Multiplying the annual attendance by the time in the library per visit, we estimate that (5,388,435)(.425) = 2,290,085 user-hours were spent in the library. A sample of user in-library activity showed that at any given time, on the average, 58 percent of the persons in the library are engaged in direct or indirect document exposure and 42 percent are engaged in other activities. It follows that 58 percent of the in-library user-hours are estimated as in-library document exposure hours: (2,290,085)(.58) = 1,328,249 hours. Adding this number to the 11,833,972 circulation exposure hours yields E = 11,833,972 + 1,328,249 = 13,162,221 exposure hours. Table 2.1 summarizes the calculation of E.

The performance measure expressed in terms of exposure hours per capita is E/N = 13,162,221/1,897,567 = 6.94 exposure hours per person.

Table 2.1. Calculation of E, the Number of Exposure Hours in the 1970 Fiscal Year, to Documents Obtained from The Free Library

$$E = \begin{pmatrix} \text{Circulation} \\ \text{exposure} \\ \text{hours} \end{pmatrix} + \begin{pmatrix} \text{In-library} \\ \text{exposure} \\ \text{hours} \end{pmatrix}$$

$$= \begin{pmatrix} \text{Number of} \\ \text{circulations} \end{pmatrix} \begin{pmatrix} \text{Exposure} \\ \text{hours per} \\ \text{circulation} \end{pmatrix} + \begin{pmatrix} \text{Attendance} \end{pmatrix} \begin{pmatrix} \text{In-library} \\ \text{time} \\ \text{per visit} \end{pmatrix} \begin{pmatrix} \text{Proportion of} \\ \text{in-library time} \\ \text{used for docu-} \\ \text{ment exposure} \end{pmatrix}$$

$$= \begin{pmatrix} 5,259,543 \\ \text{circulations} \end{pmatrix} \begin{pmatrix} 2.25 \text{ hours} \\ \text{per} \\ \text{circulation} \end{pmatrix} + \begin{pmatrix} 5,388,435 \\ \text{visits} \end{pmatrix} \begin{pmatrix} 25\tfrac{1}{2} \text{ min.,} \\ \text{or .425 hour} \\ \text{per visit} \end{pmatrix} (.58)$$

$$= \begin{pmatrix} 11,833,972 \\ \text{circulation} \\ \text{exposure hours} \end{pmatrix} + \begin{pmatrix} 1,328,249 \\ \text{in-library} \\ \text{exposure hours} \end{pmatrix}$$

$$= 13,162,221 \text{ exposure hours}$$

Costs

The Free Library operating expense budget for city library services was $8,356,655 for the 1970 fiscal year. Those expenditures that are incurred to produce a significant amount of document exposure in future periods are to be allocated to those periods: $979,847 for library materials, $160,442 for furniture and equipment, and $149,001 for materials and services related to branches that have not yet opened. The remaining portion, $7,067,365, may be associated with the current year. A small part of these expenses was devoted to promotion activities that were designed to have a carry-over effect into the next year. However, no allocation to next year is made because the amount is considered small and the carry-over of promotion activities from the prior year to the current one approximately equals the carry-over from this year to next year.

Library documents are estimated to have, on the average, a ten-year life. All expenses incurred in order to get library documents on the shelves are to be allocated over this approximate period. The expenditure of $979,847 to acquire these documents obviously is in this category. In addition, it is estimated that 15 percent of all library staff expenses and other expenses is devoted to selecting, acquiring, classifying, cataloging, and processing library materials. Therefore, 15 percent of $7,067,365 = $1,060,105 is included in the amount of current expenditures invested in document resources available for immediate use, bringing the total to $979,847 + $1,060,105 = $2,039,952. The remaining portion of the operating budget, $7,067,365 − $1,060,105 = $6,007,260, represents current expenditures devoted entirely to producing current document exposure, that is, maintenance of facilities, circulation, maintenance and weeding of documents, promotion of library use, planning and administration, and various forms of reference services.

For purposes of constructing performance measures, expenditures for library documents are entered into an asset account that is depreciated each year. The account may be initiated by sampling the documents in order to estimate the number of volumes currently owned by the library which were obtained at different accession dates. Alternatively, we analyzed annual additions and withdrawals of various types of documents for each library unit. We assumed (1) half of each annual withdrawal was from the oldest accession period(s) and (2) the other half was distributed over all accession periods proportionally with respect to the number of documents in the accession period at the time of the withdrawal. We began with 1953 balances of library documents and simulated annual additions and withdrawals through time. The results were estimates, for each library unit and type of library material, of the number of volumes currently owned by the library which were obtained annually from 1954 to 1970 or before 1954.

The current average purchase prices for library documents are shown in Table 2.2. In order to determine the current unit values of recently acquired library documents, we must add to the purchase price an estimate of per document expenses for selecting, acquiring, classifying, cataloging, and processing. We have estimated that $1,060,105 had been devoted to these document services. Let us assume that each book category (including bound serials) has the same per document cost for these services and that the expenses for other documents (predominantly uncataloged pamphlets) are 20 percent of those for books. Hence, in the fiscal year, the number of book equivalents are 27,696 Central adult books + 8014 Northeast adult books + 61,027 branch adult books + 57,271 juvenile books + 59,424 (20 percent of 297,121) other documents = 213,432 book equivalents. The per book cost to be added to the purchase price is $1,060,105/213,432 = $4.97. For other documents, the increment is 20 percent of $4.97 = $.99. In Table 2.2 we add these costs to the purchase price.

In order to estimate the current value of library materials on hand, we must take into account the fact that there is a sharp decrease in value over time because of obsolescence of content and deterioration of the physical document. We assume that the per document value to the library decreases exponentially over time.[1]

Table 2.2. Current per Unit Costs of New Library Materials

	Purchase Price	Additional Cost	Total Costs
Central adult books	$6.86	$4.97	$11.83
Northeast adult books	5.76	4.97	10.73
Branch adult books	4.64	4.97	9.61
Juvenile books	3.01	4.97	7.98
Other documents*	.62	.99	1.61

* Uncataloged pamphlets; bound documents; broadsides; clay tables; embossed volumes; films; hornbooks; large-type books; manuscripts; maps; microfiches; microfilms; microcards; boxes of music; photos, pictures, and prints; sheet music; slides; sound recordings; talking books; tapes; unbound documents; and wood blocks.

1. If t = number of years since accession, assuming that the average pre-1954 document is 25 years old, we multiplied the current unit value by e^{-At} where A was set to yield a unit value of

Finally, we obtain the current value of library material on hand by multiplying the number of documents by the corresponding unit value. Summation over accession periods and document types yields the total value of documents on hand, $15,118,845.

A certain amount of this asset is depreciated each year to include part of document resource expenses in the current matching of exposure and expense. Document use has been found to decrease exponentially with time due to obsolescence of content, deterioration of the physical document, and because the longer the document is held, the higher the probability of theft, loss, or misplacement. Therefore, we choose the declining balance method of depreciation in which a constant rate of depreciation is applied to a declining balance. We choose an annual rate of 15 percent, which results in approximately 80 percent cumulative depreciation after ten years. The depreciation for the 1970 fiscal year is 15 percent of $15,118,845 = $2,267,827. The document resource balance for the beginning of next year is $15,118,845 − $2,267,827 = $12,851,018.

Thus far, C, total costs for the 1970 fiscal year, consists of $6,007,260 of current expenditures devoted entirely to producing current document exposure and $2,267,827 of depreciation of library resources. The final elements of C are depreciation of building, equipment, and furnishings. Straight-line depreciation is used over a 50-year life for buildings (2 percent per year) and over a 15-year life for equipment and furnishings (6.67 percent per year).

The Free Library consists of 48 buildings that are currently providing city library services: the main library, Central; a regional library, Northeast; 2 special libraries, Mercantile and the Library for the Blind; and 44 branch libraries. We have compiled or estimated cost data on constructions, additions, renovations, and renewals. Expenditures made more than 50 years ago are considered completely depreciated. Depreciation for the 1970 fiscal period consists of 2 percent of all construction costs, site purchase costs, and related planning and architectural expenses. These expenditures total $12,595,100 (construction costs) + $5,027,300 (addition, renewal, or renovation costs) = $17,622,400. The 1970 depreciation is (.02)($17,622,400) = $352,448.

Expenditures for equipment and furnishings are part of both the operat-

---

$1.00 for pre-1954 branch adult books on hand: A = .091. There was librarian agreement that unit values obtained in this manner reflected the amount of current funds the library would be willing to spend to retain a typical document in its collection.

ing and capital budgets. In the past 15 years, approximately $791,000 has been allocated for this purpose from the operating budget and approximately $649,000 from the capital budget, a total of $1,440,000. Annual depreciation, on a straight-line basis, for a 15-year period, is $1,440,000/15 = $96,000.

The calculation of C is as follows:

Current expenditures devoted entirely to current document exposure	$6,007,260
Library document resource depreciation	2,267,827
Building depreciation	352,448
Equipment and furnishing depreciation	96,000
Total	$8,723,535

Table 2.3 summarizes the calculation of C.

Pertinent data elements are

$C/E = 8,723,535/13,162,221 = \$.66$ per exposure hour

$C/N = 8,723,535/1,897,567 = \$4.60$ per person

The performance measure expressed in terms of exposure hours per dollar is $E/C = 13,162,221/8,723,535 = 1.51$ exposure hours per dollar.

The Imputed Value of an Exposure Hour

As expressed previously, exposure hours enhance individual knowledge, ability, creativity, motivation, and confidence. These educational outputs in turn further progress toward the fulfillment of the objectives of society. Therefore, exposure hours have a value to society. This value may be expressed in monetary terms: $V =$ the imputed monetary value to society of one exposure hour.

Inherent in the governmental decision to invest in library services is a decision to forgo alternative governmental investments, and such nongovernmental uses of funds as private investment and consumption. According to Baumol (1969, pp. 202–212), the benefits of a governmental investment are expected to exceed costs to the extent that the resources utilized would otherwise result in benefits which exceed costs in the private sector. Since funds can be invested in the private sector with an average rate of return of 10 percent to 15 percent, governmental benefits are expected to exceed costs by this rate (see Stockfish 1969, pp. 187–201). By assuming that the average public library has benefits that exceed costs by 12.5 percent, we estimate the dollar value imputed to an exposure hour.

If we could perform E and C calculations for all public libraries in a given year, we could add them to obtain a total E value and a total C

Table 2.3. Calculation of Total Costs C

$$C = \begin{pmatrix} \text{Current expenditures} \\ \text{devoted entirely to} \\ \text{current document} \\ \text{exposure} \end{pmatrix} + \begin{pmatrix} \text{Library document} \\ \text{depreciation} \end{pmatrix} + \begin{pmatrix} \text{Building} \\ \text{depreciation} \end{pmatrix} + \begin{pmatrix} \text{Equipment and} \\ \text{furnishings depreciation} \end{pmatrix}$$

$$= \begin{pmatrix} \text{Operating budget (less) Library} \\ \text{material expenditures (less)} \\ \text{Furniture and equipment} \\ \text{expenditures (less) Materials and} \\ \text{services related to unopened} \\ \text{branches (less) Estimated expenses} \\ \text{to get new documents on shelf} \end{pmatrix} + (.15)\begin{pmatrix} \text{Current value} \\ \text{of documents} \\ \text{on hand} \end{pmatrix} + (.02)\begin{pmatrix} \text{All costs for} \\ \text{construction, additions,} \\ \text{renovations, and} \\ \text{renewals in last} \\ \text{50 years} \end{pmatrix} + \left(\frac{1}{15}\right)\begin{pmatrix} \text{Equipment and} \\ \text{furnishings} \\ \text{expenditures} \\ \text{in last 15} \\ \text{years} \end{pmatrix}$$

$$= \begin{pmatrix} \$8,356,655 \\ -979,847 \\ -160,442 \\ -149,001 \\ -1,060,105 \end{pmatrix} + (.15)(\$15,118,845) + (.02)(\$17,622,400) + \left(\frac{1}{15}\right)(\$1,440,000)$$

$$= \quad \$6,007,260 \quad + \$2,267,827 \quad\quad + \$352,448 \quad\quad + \$96,000$$

$$C = \quad \$8,723,535$$

value for the nation as a whole. Then, since we assume that the average ratio of benefits and costs for all libraries is 1.125,

$(VE)/C = V(E/C) = 1.125$
$V = 1.125/(E/C).$

Since E, C, and N values for all public libraries are not obtainable, we utilize available data to make the best possible estimates of E, C, and N. The most convenient data for this purpose may be found in *Statistics of Public Libraries Serving Areas with at Least 25,000 Inhabitants, 1968* by Ruth L. Boaz (1970). We wish to estimate the following:

1. E = 1969–1970 exposure hours
2. C = 1969–1970 total costs
3. N = 1969–1970 population served (as calculated before for The Free Library)

The most analogous available data are

4. 1968 loan transactions of all printed and audiovisual materials
5. 1968 operating expenditures
6. 1968 population served.

We assume that the ratios between 1 and 4, 2 and 5, and 3 and 6 for The Free Library of Philadelphia are the same as for the aggregate of the 35 libraries reporting that have a population of at least 500,000. These assumptions and the fact that we have calculated E, C, and N for The Free Library enable us to transform the given data into approximate values of E, C, and N for all reporting libraries. The transformation factors are presented in Table 2.4.

Table 2.4. Use of Data from The Free Library of Philadelphia to Transform Three 1968 Data Elements Published by the Office of Education into 1969–1970 Estimates of E, C, and N

	(1) 1969–1970 Calculations	(2) Analogous Office of Education 1968 Data Elements	Transformation Factor = (1)/(2)
E	13,162,221 exposure hours	5,984,642 loan transactions	2.20 fiscal 1970 exposure hours per 1968 loan transaction
C	$8,723,535	$7,994,655	1.09
N	1,897,567 persons	2,002,512 persons	.95

With these transformation factors for the reporting libraries that have a population of at least 500,000,

E = (156,420,544 loan transactions)(2.20) = 344,125,197 exposure hours

C = ($159,873,584)(1.09) = $174,262,207

E/C = 344,125,197/$174,262,207 = 1.97 exposure hours per dollar

V = 1.125/(E/C) = 1.125/1.97 = $.57

The interpretation of the latter figure is that if the average monetary value of benefits from libraries of 500,000 people or more exceeds costs by 12.5 percent then it follows that this country is imputing a value of $.57 to an average exposure hour at a large public library.

Table 2.5 shows the E/C ratio performance measure for the aggregate of reporting libraries and for libraries of various population sizes. It is quite apparent that E/C decreases significantly as the size of the population increases. Some reasons for the relatively low effectiveness of larger libraries may be lower educational levels of populations served; distance from and fear of going to the library; alternative libraries and other activities that compete for the time of potential users; higher initial costs of facilities; and higher costs for staff, which represents a significant part of total operating costs. Table 2.5 also shows the results of a separate imputed V calculation for each population size. The V value for the aggregate of reporting libraries serving over 25,000 people, for an assumption that the total library benefits exceed costs by 12.5 percent, is $.42.

Computation of the overall ratio or difference library performance measures over time would enable library managers to trace major trends in performance. It would highlight the effect of major programs, such as

Table 2.5. Ratio Performance Measure and Imputed Exposure Value by Population Size

Population Size Group	Number of Libraries Reporting	E/C	V
Total (all 25,000 and over)	1057	2.68	$.42
25,000 to 35,000	258	3.62	.31
35,000 to 50,000	250	3.46	.33
50,000 to 100,000	318	3.28	.34
100,000 to 500,000	196	2.85	.40
500,000 and over	35	1.97	.57

the opening of a new branch. It would also focus attention on the effect of changes in the environment, such as the increasing use of individual book purchases in place of library use.

The overall performance measure may also be useful in comparisons among similar libraries. Major differences in performance may aid in specifying particularly effective programs.

The illustrative computation of the performance measure was shown in terms of the entire library. However, perhaps the most important use of library performance is in terms of evaluating individual library programs or aiding in library decisions. Similar computations can relate exposure and costs associated with a program. The use of performance measures to evaluate programs is discussed in Chapter 3.

Library Standards

Thus far, we have analyzed what a library tries to accomplish (its objectives), and we have proposed library performance measures to evaluate how well the library is achieving these objectives. It is revealing to take a brief look at library standards against this background. Standards are neither objectives nor performance measures. Objectives are general statements of purpose, and performance measures are a quantitative means of relating benefits (outputs) to costs (inputs). Library standards either are descriptive rules for "proper" management or are quantitative rules for "minimum" inputs of materials, personnel, and physical facilities. However, they are often considered to be objectives or performance measures or both.

The most up-to-date presentation of public library standards is the American Library Association's *Minimum Standards for Public Library Systems, 1966* (1967). The preface states: "This document presents minimum standards; that is, it describes the least the citizen living in the last third of the twentieth century has the right to expect." There are 66 general guiding principles, organized in sections of Structure and Government of Library Service; Service; Materials: Selection, Organization, and Control; Personnel; and Physical Facilities. For each guiding principle, there are one or more standards. An example of a standard that is a descriptive rule for proper management is "22i. To ensure quality service all sources of information and all forms of materials must be consulted." An example of a standard that is a quantitative rule for "minimum input" is "39i. . . . At least one currently published periodical title should be available for each 250 people in the service area." Unit and total cost estimates for meeting these "minimum standards," for populations of different sizes, are discussed in Plain (1968).

Descriptive rules are useful to the extent that they provide reasonable advice to library administrators. The purpose of most quantitative standards is "to prod or scare most communities into raising budgets in the belief that improvement would be generated." (Beasley 1968, p. 2.) These standards are useful to the extent that they increase library receipts, resulting in an increase of library inputs of materials, personnel, and physical facilities, in turn resulting in greater document exposure.

Most university library standards have been either descriptive in nature or based upon value judgments. In contrast, the recently published data for fifty of the better university libraries in the United States and Canada by the Committee on University Standards (see Downs and Heussman 1970 and Downs 1969) are in terms of average, range, and quartiles. However, the major emphasis is still directed toward measuring inputs to the library, as opposed to measuring outputs or benefits imparted to the users. The one exception is in the area of reserve and circulation service, wherein data are presented on a per library basis as well as a per student basis. Further, the defining of input measures in areas of expenditures, document resources, personnel, and space on a per student basis represents a significant improvement in the development of input indicators (for example, volumes per student). Development of comparable measures relating to the research function of the university would represent a further significant advancement in the area of input indicators.

Unfortunately, even these standards are not very helpful in evaluating the effectiveness of any particular library. They merely serve as a guide for comparing gross input data, in the areas of expenditures, space, personnel and document resources, and circulation data of a particular library with gross input and circulation data for fifty of the better university libraries.

Both university and public library standards fail to provide a basis for meaningful evaluation of the performance of the library for the following reasons:

1. Most of the standards are descriptive in nature, making evaluation extremely difficult.
2. Most of the standards that prescribe quantitative objectives are arbitrarily formulated by value judgments.

3. The emphasis of the standards is directed toward evaluating the input resources of the library, as opposed to evaluating the difference between the output (exposure benefits imparted in the user-library interface) and the input.
4. The standards discourage experimentation with different programs and different allocations of input resources, designed to meet the needs of the library's particular population of potential users; merely meeting the standards implies, perhaps falsely, that the library is doing an adequate job.

A library performance measure is a yardstick to determine how well a library is performing, analogous to a measure such as return on investment in the private sector. If a measure were to be generally adopted, distributions of the measure could be established for libraries of similar types. These distributions could be used to establish certain performance levels as performance standards.

Conclusion

We have seen that public library objectives refer to formal education, library materials, the process of communicating with the user, and the end result of library use. University library objectives refer to the reading, reference, and research needs of users. In neither case are the objectives operationally meaningful enough to yield suitable performance measures.

We traced library benefits back from ultimate progress toward the fulfillment of society's objectives to educational effects, and we finally focused upon the coming together of individuals and documents of recorded human experience. For libraries emphasizing the reactive aspect of library service, we suggested performance measures such as the proportion of users satisfied and document retrieval time. For libraries also having a significant active or promotional aspect of library service, we suggested and discussed measures of exposure counts, item-use-days, and exposure time.

In measuring performance, we emphasized the importance of matching costs with the exposure they are intended to produce. Performance measures were established based upon the ratio of exposure benefits to costs and based upon the difference between exposure benefits and costs. A detailed example was undertaken illustrating computation of both types of measures of exposure hours for the 1970 fiscal year of The Free Library of Philadelphia. Calculations were made of the population of potential users, the number of exposure hours, and the total cost designed to produce the exposure. Under certain assumptions, we determined both a ratio performance measure and the monetary value imputed to an exposure hour for groups of public libraries of various sizes.

Finally, library standards were shown to be neither objectives nor performance measures. They are either descriptive rules for "proper" management or quantitative rules for "minimum" input.

3

A FRAMEWORK FOR LIBRARY DECISION MAKING

Introduction

In the preceding chapter, we found out *what* a library is attempting to do. In this chapter, we outline *how* a library may incorporate systematic analysis into its management system.

We identify the various aspects of a rational management system, we trace the steps involved in the planning and decision-making aspect, and we describe library program structures. Finally, we present a methodology for utilizing performance measures to evaluate programs.

Aspects of a Rational Management System

Critics of systems analysis emphasize that management depends on good judgment. However, in large organizations with complex operations, good judgment *alone* will not suffice. Decisions made solely on the basis of managerial intuition cannot possibly take into consideration the many complex interrelationships that exist.

In recent years, the general management problems of libraries have been accelerating at a dizzy pace. Rapid expansion has taken place in development of cooperative arrangements among libraries, in computerization, mechanization, and centralization of library services, in sizes of collections, and in the variety of services offered by libraries. These increasing complexities of library organizational arrangements and expansions in activities and services, along with the economic problem of allocating limited resources in such a manner as to generate maximum benefits, necessitate the development of a management system for allocating and controlling resources. A logical framework is needed in order to coordinate all that is known about various aspects of the organizational environment and in order to facilitate decision making in accordance with the overall objectives.

The main elements of a rational management system and their significant interrelationships are depicted in Figure 3.1. They are
1. Statistical data and information
2. Analytical tools
3. A process for planning and decision making

42   A Framework for Library Decision Making

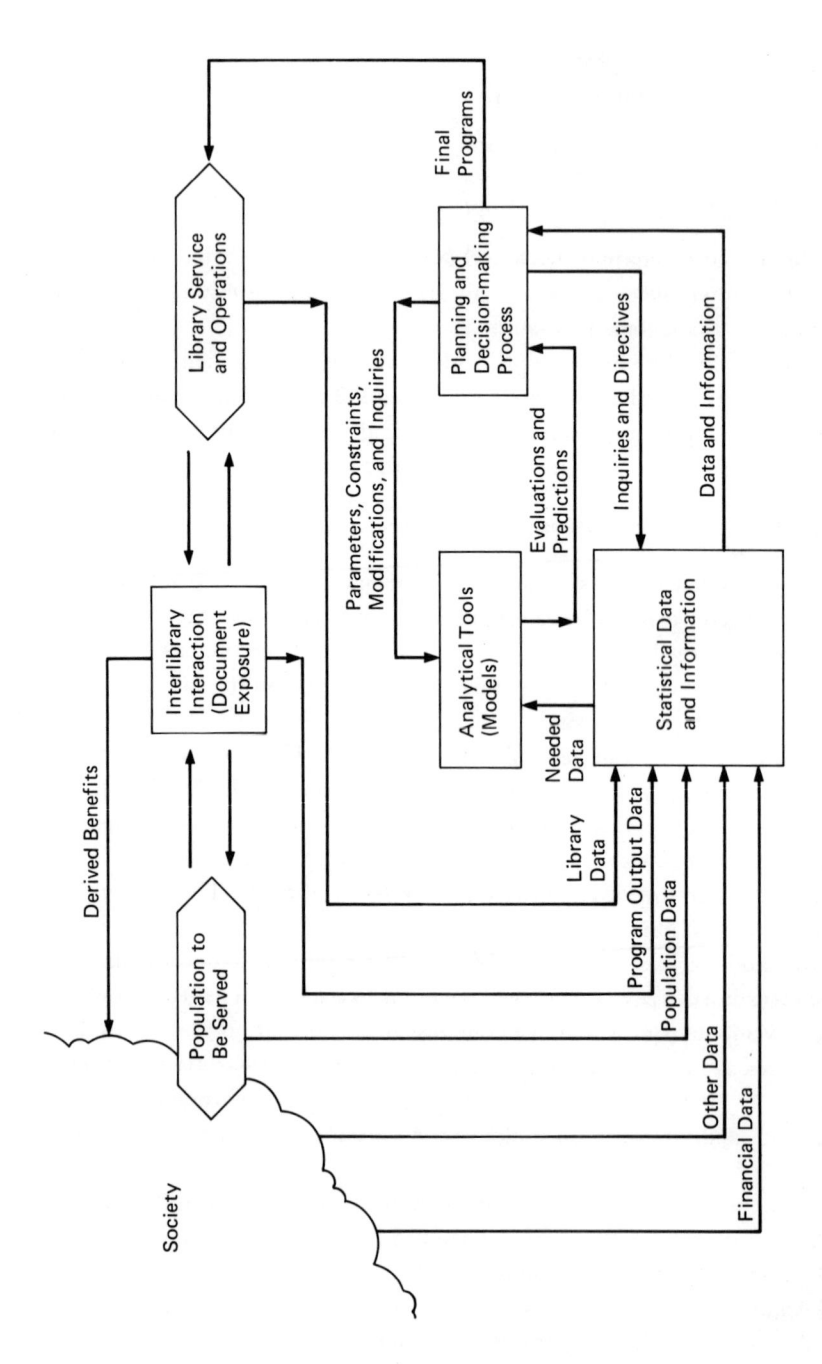

Figure 3.1. Elements of a library management system.

We noted in Chapter 2 that library services and operations are designed to bring together documents of recorded human experience and individuals in the population to be served. As depicted at the top of Figure 3.1, the resultant user-library interaction yields societal benefits.

There are many currently and potentially available analytical tools for aiding the library manager in answering "what if" questions. The manager may alter parameters and constraints, and he may inquire about any program or set of programs at various allocation levels. These analytical tools, called "models," are the subject of Chapter 4.

There is a continuous outpouring of data, and potentially measurable activities are continually occurring. Data relevant to library planning and decision making include statistics about the population to be served; library facilities, documents, and staff; the output of programs; finances; and other activities originating outside the library. These data must be made available in response to inquiries and directives from management. In Chapter 5, we provide direction for the development of an improved statistical data and information system.

In the remainder of this chapter, we outline a process of planning and decision making that utilizes statistical data and models. This process is designed to allocate funds in such a way as to attain the greatest predicted library performance.

The Process of Planning and Decision Making

The problem confronting every library is how to allocate and control scarce resources, and manage and control library activities, so as to maximize benefits imparted to society. The Planning-Programming-Budgeting-System (PPBS) represents a logical and useful planning and decision-making system to achieve this end. In brief, utilization of PPBS assists managers in making decisions and plans that are consistent with the desired objectives of the library. The major emphasis of PPBS is directed toward outputs or accomplishments as related to inputs or resources necessary to achieve these objectives. Estimates are made of both outputs and costs of various alternatives. The decision maker uses these estimates together with his experience and intuition to make decisions.

The basic elements of using PPBS or any logical framework for planning and decision making are

1. Specification of objectives
2. Derivation of performance measures to evaluate achievement of these objectives
3. Specification of a program structure oriented toward achievement of stated objectives
4. Specification of input and output indicators for programs in the program structure
5. Determination of the relationship between performance measures and input and output indicators
6. Development of a multiyear plan

Advantages of utilizing PPBS as a management tool include

1. Emphasis on achievement of objectives
2. Facilitation of consideration and evaluation of a wide range of alternative programs
3. Assistance in optimal resource allocation
4. Flexibility in adapting to idiosyncrasies of different organizations
5. Compatibility with modern management methods such as benefit-cost analysis and mathematical models
6. Provision of a rational and systematic means for decision making and planning necessary for the functioning of any management system

Further background discussion on PPBS applicable to education and libraries can be found in Hartley (1968), Raffel and Shishko (1969), and Hinrichs and Taylor (1969).

Probably the greatest criticism leveled at PPBS is that it is difficult to implement. The reality of the situation is that establishing objectives, deriving performance measures, and developing a multiyear plan do require a great deal of time and effort. If a library desires to know what outputs or benefits are being achieved per unit input and to determine how resources can be most effectively allocated, it must be willing to undertake this process or a similar one.

Another basis for criticism is the fact that PPBS is often imposed upon a lower-level agency from above. Hence, frequently those involved with developing a PPBS believe that they are doing it to meet a requirement, without realizing what a helpful management technique it can be to them.

The procedures necessary for the employment of a PPBS are outlined in Figure 3.2. The steps are shown in a specific sequence. However, at any given stage, previous steps may be repeated or reevaluated. The data and

The Process of Planning and Decision Making

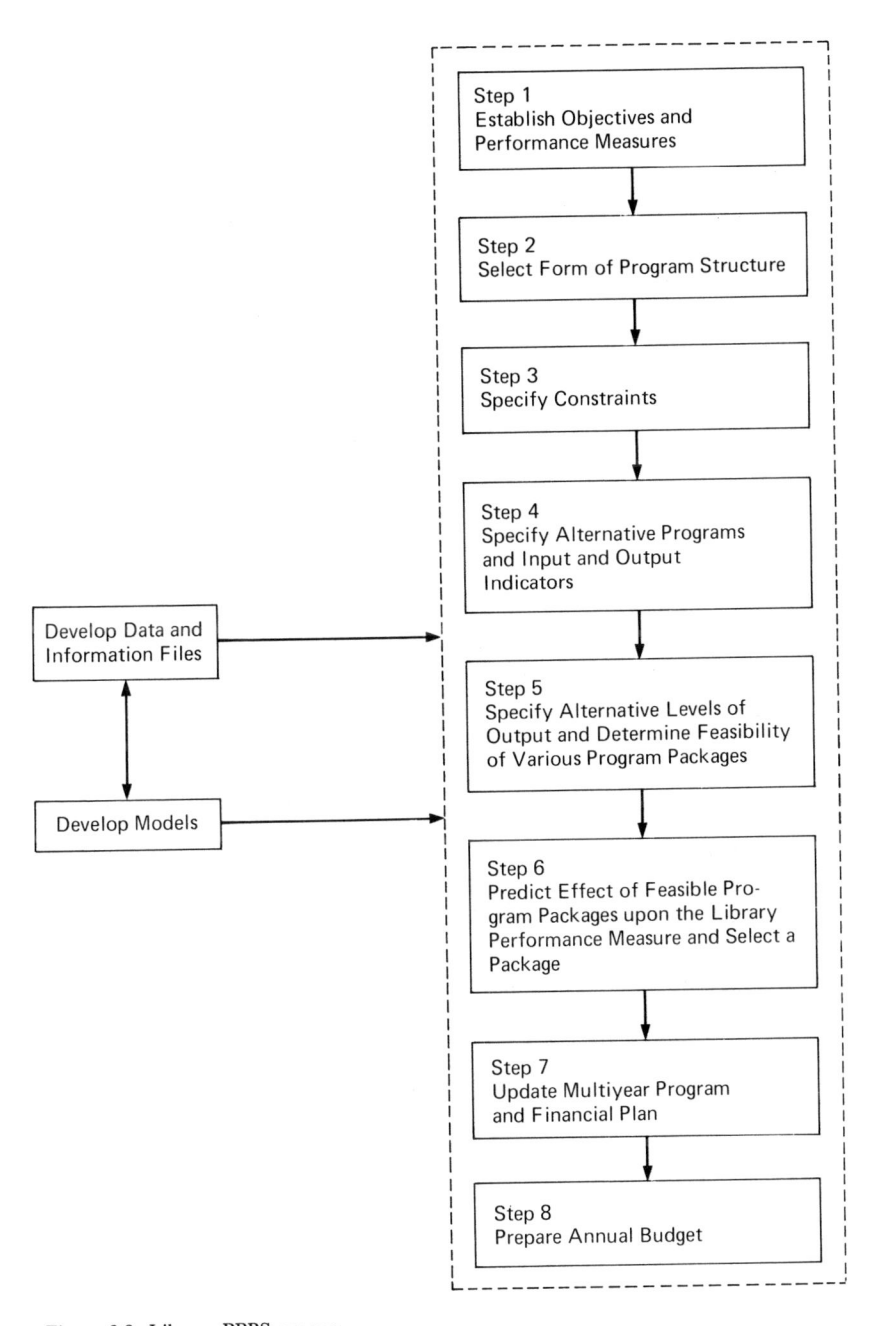

```
┌─────────────────────────────────────┐
│  Step 1                             │
│  Establish Objectives and           │
│  Performance Measures               │
└─────────────────────────────────────┘
                │
                ▼
┌─────────────────────────────────────┐
│  Step 2                             │
│  Select Form of Program Structure   │
└─────────────────────────────────────┘
                │
                ▼
┌─────────────────────────────────────┐
│  Step 3                             │
│  Specify Constraints                │
└─────────────────────────────────────┘
                │
                ▼
┌─────────────────────────────────────┐
│  Step 4                             │
│  Specify Alternative Programs       │
│  and Input and Output Indicators    │
└─────────────────────────────────────┘
                │
                ▼
┌─────────────────────────────────────┐
│  Step 5                             │
│  Specify Alternative Levels of      │
│  Output and Determine Feasibility   │
│  of Various Program Packages        │
└─────────────────────────────────────┘
                │
                ▼
┌─────────────────────────────────────┐
│  Step 6                             │
│  Predict Effect of Feasible Pro-    │
│  gram Packages upon the Library     │
│  Performance Measure and Select a   │
│  Package                            │
└─────────────────────────────────────┘
                │
                ▼
┌─────────────────────────────────────┐
│  Step 7                             │
│  Update Multiyear Program           │
│  and Financial Plan                 │
└─────────────────────────────────────┘
                │
                ▼
┌─────────────────────────────────────┐
│  Step 8                             │
│  Prepare Annual Budget              │
└─────────────────────────────────────┘
```

Side boxes (connected into Step 4 and Step 5 area):
- Develop Data and Information Files
- Develop Models

Figure 3.2. Library PPBS process.

information file and the models are seen to be basic to the entire planning and decision-making process.

Objectives and Performance Measures

The first step is to establish objectives and formulate appropriate performance measures. This step was the subject of Chapter 2. In addition to developing performance measures, it is often helpful to specify levels of achievement for the planning period (usually one-year intervals of a five-year period). Models may be used here to aid in predicting future needs of the population to be served.

Program Structure

The program structure consists of mutually exclusive, output-oriented categories, grouped according to common ends or means, which together encompass all library activity. It serves as a basic framework for presenting budgetary information and making resource allocation decisions. Programs are subdivided for managerial convenience in distinguishing between various parts of programs. Some programs may be subdivided in great detail, while others may be subdivided very little. Program structures for public and university libraries are designed in the next section.

Constraints

All limitations to the achievement of infinitely high performance are referred to as "constraints." They may be technological, legal, administrative, distributional, political, financial, budgetary, traditional, social, or religious. They must be specified over the planning period. Models are utilized here to forecast and predict the constraints. For example, the average purchase price of documents in the coming year or the expected revenue to be obtained from the parent funding agency (that is, the university, the city, and so on) might be forecast.

Alternative Programs and Their Indicators

Suggestions for different possible library activities are made and grouped with respect to programs and subdivisions within the program structure. Generally, both (1) the program categories and their subdivisions in the program structure and (2) the library activities planned for each planning period are called "programs"—somewhat of an ambiguity. Where the distinction is important, we refer to the former as "program categories" and the latter as "program activities." Otherwise, we use "programs" to refer to one or the other or both. Indicators are developed in Chapter 5 to trace input and output effects of alternative proposed activities within program categories.

Determination of Feasible Program Packages
Various proposed program activities with differing input and output levels are considered for each program category. Combinations of program activities are formed, and their feasibilities are determined based on available inputs.

Evaluation of Feasible Program Packages
With the assistance of models, the effects of various feasible program packages upon the library's performance measures are predicted. That package of feasible programs is selected which is expected to yield the greatest benefit to the population being served.

Multiyear Program and Financial Plan
A logical and compact format is needed to summarize output, cost, and financing information of a package of program activities. The activities are grouped within the program categories of the program structure. For each program activity, one or more quantifiable output measures are used to give some indication of what is to be accomplished. Best estimates, perhaps with use of models or perhaps subjective "best guesses," are made of the level of the output measures and the costs of program activities for each of the next five years. Outputs and costs are aggregated within each program category to yield an overview of library activity. Each year the plan is updated, and one year is added to the plan.

Budgeting
The budget is the financial expression of the final program activity package. The framework for the formulation and review of the budget should be the first year of the Multiyear Program and Financial Plan. A traditional line item budget may be maintained by means of a crosswalk that translates program category costs into traditional cost items.

Program Structure Design

The primary purpose of a program structure is to facilitate allocation of scarce resources among programs. Therefore, the program categories should be defined with respect to the one or more dimensions of library activity that will yield an information display of highest significance and utility to decision makers. There are four major dimensions which a library decision maker may use to classify library activity meaningfully into nonoverlapping subsets: (1) population, (2) documents, (3) functions, and (4) organization.

Program categories of a program structure may be defined according to subdimensions of a single dimension. Hence, program categories can be defined by population subsets, by document subsets, by library functions, or by library units. For example, a program category for a public library utilizing a program structure defined by population might be directed toward meeting the needs of the elderly. A public library utilizing a program structure defined by documents might have a program category to provide documents and service in the area of psychology. A public library whose program structure is defined by library functions might have a program category for publications, advertisements, and exhibits. A public library whose program structure is oriented in terms of its organization might have a program category for a particular branch library.

The program structure also may be defined along a combination of dimensions. For example, the library might have a program category geared to meet the needs of young adults and another program category for black studies. In this case, the overlap caused by the intersection of these two program categories would have to be resolved to maintain the nonoverlapping aspect of program categories. Similar examples of various program structures can be generated for a university library.

Dimensions can be subdivided in different ways. For example, for the university library, population can be subdivided according to affiliation (that is, faculty, staff, graduate student, or undergraduate student) or by subject interests (for example, anthropology, engineering, and so forth) or by both affiliation and subject matter simultaneously (e.g., faculty-anthropology, graduate student-physics, and so forth). Likewise, documents can be subdivided according to subject matter, by document type, by document form, and so on, or by all simultaneously. If we consider that the smallest unit in any program structure is defined by subdivisions of the four dimensions, we realize there are an extremely large number of these units. For example, one unit might be defined as selecting (function) psychology periodicals (document) for adults (population) for the 40th Street Branch Library (organization). Since a program can be defined as composed of a set of these units, it is apparent that there exists a tremendous number of possible program structures.

We now analyze in detail the possible methods of subdividing the four library dimensions. Then we present illustrative program structures for a university library and a public library.

Population

For some library planning and decision-making purposes, the population of potential users may remain undifferentiated. However, unless the population is unusually homogeneous, it is essential for most library-planning and decision-making purposes to segment the population into meaningful subsets. These purposes include specification of programs, measurement of performance, formulation of models, and collection of data.

The number and types of population subsets are not determined automatically and are not fixed. The creation of population subsets is a conceptualization used for managerial convenience, and in each instance it is subject to managerial control. If the subset definitions are made very broad, the subsets are few in number. At the limit, where the population is undifferentiated, one may consider the entire population as one population subset. If the subset definitions are made very narrow, the subsets are numerous. At the limit, every individual in the population is in a unique population subset. Any number of population subsets between these extremes is possible.

Various characteristics of individuals in the population may be used to define population subsets. Categories are chosen with respect to these characteristics. The choice and number of characteristics and categories determine the number and types of population subsets, which in turn depend on the purpose of the segmentation.

The populations of potential users of a *public library* typically would be defined as the set of individuals residing in the one or more governmental units that contribute local tax funds. Alternatively, it may be defined as the set of individuals residing in the municipality in which the library is located, or the set of individuals to which library service is free.

The heterogeneous nature of the public library population requires frequent segmentation. Characteristics used for segmentation into subsets include age, reading or educational level, occupation, and geographical area, as well as certain other special characteristics.

The most frequent segmentation of the public library population is by *age*, into adults and children. The age of separation could be anywhere from 12 to 17, with 14 and 15 being typical. Often, an adult is defined as an individual reaching the ninth grade or age 15, whichever occurs first.

There is no maximum age of individuals in the population. Minimum age usually is considered to be 4 or 5, although younger children could be defined as part of the population of potential users because of their use of picture books. Therefore, one possible segmentation by age, yielding two population subsets, is Adults (14 years and over) and Children (4–13 years). A somewhat different segmentation would result if the minimum age or the age of separation is shifted.

A third category with respect to the age characteristic, that of Young Adults, is often introduced. It is typically the first few years of what otherwise would be the Adult category. Therefore, if three categories along the age dimension are desired, one may use Children (4–13 years), Young Adults (14–19 years), and Adults (20 years and over). There has been a great deal of controversy in the public library community over whether to organize library programs and collect use and resource data in terms of two or three categories of age.

Three age categories are by no means the maximum that is conceptually useful for library management purposes. Indeed, there are suggestions that public library programs should be specialized in terms of many stages in the development of readers, from preschool years to senior years (see Martin, *Baltimore Reaches Out*, 1967, pp. 36–38, and Wheeler and Goldhor 1962, p. 27). In this respect, additional segmentation is particularly necessary for children and young adults, at least to distinguish between readers and nonreaders. However, this segmentation may be more conveniently accomplished with respect to reading, educational or broad occupational characteristics, rather than by age. Table 3.1 illustrates various ways of categorizing the age dimension.

Since the United States Census is the major source of population data, its delineations may set the practical upper limit for age categories. It publishes the number of individuals of each age, by individual year, from "under one" up to age 20. Therefore, by simple addition, population data are readily available for any categorization of children and young adults. In addition, the Census publishes population numbers in classes as follows: 0–4 years, 5–9 years, . . . , 80–84 years, and 85 years and over. These classes are convenient for most age categorizations.

For many years the public library has been geared to satisfying the needs of the relatively highly educated, highly motivated good reader. In the past few years, there has been increasing emphasis on encouraging use of the library by the less educated or motivated, poorer reader. Since different library programs are now being planned with respect to different

Table 3.1. Public Library Age Categories

Number of Categories	Category	Source
2	Children Adults	
3	Children Young Adults Adults	
4	Under 18 18–20 21–64 65 and over	Council of National Library Associations, *Bowker Annual* 1969
4	Under 21 21–34 35–49 50 and over	Mendelsohn and Wingerd 1967
5	Preschool (Under 5) Children (5–14) Young Adults (15–19) Adults (20–64) Senior Citizens (65 and over)	Martin 1969
6	Under 12 12–16 17–21 22–34 35–50 Over 50	Bundy—May 1967 Bundy—December 1967
7	Under 15 15–19 20–24 25–34 35–44 45–54 55 and over	Shaughnessy 1967

reading or *educational levels*, this characteristic is an important one for defining population subsets.

One possibility is to segment by reading ability. If two categories are desired, individuals may be classified as good or poor readers, depending upon whether their reading ability is above or below a chosen reading level. In this same manner, three or more categories of reading levels could be identified.

Another possibility is to segment by educational level. Some examples are presented in Table 3.2.

An individual's *occupation* consumes a good deal of his time and concern. It results in "on the job" and job-related reading, and it is often an influence for personal reading. In addition, individuals in the same occupational category have relatively similar interests and educational levels. Therefore, library programs may be formulated in terms of occupation categories (see Wheeler and Goldhor 1962, p. 28).

The U.S. Census categorizes males 14 and over and females 14 and over initially as follows: employed in the civilian labor force; unemployed in the civilian labor force; employed in the noncivilian labor force; and not in the labor force. There are then three classifications of those employed in the civilian labor force.

The first, by individual service performed, is done separately for males and females:

1. Professional, technical, and kindred workers
2. Managers, officials, and proprietors, including farmers
3. Clerical and kindred workers
4. Sales workers
5. Craftsmen, foremen, and kindred workers
6. Operatives and kindred workers
7. Private household workers
8. Service workers, excluding private household workers
9. Laborers, except farm.

The second, by employer type, does not seem relevant to libraries. The third, by industry type, might be useful: mining; construction; manufacturing (furniture and lumber and wood products; metal industries; machinery; transportation equipment; other durable goods, food and kindred products; textile and apparel products; printing, publishing, and allied industries; other durables, including unspecified manufacturing; railroad and railway express service; other transportation; community, utility, and

Table 3.2. Public Library Educational Level Categories

Number of Categories	Category	Source
3	Last attended elementary school Last attended high school Last attended college	Bundy 1968
3	Less than 9 years 9–10.9 years 11 or more years	Martin 1969
4	Eighth grade or less Some high school High school or vocational school graduate One or more years of college	Shaughnessy 1967
5	No schooling 1–7 years of grade school 8 years of grade school and 0–3 years of high school 4 years of high school and 0–3 years of college 4 or more years of college	Council of National Library Associations, Bowker Annual 1969
6	Less than high school graduation High school or business and vocational school graduation Some college but no degree College graduation Some graduate school Graduate or professional degree	Shaughnessy 1967
8	No school years completed Elementary school, 1–4 years Elementary school, 5–7 years Elementary school, 8 years High school, 1–3 years High school, 4 years College, 1–3 years College, 4 years or more	1970 Census of Population

sanitary service; wholesale trade; eating and drinking places; other retail trade; business and repair services; private households, other personal services; hospitals; educational services; other professional and related services; public administration and other industries).

The library community has referred primarily to the first classification, by individual service performed, with only minor changes. In some instances, the first two categories of the nine are grouped together into a "professional and businessmen" category; (3) and (4) are grouped together in a "white collar sales and clerical" category; (5), (6), and (9) are grouped together into a "blue collar manual worker" category; and (7) and (8) are grouped together into a "service and household worker" category. Bundy (May 1967, 1968) includes two extra categories for "farm laborers and foremen" and "farmers and farm managers."

A finer segmentation of the occupation characteristic may be utilized for some library purposes to identify such specific occupations as engineers or scientists; teachers; governmental employees; authors; clergymen; draftsmen; editors or reporters; lawyers or judges; librarians; physicians and surgeons; social welfare workers; electrical or electronic technicians; accountants or auditors; secretaries; insurance agents, brokers, or underwriters; members of the armed forces; and executive or middle management.

A more encompassing categorization of occupations may include students, housewives, and the retired. Student categories may be preschool, elementary school, high school, college, vocational school, and graduate school. The categories may be made finer by breakdowns of individual grades and by type of school.

Individuals rarely will travel long distances for library services. (See, for example, Bundy 1968, pp. 43–44.) The branch system is designed to bring library services closer to more people. Also, individuals living close together tend to be relatively homogeneous with respect to any socioeconomic variables and interests. They are more likely to be involved in similar community organizations. For these reasons, *geographical area* is an important characteristic for population subsets. The categories may be determined in any manner. They may be along lines of political jurisdictions, such as county, township, or city. They may follow broad popular designations, such as Northeast Philadelphia, Northwest Philadelphia, North Central Philadelphia, West Philadelphia, South Philadelphia, and Center City. Such popular designations may be very narrow, perhaps even indicating specific neighborhoods.

Two particularly convenient methods of delineating geographical areas are by zip codes and by census tracts. Zip codes have the advantage of being part of the full addresses of users, thereby making it easier to relate library users to geographical areas. Census tracts are convenient, in that U.S. Census population data are in this form. If census tracts are too small and numerous for library purposes, they may be grouped together. Most cities combine census tracts into planning areas. For instance, the city of Philadelphia uses planning analysis sections and subsections, each of the latter including, on the average, eight census tracts. The city has 12 sections, 46 subsections, and 370 census tracts.

Certain other groups of individuals may be identified in creating population subsets. They include males, females, parents, the disadvantaged (although this class may be sufficiently defined on dimensions of educational or occupational level and geographical area), the blind, the physically handicapped, persons in hospitals and institutions, persons of different races, persons of different national origins, and persons speaking a language other than English.

Population subsets may be defined as categories with respect to any single characteristic as for instance, "adults" and "children." Also, subsets may be defined by associating categories with respect to different characteristics. Some of the many possibilities are "preschoolers in a specific geographical area," "adults in a specific geographical area who speak Spanish," "juvenile nonreaders," and "adults having a low reading level." Definitions of subsets may vary for different managerial purposes.

As in the case of the population served by the public library, the population served by the *university library* has been categorized into subsets. For members of the university community, two ways of subdividing the population seem significant. The first way is in terms of university affiliation: undergraduate student, graduate student, staff, and faculty. The second way is in terms of subject area of interest. For purposes of this classification, *subject areas* are defined as subdivisions of an academic discipline in which the subject matter or knowledge of any particular subject area is rather homogeneous. These subject areas are nonoverlapping and attempt to cover all areas of knowledge. The academic disciplines are referred to as *subject categories*. For example, physics is a subject category, whereas nuclear physics, high energy physics, solid state physics, gravitation, and astrophysics define subject areas within physics. In our studies, subject areas were defined in coordination with professors in the respective academic disciplines and library personnel at the University of Pennsylvania. The criteria for defining a subject area consisted of a combination of the way the discipline was viewed by the academic profession and what seemed to comprise a meaningful area for document selection purposes. Some consideration was also given to how these areas correspond to areas defined by the D.D. and L.C. classification systems. Appendix I is a listing of tentative subject categories developed at the University of Pennsylvania, for which instruction is offered and research is conducted. Medicine and law were excluded from the study. This listing does not presume to be a comprehensive enumeration for all academic disciplines.

When we relate the university affiliation subsets with the subject area subsets, one idiosyncrasy arises. Demand for library service seems to be more nearly linked to the activities in which the user is engaged than to the position of the user in the university community. This finding has been presented in research by McGrath, Huntsinger, and Barber (1969), and has been borne out by our own observations. For example, an undergraduate physics major consults a history document because he is enrolled in a history course, not because he is a physics major. A statistics professor borrows a library science document because he is engaged in a library science research project, not because he is a member of the statistics faculty. Each user exhibits a multiplicity of demands, most of which are related to his involvement in research and teaching aspects of the university. Hence, when these two ways of subdividing the university community are utilized simultaneously, the resulting relevant subsets are number of undergraduate students enrolled in courses that related to a particular subject area, graduate students in courses that relate to a particular subject area, full time equivalent (f.t.e.) staff conducting research relating to a particular subject area, and f.t.e. faculty teaching classes or conducting research relevant to a particular subject area. Additional subsets might be devised; for example, one could separate basic undergraduate students from advanced undergraduate students and/or establish a separate subset composed of Ph.D. candidates writing dissertations in a particular subject area.

If the university library serves members of other academic institutions and/or residents of the neighboring community, additional subsets can be defined. In these instances, subsets for members of other academic institutions can be defined in ways similar to those presented for the university community, and subsets for members of the neighboring community can

be defined in the same manner as those presented for the public library community.
Documents
Since the library objective is to maximize exposure of individuals to documents of recorded human experience, it is essential for most library-planning and decision-making purposes not only to segment the population of potential users into population subsets but also to segment the set of all documents of recorded human experience into document subsets. Just as in the case of population subsets, the creation of document subsets is a conceptualization used for managerial convenience, and, in each instance, any number and type are possible. Characteristics that could be used for segmentation include form, subject matter, reading level, language, publication date and accession date.

A segmentation of documents made almost automatically is by physical *form* or type of document. Procedures for acquisition, classification, cataloging, storage, use, and control may vary according to document form. A broad categorization of documents by form may be: books, periodicals, microforms, nonbook materials not needing special equipment for use, audiovisual materials (nonbook materials, other than microforms, needing special equipment), and materials for the blind.

A "book" is defined by the American Library Association (1966) as

A unit of publication, either bibliographically independent or a volume in a series published under the same title, consisting of leaves, sheets, or signatures sewn or otherwise bound together, covered or uncovered. Bound volumes of periodicals and newspapers are not considered books.

It is defined by the United States of America Standards Institute (1969) as

A nonperiodical printed publication of at least 49 pages, exclusive of the cover pages, published within the country and made available to the public; or a juvenile of less than 49 pages bound in hard boards whether cloth or paper covered.

The Institute defined a "nonperiodical" as a document "published at one time, or at intervals, by volumes, the number of which is generally determined in advance."

Books have been categorized broadly into "general," "textbooks," and "subscription-only reference"; into "hardbound" and "paperbook"; and into "first editions" and "re-editions." More detailed book categories may be any of the following: paperback—mass market; paperback—not mass market; imports; adult trade—hardbound; adult trade—paperbound; professional books—law; professional books—medicine; professional books—business; professional books—technical, scientific, and vocational; university press; encyclopedias; textbooks—hardbound; textbooks—teachers' editions; textbooks—paperbound; workbooks; objective tests; manuals; juvenile—under $1; juvenile—$1 and over; picture books; translations into English—by language; works in two or more languages; telephone books; and rare books.

The "periodicals collection" is defined by the American Library Association (1966) as "a library's collection of periodicals, newspapers, and other serials treated like periodicals, whether bound, unbound, or in microform." A broad categorization may be "periodicals," "newspapers," and "serials." A finer breakdown could include any of the following: professional journals, current serious feature journals, technical special audience journals; news magazines, current popular feature periodicals, sponsored periodicals, unbound periodicals, bound periodicals; reports, yearbooks (annuals), conference proceedings, and transactions of societies.

A "microform" is defined by the American Library Association (1966) as "any library material which has been photographically reduced in size for storage and protection purposes, and which must be read with the help of enlarging instruments. . . ." A microform could be considered a distinct category of document form or it could be included in the other categories of books, periodical collections, and so forth. If considered separately, finer categories may be microfilms, microcards, and microfiches.

"Nonbook material not needing special equipment for use" includes any of the following: government documents, pamphlets, theses and dissertations, catalogs (college and trade), technical reports, manuscripts, typescripts, political campaign material, community material, private archives, maps, pictures, clipping files, photographs, prints, patents, engravings, broadsheets, posters, plates, and sheet music scores. "Audiovisual material" categories may be phonograph records, tape recordings, video tapes, slides, films, filmstrips, transparencies, teaching machines, closed circuit television, and educational television. Finally, "materials for the blind" are Braille materials, large-type books, and talking book containers (discs and tapes).

Subject matter, or document content, is the most important characteristic for document segmentation. It has already been used to segment the university library population by activity. The categories with respect to this characteristic can be made very broad or extremely narrow, depending on the purpose of the segmentation. The broadest is the division into the two categories of fiction and nonfiction. The narrowest would make use of a detailed list of subject headings, such as the *Sears List of Subject Headings*, edited by Barbara Marietta Westly (1965). The various possibilities in between are indicated by the progression of categories presented in Appendix II.

Other characteristics that are useful for segmenting documents are reading or educational level, language, publication date, and accession date. The first two have also been used to segment population. Documents may be classified in exactly the same manner with respect to these two characteristics. They may also be classified according to the *reading or educational level* assumed by the author, or by *language*.

Like document form, publication date and accession date are characteristics unique to document segmentation, as opposed to population segmentation. *Publication date* is important because the usefulness of documents often declines with age. Of course, in some cases, for instance for rare books, the opposite is true.

Time may be classified in any manner to obtain categories useful for document segmentation. An appropriate set of categories for 1971 may be before 1901, 1901–1930, 1931–1950, 1951–1960, 1961–1965, 1966–1968, 1969–1970, 1971.

Accession date may be a useful characteristic for document segmentation because of its relationship to the physical deterioration of documents. Any classification of time, such as the preceding one, may be sufficient.

Document subsets may be defined with respect to any single characteristic or with respect to any combination of characteristics. Some possibilities are "books," "professional journals in the social sciences," "films on biology for high school students," "college textbooks in mathematics published on or after 1960," and "Spanish language documents."

Functions

In the process of bringing together users and documents, certain activities are performed, in one way or another, by all libraries. It is conceptually convenient to divide library activity into specific functions. We have identified seventeen functions, which are a combination of services offered to users and operations necessary for internal library use. The functions are so defined that they do not overlap and they cover all possible library activities. Hence, virtually every activity a library performs can be classified under one and only one function. Table 3.3 lists and groups these functions into five major areas: providing physical facilities; providing access to documents within the library; providing access to documents in other libraries; promoting library use; and planning, administration, and support. These major areas evolved by grouping the functions according to similarity of the output of each function.

A sixth major area may be formed if it is deemed necessary to group together all library activity that is aimed at identifying and locating documents and conveying information, as opposed to providing access to documents. The area would include function 7, classification and cataloging; the part of the activity in functions 4, 5, 6, 8, 9, and 10, which involves indexes (bibliographies, abstracts, book indexes, periodical indexes, computer citation services, and so forth); function 11, provision of aids to locate documents in other libraries; and function 13, personal assistance for

Table 3.3. Library Functions

Providing Physical Facilities
1. Provision of building area
2. Provision of user furnishings
3. Maintenance of facilities

Providing Access to Documents within the Library
4. Selection of documents and indexes
5. Acquisition of documents and indexes
6. Processing of documents and indexes
7. Classification and cataloging of documents and indexes
8. Control of document and index location and use
9. Facilitation of document and index use
10. Maintenance and weeding of documents and indexes

Providing Access to Documents in Other Libraries
11. Provision of aids primarily to locate documents in other libraries
12. Facilitation of access to documents in other libraries

Promoting Library Use
13. Personal assistance for document identification and location and for conveying information
14. Publications, advertisements, and exhibits
15. Personal communication at the initiative of the library with members of the population being served

Planning, Administration, and Support
16. Planning and administration
17. Support

document identification and location and for conveying information.

The activities performed and decisions made by most libraries will now be enumerated utilizing the set of functions as a framework.

1. PROVISION OF BUILDING AREA. This function is addressed primarily to the provision of library units over a long-range planning horizon. A library unit is defined as an individual building or as a segment of a large building which the library prefers to consider separately. Expenditures in this area are capital in nature and include all costs required to prepare a building for occupancy. Activities in this function include provision of user study area, user recreation and service area (snack bar, rest rooms, telephones, and so on), lecture and meeting rooms, document storage area, library staff area, heating equipment, air-conditioning equipment, lighting fixtures, and other equipment normally considered to be a permanent part of the building.

Decisions relevant to this library function include those concerning

(a) Number of library units
(b) Location of each library unit
(c) Size and arrangement of user area, document storage area, and staff area for each library unit
(d) Number, type, size, and routing of mobile units (public libraries)
(e) Temperature control, humidity control, and lighting equipment for each library unit
(f) Number of hours open per time period for each library unit
(g) Design and construction of new library units

2. PROVISION OF USER FURNISHINGS. Included in this function are those furnishings demanded by patrons when using the library. Desk-chair combinations (carrels), table-chair arrangements, and lounge chairs represent the major items of user furnishings. Other items provided for user comfort might include coatracks, rugs, individual table lamps, curtains, and so on. As in the case of providing building area, outlays within this function are considered to be capital expenditures.

Decisions within this function are made concerning

(a) Number and types of seating to be provided (desk-chairs, table-chairs, and lounge chairs)
(b) Other user furnishings to be provided

3. MAINTENANCE OF FACILITIES. Subsumed under this function are those ac-

tivities generally considered necessary for the operation of a building including janitorial service, heating, air conditioning, lighting, insurance, and equipment and building repairs.

Decisions are required regarding
(a) Janitorial services
(b) Temperature control
(c) Lighting control
(d) Insurance (building)
(e) Repair of equipment and building

4. SELECTION OF DOCUMENTS AND INDEXES. This function is addressed to the process of determining which documents and indexes will be added to the library collection.

Within this function, decisions are made concerning
(a) Choice of documents with regard to subject matter, type, form, comprehension level, language, and publication date
(b) Document purchase price
(c) Duplicate copies
(d) Choice of selection mechanism (reviews, examination copies, patron recommendations, committees, and so on)
(e) Time duration between publication date and selection date
(f) Selection of indexes

5. ACQUISITION OF DOCUMENTS AND INDEXES. Activities here include ordering, monitoring orders, receiving, and payment procedures for those documents and indexes selected.

Decisions relevant to this function include those concerning
(a) Choice of source of documents and indexes (jobbers, direct from publisher, and so on)
(b) Ordering procedure (coordination of orders, priorities, and so on)
(c) Time duration between selection and ordering of documents
(d) Receipt and payment procedures

6. PROCESSING OF DOCUMENTS AND INDEXES. Activities within this function are addressed to preparations required to increase the longevity of these documents and indexes to make them easier to handle and use. Additional activities include the marking of call numbers, the pasting of charge slips, and so on.

Decisions in this area are concerned with
(a) Binding of new documents and indexes (choice of binder, type of binding, and so on)

(b) Marking and labeling of new documents
(c) Jacketing of new documents
(d) Time duration for document preparation

7. CLASSIFICATION AND CATALOGING OF DOCUMENTS AND INDEXES. Included in this function are classification systems for assisting user browsing, catalogs listing library documents by author, title, and subject relevance, directional signs and explanatory placards, and any system that communicates current status of a given document to the patron.

Within this function, decisions are required concerning
(a) Choice of classification system (Dewey Decimal, Library of Congress, other, none)
(b) Use of preprinted cards
(c) Desired precision of individual document classification
(d) Number, location, form, and coverage of catalogs
(e) Directional signs and placards
(f) Communication to users regarding status of document not in specified location

8. CONTROL OF DOCUMENT AND INDEX LOCATION AND USE. Activities in this function include registration of patrons, storage of documents, circulation service, document loans to other libraries, periodical control, reserve service, reshelving of documents and security of documents.

Decisions in this area are concerned with
(a) Who may use the library
(b) Mechanism for granting user privileges
(c) Alternative document storage locations
(d) Number and type of shelves for storage locations
(e) Organization of documents on shelves
(f) Whether each storage location should be open or closed access
(g) Alternative use periods (including whether or not document can be removed from the library and renewal policy)
(h) Determination of storage location and use period for each document
(i) Choice and implementation of charging systems
(j) Limit on number of documents that can be taken out on loan by one user
(k) Overdue notices, penalties, and enforcement of penalties
(l) User requests for documents out on loan
(m) Routing of documents upon return
(n) Shelving and reshelving of documents

(o) Lost or damaged documents or cards
(p) Security of documents (guards, detection system, and so on)

9. FACILITATION OF DOCUMENT AND INDEX USE. Included in this function are microform readers, tape recorders, record players, movie projectors, slide projectors, and other equipment necessary for patron use of special document forms. In addition, other activities facilitating a patron's use of documents are included here such as microform copiers, photocopy service, document delivery service, and so forth.

Decisions in this function include those concerning
(a) Microform equipment
(b) Audio equipment
(c) Visual aid equipment
(d) Photocopy service
(e) Document delivery service

10. MAINTENANCE AND WEEDING OF DOCUMENTS AND INDEXES. This function covers the activities required to insure a vibrant document collection. Included here are weeding of documents whose subject matter is obsolete, binding of documents that have physically deteriorated, and tracing documents that are missing.

Decisions relevant to this function include those concerning
(a) Prevention of document deterioration
(b) Criteria for repairing, discarding, removing to a different location, preserving document content via microfilming, and so on
(c) Frequency and intensity of effort
(d) Choice of binding, bindery, and so on
(e) Tracing of lost documents

11. PROVISION OF AIDS PRIMARILY TO LOCATE DOCUMENTS IN OTHER LIBRARIES. This function includes those activities necessary to obtain indexes and catalogs describing individual library holdings. Also included here is activity directed toward compiling and updating holdings of libraries within a regional interlibrary cooperative system.

Decisions in this function are concerned with
(a) Choice of indexes and catalogs of holdings of one or more libraries (subject area covered, types of documents covered, dates covered, and libraries)
(b) Cooperation in compiling interlibrary catalogs of holdings

12. FACILITATION OF ACCESS TO DOCUMENTS IN OTHER LIBRARIES. Activities in this function define the library's ability to reach out to other libraries to

satisfy user needs that cannot be met directly by the user's library. Included in this function are interlibrary document loan service, user reciprocity agreements and photocopy service.

Decisions relevant to this function are those concerning
(a) Choice of libraries to be dealt with
(b) Types of service (user reciprocity, document loan service, photocopy service, and so on)
(c) Interlibrary payments
(d) Assistance offered in aiding user to obtain documents
(e) Choice of mechanism for requesting, receiving, controlling, and returning documents

13. PERSONAL ASSISTANCE FOR DOCUMENT IDENTIFICATION AND LOCATION AND FOR PROVIDING INFORMATION. Activities within this function correspond to what is generally considered to be reference service. These activities include assisting patrons in the use of indexes and catalogs, assisting users to complete or verify an individual citation, compiling a bibliography, directing a patron to a particular document, and providing specific information either directly to the user or via telephone.

Decisions must be made concerning
(a) Intensity of reference service
(b) Specialization of reference personnel
(c) Telephone service

14. PUBLICATIONS, ADVERTISEMENTS, AND EXHIBITS. Activities in this function can be characterized as promotion of library use by means of methods other than direct personal contact. Examples include publications, advertisements, and exhibits, all designed to inform the population being served as well as to stimulate its interest in using the library.

Decisions in this function include those concerning
(a) Publication of user guides, acquisition lists, current awareness lists, calendars of events, and so on
(b) Advertisements in various media
(c) Exhibits

15. PERSONAL COMMUNICATION AT THE INITIATIVE OF THE LIBRARY WITH MEMBERS OF THE POPULATION BEING SERVED. Activities in this function are concerned with promotion of library use by means of personal communication. Included are such activities as communication and liaison visits to organizations comprised of members of the population being served; lectures, classes, and events designed to bring members of the population to

the library; and tours and courses designed to explain what the library offers and how a person might utilize library services.

Decisions in this function include those concerning
(a) Communication with schools, businesses, community organizations and individuals (public library)
(b) Liaison visits with faculty and student groups (university library)
(c) Lectures, classes, and events
(d) Tours and instruction on library use

16. PLANNING AND ADMINISTRATION. Activities in this function include those for overall library planning, for budgeting, procuring, allocating, controlling, and accounting of funds, for specification of staff positions, for recruitment, processing, training, and administration of personnel, and for general administration of activities that are either of a recurring or special nature.

Decisions here include those concerning
(a) Choice of programs and projects
(b) Budgeting
(c) Obtaining funds
(d) Accounting and controlling of funds
(e) Reports
(f) Specification of staff positions
(g) Recruitment and selection of personnel
(h) Salary and fringe benefits
(i) Personnel promotions
(j) Personnel training
(k) Insurance

17. SUPPORT. Activities within this function include printing and duplication service, internal communication, purchase and distribution of office supplies, and other supporting activities.

Decisions must be made regarding
(a) Printing and duplication
(b) Internal communications (mail, interoffice telephones, and so on)
(c) Purchase and distribution of office supplies and equipment

Organization

The manner in which library activities are administratively grouped differs from library to library. In public libraries, library units sometimes conform to population categories (special user departments), document categories (newspapers, films, subject departments, and so on), or functions (acquisitions, cataloging, binding, circulation, public relations, and so on). Other library units, such as branches, may be uniquely defined on the organization dimension (although a branch may be thought of as serving a specific population category defined geographically).

In a typical university library, the library units are composed of departmental libraries and technical processing operations. Other library units might be specified to include certain administrative support units such as data processing, payroll and accounting, and so forth.

Example of a Public Library Program Structure

An example of a program structure for a large public library is given in Appendix III. Program categories are grouped into four major areas, by function (the functional major areas of promoting library use and providing access to documents within the library are initially grouped together in order to subdivide them first by population):

1. Programs to provide physical facilities
2. Programs to promote library use and to provide access to documents within the library
3. Programs to provide access to documents in other libraries
4. Programs to provide general planning, administrative, and support activities

Programs are also subdivided for managerial convenience in distinguishing between various parts of programs. Some programs are subdivided in great detail along many dimensions, while others are subdivided very little. For identification convenience, let us call the subdivisions, in the order of greatest aggregation: program, subprogram, element, component, task, subelement, subcomponent, and subtask. These names are given to subdivisions merely for convenience in referring to various parts of a program. There is no implication that, for instance, all components of various programs, or even the programs themselves, are of equal importance.

The purpose of program group 1 is to provide physical facilities. Programs are formulated by geographical area, which is a population subset. Subprograms are classified by each physically separate library unit that either exists or is proposed in the geographical area. Elements are building area, user furnishings, and maintenance. Building area components are user, document storage, and staff areas. User area tasks are document exposure area and user service area (rest rooms, snack bar, telephones, and so forth). Document exposure area subelements, as well as document storage area and staff area tasks, are physical area and environment (heating, air conditioning, and lighting). User furnishing components are seating and other furnishings. Seating tasks include carrels, table-chair combinations, and lounge chairs. Maintenance components are janitorial service and repair and replacement.

Program group 2, whose purpose is to promote library use and to provide access to documents within the library, has four programs. The first three programs apply to three population groups:
(a) Adults and young adults
(b) Children
(c) Special population subsets

The fourth program includes document access activities, a group of functions that are typically undifferentiated by population subset.

Program 2.1 is to promote library use and select documents for the general adult and young adult population. Program 2.2 is to promote library use and select documents for the general population of children. Both programs are subdivided in the same manner. Subprograms are the promotion of library use and the selection of documents and indexes. Promotion of library use elements are providing publications, advertisements, and exhibits (each of which is a component), and personal communication. Publication tasks are user guides, selected bibliographies, and calendars of events. Each of these tasks has a subelement for the whole library and for each library unit. Exhibit tasks are also classified by library unit.

Components of the personal communication element in the first two programs are (1) library initiative and (2) assistance for document identification and location, and for information. Library initiative tasks are divided by geographical area. Subelements within each geographical area are communication outside the library (with schools, businesses, community organizations, and individuals) and are then classified by library unit. Tasks for the "assistance" component are shown by library units; subelements are in-person service and telephone service; and in-person service subcomponents are general service and subject matter.

The second subprogram in programs 2.1 and 2.2. is the selection of documents and indexes. Elements are the organization of the selection procedure and its implementation. The latter element is further subdivided first by library unit, then by document subset (defined by form, subject matter, reading or educational level, language, or publication date), and finally into documents and indexes.

Program 2.3 is the promotion of library use and the selection of documents for special population subsets. Subprograms are defined by the various special population subsets, such as the blind; the disadvantaged; persons of different languages, national origins, or races; the physically handicapped; persons in hospitals and institutions; and so forth.

Program 2.4 is the performance of necessary document access activities that are typically undifferentiated by population subset. Subprograms are the acquisition of documents; the aiding of document search within the library by classifying, cataloging, and placarding; the processing of documents; the control of location and use of documents; the facilitation of document use; and the maintenance and weeding of documents. Acquisition elements are the ordering of documents and the reception of documents. Elements to aid document search are classifying, cataloging, and providing directional and explanatory placards. Cataloging components are individual entries and processing, the latter including tasks for preparation, dissemination, and maintenance. Components for placards are shown by library unit. Processing elements are binding and marking, labeling, and pasting. Elements of the control of location and use are classified by library unit, and components are storage, circulation, and security. Circulation tasks are granting user privileges, charging documents to users, and loans to other libraries. Elements for facilitation of document use are given by library unit, and components are accessory equipment (tasks are microform readers and audiovisual equipment), copy service, and other facilitation services. Elements of maintenance and weeding are the determination of documents needing special action (components by library unit) and acting upon specific documents. Components for the latter are rebinding and repairs, relocating, discarding, and tracing.

Program group 3 is the provision of access to documents in other libraries. Program 3.1 is the formation of interlibrary catalogs of holdings. Subprograms are assistance in the compilation of interlibrary catalogs and arrangement for use of interlibrary catalogs by users of the library. Program 3.2 is the coordination and administration of interlibrary access agreements. Program 3.3. is the assistance of users in obtaining documents from other libraries. Subprograms are requesting, receiving, controlling, and returning documents.

The purpose of program group 4 is to provide general planning, administrative, and support activities. Programs are planning and administering library service and providing support services. Subprograms for the former are preparing programs, projects, and budgets; performing financial administration (elements are handling payments and receipts, and performing accounting procedures); preparing reports; administering personnel activities (elements are specifying staff positions, recruiting and selecting personnel, establishing salary and fringe benefits, promoting, and training); and performing other administrative services, as required. Finally, subprograms of the support services program are providing office supplies (elements are purchase and distribution); providing printing and duplication service; and providing internal communications (elements are telephones and mail).

The full program structure is presented in outline form as Appendix III.

Example of a University Library Program Structure

In this section an example is given of how a university library program structure might be developed. There are six programs in all, five of which are user-oriented programs. The last program is composed of activities that are not easily related to user service.

Program I is directed toward providing space and furnishings for use by library patrons (student and faculty). At the subprogram level, provision of user area and furnishings are considered by library units (that is, departmental libraries, and so on). Provision and maintenance of physical facilities for areas utilized for document storage and for areas used by library staff are not considered part of Program I.

Providing access to documents within the library is the substance of Program II. The subprogram of managing document collections is further subdivided in terms of the subject categories defined in Appendix I. The subprograms of controlling use and location of documents and facilitating document use are subdivided on a library unit basis. Providing indexes, classifying documents and providing catalogs are not considered part of this program. These activities appear in Program IV.

Program III deals with activities necessary to provide access to documents in other libraries. This program, except under special circumstances, would not normally be subdivided by library units.

Program IV is concerned with providing aids to assist patrons in identifying and locating documents to satisfy an information need. In addition, the service of providing personal assistance for document identification and location and that of providing information are included here. These services are defined as subprograms on a library unit basis with two exceptions. Assistance in compiling an interlibrary catalog of holdings would be provided on a library-wide basis. Further provision of indexes might be accomplished on a subject category or group of subject categories basis.

Promotion of library use comprises Program V. The subprograms of publications, advertisements, and exhibits; and personal communication would be further divided by library units.

The last program, Program VI, is composed of library-wide administrative and planning activities, support activities, and provision and maintenance of area utilized by the library staff. Only library-wide planning and administration activity is included here. For example, supervision of circulation service would be included in Program II. For the most part, it is difficult to relate activities included in this program with service requested by or offered to users.

It may be noted that this program structure cuts across organizational lines in some instances. As indicated previously, this is not important. What is important is to be able to determine benefits imparted to users in relation to resource inputs. This program structure is presented in outline form as Appendix IV.

Program Evaluation

In Chapter 2, we developed difference and ratio measures of library performance for the entire library. Now we will extend these measures to relate exposure and costs associated with any identifiable subset of library activity. A program (activity, category, or package of program activities) may be evaluated by predicting its effect on exposure and costs over time. In this context, allocation decisions must be made in order to identify the specific exposure, costs, and population associated with the program. Analysis of past effects of programs on benefits and costs may be useful in predicting future effects.

Generally, the initiation of a program (activity) or a change in the program affects the level of library service. A change in the level of library service means a change in the same direction of library activity, which in turn means a change in the extent of document exposure. In addition, an increase in document exposure may necessitate an increase in the level of service and in costs for document control (circulation, in-library use, periodical control, and so on). In order to evaluate any program change or program package, we must estimate the exposure and cost changes caused by the program change or associated with the program package. The estimation must include effects that occur not only in the present year but also in future years. A discounting procedure is needed to combine estimated exposure and cost changes over time into one measure.

We define

E_t = exposure in year t (where $t = 0$ for current year, $t = 1$ for next year, and so on) attributed to a given program or program package

C_t = cost in year t attributed to a given program or program package

r = the interest rate applicable to government projects

V = the imputed monetary value to society of one exposure hour

Receipts (or payments) of X dollars or something having a value of X dollars, today, next year, and t years from now are not the same things. The sooner money, or something having a monetary value, is received, the sooner it can be put to work to earn money. The later money is to be paid, fewer current dollars need to be set aside to ensure the payment. In fact, P_0 dollars (or dollar value) today is equivalent to $P_0 (1 + r)$ dollars next year, and to $P_t = P_0(1 + r)^t$ dollars t years from now. Therefore, in order to convert dollars or dollar value received or paid in year t to dollars received or paid today, we must divide by $(1 + r)^t$. The result is the discounted present value of future receipts or payments.

As stated in Chapter 2, exposure has an imputed monetary value. Therefore, predicted exposure over time must be discounted. The discounted present value of exposure attributed to a given program or program package is

$$\sum_t \left[\frac{V}{(1+r)^t}\right] E_t = V \sum_t \frac{E_t}{(1+r)^t}. \tag{3.1}$$

Similarly, the discounted present cost attributed to a given program or program package is

$$\sum_t \frac{C_t}{(1+r)^t}. \tag{3.2}$$

The difference measure is

$$\sum_t \frac{VE_t}{(1+r)^t} - \sum_t \frac{C_t}{(1+r)^t} = \sum_t \frac{VE_t - C_t}{(1+r)^t}. \tag{3.3}$$

The ratio measure is

$$\frac{V \sum_{t} \frac{E_t}{(1+r)^t}}{\sum_{t} \frac{C_t}{(1+r)^t}}. \tag{3.4}$$

In the ratio measure, the V value may be eliminated; V is needed only in the difference measure, where subtraction is required. There V affects the subtraction by allowing us to express benefits in the same monetary unit as costs. Since there is no subtraction in the ratio measure, use of V is optional. If V is used, the ratio measure expresses the average dollar value of benefits per dollar of costs. If V is not used, the ratio measure expresses the average number of exposures (or exposure time) per dollar of costs.[1]

Programs or program packages with the highest expected discounted benefits less costs or benefits per unit cost are adopted.

The preceding measures may be used if all exposures (counts, item-use-days, or hours) are given equal weight. In Chapter 2, we stated that a library manager may choose to weight exposures. Weighting may be accomplished by delineating exposure into population and document subsets and by making relative value judgments for each exposure type. If M population subsets and N document subsets are formulated, then $M \times N$ estimates of exposure, relative value, and costs are made, one for each pair of population and document subsets.

Let E_{ijt} = change in exposure (number of exposures, item-use-days, or exposure hours) of persons in population subset i to documents of document subset j in year t, where t runs from 0 (present year) to T (last year in planning period), associated with a program change.

V_{ij} = the relative social value of an exposure, an item-use-day, or an exposure hour by a person in population subset i to a document of document subset j.

The V_{ij} are conceptual variables, ranging from zero to one, that incorporate into the library performance measure all that is known about the relative social value of exposure between individuals and documents. The library director may attribute $V_{ij} = 0$ to exposures that, in his opinion, have

1. It may be noted that, for simplicity, the same V value has been assumed over time in this model. This assumption was made because of the difficulty in predicting temporal changes in the imputed monetary value to society of an exposure hour. Of course, the model can be generalized to take such changes into account by the use of V_t rather than V.

no social value. For instance, the document subset(s) relating to very cheap novels may have a zero or close to zero relative value, perhaps regardless of the population subset. On the other hand, the director may consider that if adults of a very low reading level were to be exposed to these novels, the positive experience may be an incentive to further document exposure. In this case, a higher V_{ij} may be attributed to this exposure. He may assign $V_{ij} = 1$ to exposures that he considers to have the highest social values.

In this case, the difference measure is

$$\sum_t \frac{\sum_i \sum_j (V_{ij} E_{ijt}) - C_t}{(1+r)^t}. \tag{3.5}$$

The ratio measure is

$$\frac{\sum_i \sum_j \sum_t \frac{V_{ij} E_{ijt}}{(1+r)^t}}{\sum_t \frac{C_t}{(1+r)^t}}. \tag{3.6}$$

The major task in utilizing these program evaluation procedures is to estimate the changes in exposure and costs resulting from a program change, a specific library decision, or a program package. In Chapter 4, we will investigate how mathematical models may be used to trace the impact of various decision alternatives upon performance and to select the one alternative that yields the best performance.

Conclusion

The main components of a management system are statistical data and information, analytical tools, and a process for planning and decision making. Elements of a systematic process for planning and decision making, of which PPBS is a good example, are establishing objectives and performance measures, selecting the form of the program structure, specifying constraints, specifying alternative programs and input and output indicators, specifying alternative levels of output and determining the feasibility of various program packages, predicting the effect of feasible program packages on the library performance measure and selecting one package, updating a multiyear program and financial plan, and preparing the annual budget.

A library may design its program structure along dimensions of population, documents, functions, and organization. Characteristics used to distinguish the population of public library users are age, reading or educational levels, occupation, geographical area, and such specially identifiable groups as males, females, parents, the disadvantaged, the blind, the physically handicapped, persons in hospitals and institutions, persons of different races or national origins, or persons speaking a language other than English. For the university library, population characteristics are university affiliation or activity and subject matter. Document characteristics are form, subject matter, reading or educational level, language, publication date, and accession date. We have delineated 17 functions: 3 for providing physical facilities, 7 for providing access to documents within the library; 3 for providing access to documents in other libraries; 2 for promoting library use; and 2 for planning, administration, and support. Finally, programs may be defined with respect to library units in the organizational structure. Typical public library and university library program structures have been presented.

A program activity, a program package, or a decision variable affecting a change in a program activity may be evaluated by identifying and estimating incremental changes in exposure and costs over time. The measures are expected discounted benefits less costs or benefits per unit cost. In addition to discounting the value of exposures and costs over time, different types of exposure may be given different weights. In the next chapter, we explore the library decision areas in which mathematical models may be used to predict the changes in library performance that are the result of program changes.

4

LIBRARY MODELS AND EMPIRICAL FINDINGS

Introduction

In today's large organizations, decisions made solely on the basis of managerial intuition cannot possibly take into consideration the many infinitely complex interrelationships that exist. A logical framework is needed in order to coordinate all that is known about various aspects of the organizational environment and in order to facilitate decision making in accordance with overall objectives.

The essence of a more scientific approach to decision making is the construction of models. The most useful models are representations of the relevant properties of reality, and are usually mathematical in nature. In general, important system variables are defined and measured, and observations of reality and managerial insight are combined to form relationships. These relationships may be used to describe and explain the past, to exercise control in the present, and to predict the future.

Models may be used to trace the impact of various decision alternatives upon the performance of the organization and to choose the one alternative that yields the best performance. In order to achieve these results, a model must contain five basic elements:

1. A performance measure that ascertains the degree of attainment of objectives (objective function)
2. The variables that are subject to the control of the decision maker (controllable decision variables or alternatives)
3. The factors that affect performance but are not subject to the control of the decision maker (uncontrollable variables or parameters)
4. A functional relationship between the controllable variables, the parameters, and the measure of performance
5. A specification of constraints on the controllable variables.

The more relevant details included in a model, the more accurate is its representation of reality likely to be. However, too much complexity impedes derivation of solutions to decision problems. Therefore, model building involves a delicate balance between accuracy and manageability.

A particularly useful characteristic of a decision model is that it indicates the data that are relevant for analyzing the decision alternatives. In this respect, models are helpful in the design of a data system (see Chapter

5). However, it is not true that models automatically determine the data to be collected. An additional balance in model building is between collection of "ideal" data and use of available data; models may be modified to take advantage of available data.

It is important to realize that scientific decision making does not eliminate the use of management intuition. An effective combination of decision models and management insight results in better decision models and a higher level of insight. The manager then is able to ask "what if" type questions, in which he hypothesizes the implementation of various policy alternatives and evaluates their effects on performance.

University and large public libraries are complex organizations. Library managers allocate resources to a very wide variety of services for users. In Chapter 3, we stated the major library functions, and for each function we enumerated the important decisions involved. Mathematical decision models may be useful in connection with any of these decisions.

In this chapter, we summarize some of the more significant existing library models and quantitative formulations of empirical findings.[1] These models are presented according to their application to appropriate library decisions and functions. We make every attempt to summarize the quantitative material in a manner that can be comprehended by a librarian. These summaries are intended to give the reader a feel for the research performed in this area. The goal is to present available tools so that the library will be motivated to involve quantitatively oriented people in the solution of its problems and so that librarians will be able to communicate effectively with these people. Readers interested in further depth or in a particular model should consult the basic reference.

Provision of Building Area

Centralization versus Decentralization

An important decision is the determination of the viability of a branch of a public library or a university departmental library. The main library can more easily satisfy requests by a variety of users for a variety of library materials but generally at the expense of greater user transportation effort. The branch library or departmental library is located more conveniently to many users and may have other convenience aspects for users who need

---

1. The cutoff date for inclusion in this review is January 1972. Of course, there have been a number of significant contributions since that date.

only certain specialized library services, but it is less likely than the main library to be able to satisfy a given request.

1. Brookes (1970, *J. of Librarianship;* 1970, *Information Storage and Retrieval*) makes an admirable first attempt at quantifying some of the significant factors inherent in this area. He looks at the situation in which the user can either visit the main library or the branch to satisfy his request. He assumes that the main library can satisfy all requests but that the branch can satisfy, on the average, only a certain proportion p of all requests (p is the probability of satisfying any given request). For a given user, there is a certain cost c in time, money, and effort of getting to the branch, which may be expressed in any convenient unit. Useful results may be obtained without calculating c directly, a fortunate situation because of foreseeable measurement problems. There is also a cost in visiting the main library. The ratio a of the cost of visiting the main library to the cost of visiting the branch is utilized. An additional variable B is the expected proportion of users who will visit the branch first. (The symbol B is also the probability that a given user will visit the branch first.)

Brookes calculates the expected user cost of satisfying a request. It is expressed in terms of probabilities of visiting the main library or the branch first, the probability of satisfaction at the branch, the cost of visiting the branch, and the relative cost of visiting the main library instead of the branch. That is, it is expressed in terms of B, p, c, and a.

If we assume that a user tries to minimize the expected cost of satisfying his request, it is shown that he will go to the branch first only if the branch has sufficient resources so that the probability of it satisfying his request is greater than the reciprocal of the ratio of costs ($p > 1/a$). If all potential users have the same cost ratio, then the branch must satisfy at least the reciprocal of the ratio ($1/a$) for it to be used at all by rational users. Assuming that potential library documents are successfully ordered in terms of relative popularity, then the Bradford-Zipf law of scattering is used to show that a minimum viable library collection, satisfying $1/a$ of the demands, is $s(N/s)^{1/a}$, where N is the set of all possible library documents considered and s is a characteristic of the specificity of the subject matter. (See Equation 4.4 and the related discussion of the Bradford law of scattering.)

Brookes illustrates use of a macroeconomic approach to model construction. He believes that a good deal can be learned about the library by hypothesizing relationships between a small number of significant variables.

Increasing detail may be added specifically when needed. This approach is in contrast to that of simulation, which attempts to imitate reality by piecing together into a model all identifiable details.

2. Brookes also applies the Bradford-Zipf law to another aspect of the extent of decentralization in Brookes (Mackenzie and Stuart, eds., 1969). For a library system with a central library containing N periodicals relevant to a given subject, a total population of R potential users, and r branches, he determines the number of the most frequently used titles to be kept at each of the branches in order to minimize total user and purchase cost.

The Bradford-Zipf law states that if N periodical titles are ranked according to usefulness, then the number of uses of the n most used periodicals is $N \log(n/s)$, where s is a characteristic of the subject matter. Therefore, if a branch holds the n most useful titles, it accounts for $N \log(n/s)$ uses, and the remaining $N \log(N/s) - N \log(n/s) = N \log(N/n)$ uses are at the central library. If user cost for visiting a branch is α and for visiting the central library is β, then total user cost is $R(\alpha N \log(n/s) + \beta N \log(N/n))$. If A is the average procurement cost of a title, then the purchase cost is $A(m + N)$. The proportion of titles to be kept at each branch, which results in minimum total cost, is $n/N = (R/r)(\beta - \alpha)/A$. In other words, in order to minimize total cost, the model suggests more decentralization (and more duplication of titles) as the number of uses per branch library increases, as the difference between user costs of the central and branch libraries increases, and as the cost of procurement decreases.

3. Morse (1972) investigates the effects of decentralization on different classes of university library users. Reliance on storage of library materials at decentralized levels makes the materials more accessible to most users, thereby reducing user time, effort, and cost. Decentralization, on the other hand, is accomplished at the expense of duplicating costs of purchase and storage and at the expense of additional cost to the interdisciplinary users. Morse demonstrates that the geometric probability distribution[2] represents

2. A probability distribution is a convenient way of expressing the likelihood of various events. It is one of the most basic and important tools in quantitative analysis. Events usually are expressed numerically by means of a random variable, which takes on numerical values, each of which is uniquely associated with an event. In this case, the events are: a user performs no tasks during a visit (random variable = 0); a user performs a task in a visit (random variable = 1); a user performs two tasks (random variable = 2); and so on. Each probability distribution is a compact, mathematical expression of the nature of the process underlying the likelihood of the events. There are a number of special probability distributions that are often used to describe certain types of processes. Some of these distributions to which reference is

the number of tasks of a specific kind performed by a user during a visit. He samples to determine the average number of times a user affiliated with subject class 1 uses subject class 2, and vice versa, in a library containing both subject classes (for instance, chemists using physics books and physicists using chemistry books). From these data and simple inferences based on the geometric probability distribution, he obtains the fraction of trips, for each user type, in which the user consults the other subject class. These fractions, multiplied by the average number of visits by users of each type, yield the additional numbers of trips caused by decentralization of the subject classes into two departmental libraries.

4. Buckland, Hindle, Mackenzie, and Woodburn (1970) consider satisfaction of user demand at various library levels. The university library user is viewed as having four distinct levels of accessibility: (1) a personal collection; (2) a departmental collection; (3) a university library; and (4) other university libraries and national libraries. Each individual holds a title in his personal collection if his demand or use rate is at least at a certain minimum level. Each departmental library holds a title if the residual demand rate for the title, that is, demand in excess of that which is satisfied by personal collections, exceeds a certain minimum level (which, of course, is lower than the minimum for personal collections). Analogously, a university library holds a title if the residual demand rate, consisting of demand not satisfied at lower levels, is at least at a certain marginal level. Finally, it is assumed that the national library holds all titles.

If one specifies marginal levels of demand for personal collections, departments, and universities, an overall storage and demand satisfaction policy is defined. The hierarchical model is used to analyze the relationship between the marginal levels of demand, and both overall and level operating costs, access times, and user costs.

5. Kochen and Deutsch (1969) make an attempt at a general quantitative theory of decentralization, which may be applicable to libraries. The models developed have been applied only to relatively simple situations. They express the number of facilities as a function of demand rates, distances, speed and costs of transport, the value of waiting or traveling times, and the costs of new facilities. A tentative result of their initial analysis is

---

made in this chapter are the geometric, the Poisson, the normal, the lognormal, the binomial, and the exponential. For a further description of probability distributions, see an introductory book on probability or statistics, such as Hamburg (1970).

that the models suggest smaller, more numerous, and more dispersed facilities than otherwise might be planned.

6. Summary. The extent of decentralization of library facilities is a difficult problem involving many different factors. The models referred to include some of the more quantifiable factors: relative user costs, probabilities of visits, probabilities of user satisfaction, numbers of library documents kept at branches, specificity of subject matter, procurement costs of library materials, use of various subject classes by different types of users, demand rates for titles, and costs of new facilities. These models, together with consideration of other factors, may be of great utility for decision making about decentralization of both public and university libraries.

Branch Location

1. Early operations research models have dealt with the building and locating of warehouses or plants in order to minimize the sum of the transportation costs and the investment costs. Similar models have been applied to the problem of locating public facilities in order to minimize a surrogate of social cost, subject to a constraint on the number of facilities or the amount of investment. ReVelle, Marks, and Leibman (1970) review both private and public sector location models.

Most location models are a conceptualization of a finite number of points in a network, as centers of population and facilities. For public libraries, these points could be communities (population areas) and possible branch sites. Branches are assigned to points, and people are associated with the branch placements. The assignments of branches may be made as follows:

(1) To minimize the average distance or time traveled to the library.
(2) To minimize the maximum distance or time traveled between a community and a branch.
(3) To maximize use of library facilities.

The last criterion recognizes the fact that the existence of a branch at a certain location affects the extent of demand for library service.

2. ReVelle and Swain (1970) present a simple linear programming algorithm[3] (procedure) for evaluating potential branch sites. In the algorithm,

---

3. A linear function is the sum of the product of numbers times variables. For instance, if $x, y,$ and z are variables, and $a, b,$ and c are any numbers, then $ax + by + cz$ is a linear function. For linear programming, a criterion for determining how well an organization performs is stated as a linear function of certain variables of interest. Also, any constraints which limit

m facilities are chosen for n communities, where $n \geq m$, such that each community is assigned to one and only one facility, and the average or total distance traveled is minimized. Existing facilities may be preassigned at the beginning of the algorithm. An important output is the change in distance traveled as a result of having $m + 1$ facilities instead of m.[4]

3. Osborn (1971) presents a technique for analyzing the implications for branch location of interrelationships among community activities. Specific community activities are identified, including public library activity. Judgments are made in a matrix analysis on the relative degree of dependency of each pair of activities. Activities are grouped by means of a linear graph or network consisting of a set of nodes and arcs connecting the nodes.

The analysis was performed for Thamesmead in Greater London. Although libraries were not highly related to any one specific group of activities, they did have some significant relationship to the location of shopping, education, and civic administration activities.

4. Coughlin, Taieb, and Stevens (1972), in surveying seven branches of The Free Library of Philadelphia, have developed measures useful in describing and explaining branch location. The market area of a branch is defined as the distance within which 80 percent of the users of a branch travel. Most branches surveyed have a market area of $1\frac{1}{8}$ to $1\frac{7}{8}$ miles. This area ranges between 0.4 mile and 1.2 miles for children, a somewhat higher range for teen-agers, a somewhat higher range for adults, and higher within these ranges for upper-class areas. The use rate of residents within $\frac{1}{4}$ mile of the branch is higher in upper-class areas, especially for adults. Generally, users consider the branches studied as essentially equivalent and, therefore, tend to go to the nearest one.

The base-level use rate is defined as the number of visits per year per thousand residents within $\frac{1}{4}$ mile of the library, an area in which distance does not impede use. This rate is higher for higher economic and social class areas. The variation among different economic and social class areas is much higher for adults than for children.

---

the values that the variables can take on are expressed as linear functions of one or more of the variables. The linear programming algorithm finds nonnegative values of the variables which satisfy the constraints and maximize or minimize the criterion.

4. The outputs of most computer routines for linear programming express the value of a dual variable for each constraint. If the constraint is the limitation of a resource, then the dual variable expresses the value, in terms of the criterion, of increasing the resource one unit beyond the constraint.

An alternative measure of the breadth of library services is based upon the base-level use rate. The effective service radius is defined as the distance from the library for which visits per year per thousand residents is 10 percent of the base-level use rate.

The effects of accessibility to schools and commercial areas are explored by means of two indices. For each library, a school access index is created by identifying all schools in the area, dividing the square of the distance between school and library into the number of students enrolled, and summing over all schools. Also, for each library, a commercial access index is created by drawing concentric rings around the library, dividing the average distance of the ring from the library into the acreage in the ring used for commercial land use, and summing over all rings.

Library overlap and lack of service may be highlighted by means of a visual display of market areas and effective service radii. Effective or ineffective branch characteristics may be identified by noting the proportion of the users of a particular branch who live closer to other branches or the proportion of users in the market area of a branch who use more distant branches.

For individual branches, the authors find a high correlation between per capita circulation and education, income, and professional employment variables. They indicate that the most important factor in determining branch use is the social and economic level of residents in the area, with bookstock the next important factor, and with location near a school or a shopping center as less important variables. They find that use rate by juveniles and young adults is five times higher than that of adults for upper-class areas and twenty times higher for lower-class areas.

Although the analysis is a useful first step in creating a decision model, there is no attempt to formulate a model. There is too much emphasis on gross correlation analysis, much of it with only seven data points (the seven branches), from which the authors conclude that public library use is essentially a function of the status of the neighborhood. This conclusion tends to de-emphasize any potentiality to influence library use, and, together with the lack of a decision model, gives the impression that library management is not relevant to library use.

5. Roberts (1966) describes an application of Reilly's Law, a law of retail gravitation used by market researchers in evaluating alternative sites for retail establishments, for the location of public libraries in Scunthorpe, England. Although the law has been stated in various forms, basically it

describes the market area or buying power of alternative sites as a function of the population of the geographical areas or the shopping areas of the sites and the distance between the geographical areas and the sites.

6. Summary. Quantitative managerial tools that appear useful for library branch location include general operations research location models; study of the interrelationships of community activities; measures of library market area, use rate, service radius, accessibility to schools, accessibility to commercial areas, and overlap; and retail gravitation models.

Hours

Morse (1968) performs an analysis of data on arrivals and lengths of stay of users of the M.I.T. Science Library. He shows that a Poisson distribution fits the data for arrivals, and an exponential distribution is appropriate for length of stay. These distributions can be used to determine the number of people in the library at any given period or instant of time, and the number of arrivals and departures.

Seating and Space Utilization

1. Cook (1968) maneuvered the furniture of the Undergraduate Library Building of the University of Michigan into various alternative arrangements. The results of a simulation were used to design an overall plan for space utilization in order to increase seating capacity without reducing collection size or limiting service or operating efficiency.

2. Raffel and Shishko (1969) (pp. 29–34) propose linear programming as a method for exploring the mix between different types of library seating. There is a capacity constraint, in that a certain minimum number of seats must be provided. There are preference constraints in that certain types of seating are preferred to others, with the parameters determined by sampling users. The objective is to minimize the cost needed to satisfy the constraints.

Maintenance

All equipment deteriorates or fails with usage. Maintenance activity usually permits equipment to be run at higher performance and at lower cost, but maintenance activity itself may be expensive. It may be done only upon breakdown, or a strategy of preventive maintenance may be adopted. An alternative to reparing equipment is to replace it. Replacement may be necessary when obsolescence is high or when equipment is impossible or uneconomical to replace. If there is a large number of small items that fail, a typical preventive maintenance policy is to replace them periodically, usually before breakdown.

Operations research analysts have addressed themselves to the problems of equipment maintenance and replacement that are inherent in all organizations. Techniques found to be particularly useful in this area are stochastic processes and dynamic programming.

Jardine (1970) summarizes a great deal of the work to date. It includes equipment replacement decisions, preventive maintenance and inspection decisions, spare parts supplying decisions, and renting versus owning decisions.

Libraries have their share of equipment maintenance and replacement problems. Some areas of application are audiovisual equipment, photographic reproduction equipment, bookmobiles, charging equipment, air-conditioning equipment, and even light bulbs.

Selection of Documents

Choice of Book Subject Matter and Year

1. The most significant pioneering library model-building effort is *Library Effectiveness: A Systems Approach* by P. M. Morse (MIT Press, Cambridge, Mass., 1968). It is the result of thirteen years of data gathering and analysis at the M.I.T. Science Library, and it utilizes the efforts of library operations research course projects. The models in this book are applied directly to a variety of library policy decisions. These include hours, acquisition allocation among subject fields, determination of the number of duplicate copies, storage in locations of differing accessibility, specification of circulation period or restriction to in-library use, and provision of security to reduce the number of lost documents.

Morse describes book use from a library, or the use of any library document, as a type of queuing situation. Customers arrive at a certain rate to use a book. Each copy is a service channel. The period of time between the withdrawal of a book and its return to the shelf is the service time, the reciprocal of the service rate. The queue discipline usually is first come, first served, and, when all copies are being used, a certain proportion of customers queue up by putting a "reserve" on the book.

Arrivals of users are, to a certain extent, predictable. Examination periods are particularly busy, and summer sessions are particularly slow. The rate of arrivals differs by month, week, day, time of day, and so forth. However, for initial ease of model manipulation, Morse uses one overall demand rate under the assumption of random arrivals described by the Poisson probability distribution. All books are segmented into very general subject matter subsets, and all parameters[5] are determined for each subset. An additional assumption, shown to be satisfactory in most similar situations, is that service time is distributed exponentially. In each subset, the average service time is estimated from the average number of circulations per book per year, the average number of books out on loan or to be shelved at a given time, and the number of books owned by the library.

Four different queuing models are applied to book use: two simple ones and two more complicated ones. The first model is based on the assumption that a demand is lost every time an arrival does not find the book sought; in other words, no one waits for the book. It is used throughout because of its relative ease of mathematical manipulation and because it appears to be an adequate approximation. The second model is based on the assumption that everyone who desires the book during the year puts a reserve on it and eventually obtains it. The third assumes that all wait but that there is an exponentially distributed discouragement time. The fourth is one in which a fraction of those arriving when the book is not on the shelf wait until they obtain it.

It is shown that the fraction of time a book is off the shelf can be computed from the number of circulations and the service rate. In all queuing models, this fraction is an important determinant of unsatisfied demand. Therefore, a possible managerial rule of thumb could be to purchase another copy or limit the circulation time if the fraction rises above a certain point for a period of time.

Morse then presents a Markov model of book use, along with very substantial evidence for verification with respect to the M.I.T. Science Library. Basically, the Markov model represents a system that could be in a number of different states, but the state in any given time period is dependent only on the state in the immediately preceding period. For book use, the number of circulations in a given period depends on the number

---

5. Each type of probability distribution is really a family of distributions, one for each value of the one or more uncontrollable variables, called parameters, which are used to describe each individual population of items.

in the prior period. The relationship between circulation in two successive years is plotted for each subset of books, and a linear approximation is shown to provide a good fit for all year pairs; the expected circulation in a year is a linear function of the circulation in the preceding year. Since the process of book circulation is random, the actual transition probability of circulation in two successive years has a Poisson distribution.

A number of assumptions and approximations are made in order to infer demand or number of unsatisfied users from circulation. The task, mathematically, is quite complex, but Morse's efforts appear to have yielded formulas that are sufficiently accurate for a librarian's purposes. Basically, circulation figures of books may be an automatic by-product of an adequately designed computer system. What cannot be observed are demand and unsatisfied demand. Therefore, a crucial managerial tool is a measure of the expected unsatisfied demand, given circulation is at a certain level. Morse estimates this value and then sums over all possible circulation levels to obtain the expected unsatisfied demand for one book in a subset. Multiplication by the number of books in the subset yields total unsatisfied demand for a subset of books, given certain managerial decisions.

These formulas are used to predict changes in expected unsatisfied demand upon the incorporation of specific management policies. Some policies evaluated in this manner are duplication of all books, duplication of all books circulating M or more times, reduction of the loan period on all books, and reduction of the loan period on all books circulating M or more times. This analysis may be an invaluable aid to library directors in evaluating possible alternatives in these areas.

Morse then extends the foregoing analysis to predict changes beyond the next year. In particular, he relates expected unsatisfied demand in any year and cumulative unsatisfied demand in any number of years to the circulation of a book in its first year. One use of this result is to specify the highest tolerable value of expected cumulative unsatisfied demand and then to determine the minimum implied first-year circulation for which action (duplication or change in loan period) should be taken. In other words, at the first indication that a particular book will have a first-year circulation above this value, it may be duplicated.

Alternatively, actual first-year circulation could be used to determine the expected cumulative unsatisfied demand for T years. If the probability distribution of first-year circulation is known for various document subsets, predictions of expected cumulative unsatisfied demand may be made without waiting for the actual first-year circulation, thereby estimating upon purchase the proportion of books in each subset that should be duplicated. Analysis of circulation of new books indicates that the geometric probability distribution is applicable.

Most of the data underlying these models may be obtained from circulation records. First, circulation rates are used to determine the parameter of the first-year book-use model and the parameters of the future year's Markov book-use model. Second, the critical demand variables are inferred from circulation. Third, the service rate may be determined indirectly from circulation counts or directly if the circulation records include the time between a book charge and return.

The final outputs of the models are estimates of unsatisfied demand. The models could be used to determine strategies that would keep the unsatisfied demand below some tolerable limit. Alternatively, by comparison of library expenditures and estimated cost of an unsatisfied demand, the models could be used to suggest optimal decisions. Different types of library use may be compared by estimating time spent with a book (in-library use versus home use) or by making subjective assignments of utility (for different documents or users).

Although Morse's analysis represents a major contribution, there are a number of limitations.

(1) Future demand for circulation is assumed to be solely a function of past circulation. Factors in the environment that influence demand, such as the magnitude and composition of the teaching and research efforts of the university community, are not included in the analysis.
(2) The demand rate is assumed to be constant over time. Hence, this analysis would yield questionable results in a situation in which the demand rate fluctuates over time.
(3) The part of the analysis that predicts unsatisfied demand from circulation applies only to unduplicated monographs. Hence, in a library system in which a substantial amount of duplication is present, this analysis would yield questionable results.
(4) The sole measure of library performance is unsatisfied demand. As discussed in Chapter 2, this measure ignores the aspect of library service that promotes library use.

Empirical findings and intermediate results that were incorporated into Morse's book are Bush, Galliher, and Morse (1956); Silver (1962); Rothkopf (1962); Ayres, Norris, and Robinson (1962); Scott, Sonnenblick, and

Uller (1962); Morse (1964); and Morse (1965). In addition, Elston (1966) analyzed samples of science journals left on tables in the M.I.T. Science Library. For different subjects, she analyzed use as a function of years since publication and found that the rate of decrease in use is approximately exponential; that is, the logarithm of use is linearly related to the number of years since publication. Morse and Elston (1969) contains mathematical details of the Markov model. Kraft (1970) suggests a substitution into the Markov model to make one of the linear parameters dependent on time. Morse (1972) summarizes, extends, and provides a number of practical graphical tools for use of a number of the models in his book.

2. Bommer (1971), in a doctoral dissertation written under sponsorship of the same research project as the present volume, builds upon some of the library use models developed by Morse and attempts to overcome some of their limitations. He constructs models to predict the demand rate for circulation use of titles in a subject area as a function of the circulation use rate and measures of teaching and research activity of a university, and to determine the number of new titles to purchase for a subject area, the number of multiple copies of a title to purchase for a subject area, and the number of copies of a title to place on reserve. These models have been listed and verified and relevant parameters estimated as applied to the Lippincott Library, the business departmental library that serves the Wharton School of the University of Pennsylvania.

A title selection model is developed to estimate the number of new titles to be purchased in a subject area for the highest overall library exposure per dollar. Exposure to books in a subject area is found to be a function of the number of faculty members with interests in the subject area and the number of students in courses in the subject area. Another factor affecting use is the exponential law of obsolescence. This was developed initially in the library context by analysis of journal use, but it has also been shown to represent monograph use. (See discussion under "Journal Weeding" later in this chapter.) The essence of the law is that use of a library document decreases exponentially over time. Another term reflects a law of scattering, which states that, although exposure increases with an increasing number of titles in a subject area, the incremental use of each additional title is successively smaller. The change in accumulated exposure over time due to an additional title divided by the cost of the title is equated with an estimate of the overall library benefit-cost ratio to determine the optimal number of new titles in each subject area.

3. Sinha (1971) presents an overall comprehensive collection control model for acquisition and weeding decisions. The model is used to determine how many books in each subject class, of each possible age, should be held by the library in order to maximize circulation, subject to space and budget limitations. If the model indicates that a greater number of titles for a subject class and age is required in the collection, acquisitions are in order. On the other hand, the model suggests weeding if space is needed for newer, more popular books. Specific solutions are obtained for several special cases of the general model.

4. For university libraries, McGrath, Huntsinger, and Barber (1969) relate circulation per subject category to various variables external to the library system. High positive direct correlations are observed between the number of books circulated in each subject category and the number of books published in the United States per subject category, the number of books held by the library in each subject category, the number of faculty members in departments related to each subject category, and the number of credit hours taught related to each subject category. The findings of this study suggest that variables external to the library system related to the research and teaching functions of a university can be utilized to predict demand for library services.

5. Consad Research Corporation (1968) performs a factor analysis based on usage at the Pratt Free Library in Baltimore, described by fifty-two document subjects and fifteen user occupational areas. Four underlying factors are identified which explain the variability in use over document subjects and user occupational areas. They are (1) school subjects by high school students (73.4 percent of variance explained), (2) professional subjects by professional and technical people (11.5 percent), (3) home arts by housewives (6.9 percent), and (4) college studies by college students (3.9 percent).

6. Summary. The models presented in this section enhance the librarian's decision-making capability by relating his choice of books with present and future expected unsatisfied demand, exposure, or circulation. Important considerations of these models are past circulations, the time a book is off the shelf, obsolescence, faculty interests, courses, diminishing returns of additional titles, and space and budget limitations.

Number of Copies

1. In the previous section, we described queuing models developed in Morse (1968) and in Morse (1972). The queuing models, together with

predictions of mean arrival (demand) rates and mean use time, yield estimates of unsatisfied demand for each number of copies of a book. These estimates may be used, in conjunction with managerial judgment, to determine whether or not additional copies should be purchased. If an estimate of cost of user frustration could be obtained, to be compared with the cost of book purchase, an optimal number of copies could be determined. Alternatively, division of the total number of volumes by annual circulation yields the average annual circulation of a book. Under the assumption that a book of average circulation justifies its cost, a copy should be purchased if it would satisfy a number of otherwise frustrated users that is higher than average circulation.

2. Sinha (1971) begins a cost analysis with the Morse queuing estimates of unsatisfied demand for each number of copies of a book, for the life of the title. The imputed penalty cost to the library for not satisfying a demand is the ratio between the cost of placing a given number of copies on the shelf and the cumulated unsatisfied demand estimates for that number of copies. The imputed penalty cost may be determined, for any given level of service, in terms of the maximum allowable fraction of time a title is permitted off the shelf before further duplication of copies is deemed necessary.

3. Arora and Rameshwar (1969) use marginal analysis to determine a simple mathematical expression for the optimal number of copies of titles. Grant (1971) discusses another simple mathematical expression for multiple copy determination. Neither expression has a strong logical foundation.

4. Bommer (1971) constructs a circulation demand regression model to predict the demand rate for circulation use of titles in a subject area as a function of the circulation use rate and measures of teaching and research activity of a university. He incorporates this function into a model that determines the proportion of titles to duplicate in a subject area and into another model that determines the number of copies to obtain of a title designated for reserve because of course use.

The number of circulations per title in a subject area is considered to be determined by both the extent of the demand for titles and the extent of the supply of copies. The specific factors determining circulation per title are probability distributions of demand, of multiple copies, and of existence on the shelf at any given time. For the probability distribution of demand, a truncated exponential distribution with a special probability for zero demand fits circulation data for all subject areas.

A model is constructed relating these probability functions. It can be solved to provide estimates of the mean demand rate for a collection as a function of the mean circulation rate of the collection, the distribution of multiple copies, and the mean loan period. The difference between the mean demand rate and the mean circulation rate yields the mean rate at which demands were not satisfied, a variable that is both very important in the selection process and very elusive in measurements.

In general, it is observed that demand (and circulation) increases during the first portion of a semester and then declines during the latter portion of the semester. Although time dependencies introduce further complexities, Bommer has derived a method for estimating demand (and unsatisfied demand) as it varies over a time period.

A regression analysis is performed relating the demand per title with the number of graduate students in courses in the subject area and the number of faculty with interests in the subject area. The result is a regression equation that expresses the demand per title as a function of the other two variables. In this manner, one can predict the change in demand due to imminent or hypothetical changes in courses, faculty, or faculty interests.

The circulation demand model just described produces estimates of mean yearly demand rates for each subject area. These estimates of demand are used as inputs to a multiple copy selection model. Other variables in the model include a function that reflects the exponential decrease in demand as a book ages; the mean loan period; and a queuing function that estimates the conditional probability that at least one copy of a title is on the shelf at a particular time, given the library holds n copies of the title. This model can be solved to yield an estimate of the additional number of circulations incurred by the title upon the addition of a second copy, third copy, and so on, over the useful life of the title.

The change in circulation attributed to additional copies in a subject area is expressed as a function of the proportion of titles duplicated, triplicated, and so forth. The amount of exposure per circulation and the cost of placing a copy on the shelf are utilized in constructing an incremental benefit-cost measure describing the change in exposure per dollar as a function of a change in the proportion of titles duplicated. Use of an overall library marginal benefit-cost ratio would permit the determination of an optimal multiple copy procurement strategy.

A separate model is constructed for the determination of the number of copies of a title to place on reserve. A regression analysis is performed for titles on reserve to determine the demand for these titles in the latter portion of the term, which is peak time, as a function of the number of students enrolled in the course or courses for which the book is used.

A queuing model is established that utilizes the peak time demand, the effective reserve loan period, and the maximum amount of time a student will wait for the return of a book before the demand is lost. The output of the model is the estimated number of waiting periods beyond maximum, that is, the estimated number of demands lost. A marginal benefit-cost analysis is then performed using the demand lost per term, the cost of an additional copy, and the overall library benefit-cost ratio. This analysis yields the estimated optimal number of reserve copies.

5. Another comprehensive modeling effort is Buckland, Hindle, Mackenzie, and Woodburn (1970). With regard to loan and duplication policies, both analytical and simulation models are presented. The analytical approach, details of which are in Buckland and Woodburn (June 1968), is similar to Morse's queuing model formulation but is less extensive. For a closed-access reserve collection with a fixed loan period, a Poisson probability distribution is used to relate the performance measure of the percentage of titles sought that are currently available with a given number of requests, a given loan period, and a given number of copies. Results for various combinations of these factors may be used by library managers to determine the best number of copies for each title.

In a second model, the authors include a greater degree of detail so that it will correspond more closely with the complexities of a general open-access collection. Therefore, they resort to a computer simulation model, which includes many more relationships than an analytical model but sacrifices mathematical manageability and the capability of obtaining an optimal solution to the decision problem. Morse deals with the same decision problem by formulating mathematical relationships which intuitively do not appear to correspond with reality but which yield more insight than does simulation of the relationship between such managerial decision variables as loan period and satisfied or unsatisfied demand. In contrast, the simulation is a motion picture of reality; the computer advances time in discrete intervals, and various events occur with respect to a particular book. The computer is programmed to portray the logical effects of each event. The inputs (controllable and uncontrollable variables) to the simulation are the number of demands to be simulated; the number of copies of a book; the maximum allowable reservations per book; the pattern of demand (intervals between requests); the ratio of borrowing to reference use; the loan policy, as defined by return times; the proportion of unsatisfied users who make reservations; and the delays in recalls. The computer output is the number of reference demands made, the percentage of reference demands satisfied, the number of loan demands, the percentage of loan demands satisfied eventually, the percentage of loan demands satisfied immediately, and the pattern of delays after reservations. The library manager may employ many computer runs to evaluate the outcomes resulting from various combinations of input.

6. Summary. The models used to aid in determining the number of copies of individual titles are similar to the queuing models developed for choosing books. Each of the modeling efforts presented is an attempt to create a foundation of model development which can be used simultaneously to aid in both book selection and multiple-copy determination.

Theoretical Foundation of Journal Selection

1. S. C. Bradford, while searching for papers on applied geophysics and on lubrication as director of the Science Museum Library, recognized a common pattern in the scatter of these papers among the scientific journals. He performed an analysis of these papers which he first published in Bradford (1934) and then in the book that is now very well known in the library field, *Documentation* (1948, pp. 110–120).

Bradford arranged the 326 journals containing 1332 articles on applied geophysics in descending order of the number of articles each carried on the subject, and he did the same thing for the 164 journals containing 395 articles on lubrication. In each case, he noticed a few periodicals containing a large number of articles, more periodicals containing a few articles, and many periodicals containing only one article.

Bradford ranked the journals in order of the number of articles in each. That is, the journal containing the most articles had rank 1, the second most had rank 2, and so on. For each rank, he then accumulated numbers of articles in the journal of that rank and in higher-ranked (lower numbers) journals. He then took the common logarithms (base 10) of the ranks and plotted them against the accumulated number of articles associated with the ranks.[6] That is, against the common logarithm of the accumu-

---

6. The logarithm to the base 10 of a number is the power to which 10 has to be raised to equal the number. In other words, the common logarithm of a number N, written $\log_{10} N$, is the power x that satisfies $10^x = N$. There are standard tables that are used to determine the common logarithm of any number.

lated sum of journals in order of decreasing productivity, he plotted the accumulated number of articles in these journals, resulting in a curve of the form shown in Figure 4.1. The curve rises slowly and then becomes remarkably close to a straight line. The journals ranked x or less, where x is the point at which the curve straightens out, are termed the "nucleus" of the subject in that they are the most productive journals in the subject.

Bradford defined the nucleus group as (1) those journals producing more than four references a year, and he defined two other groups as (2) those journals containing more than one but not more than four references a year and (3) those journals producing one or less a year (fractional articles are possible if the results of more than one year are averaged). The group delineations were made in this manner so that each group contained approximately the same number of articles. Bradford then noticed that the numbers of journals in the three groups, for each subject, created a geometric progression of form $1:n:n^2$. That is, the number of journals in a group is n times that of the preceding group. Thus, Bradford defined his "law of distribution of papers on a given subject in scientific periodicals" (1934, p. 86; 1948, p. 116):

If scientific journals are arranged in order of decreasing productivity of articles on a given subject, they may be divided into a nucleus of periodicals more particularly devoted to the subject and several groups or zones containing the same number of articles as the nucleus, then the numbers of periodicals in the nucleus and succeeding zones will be as $1:n:n^2$. . . .

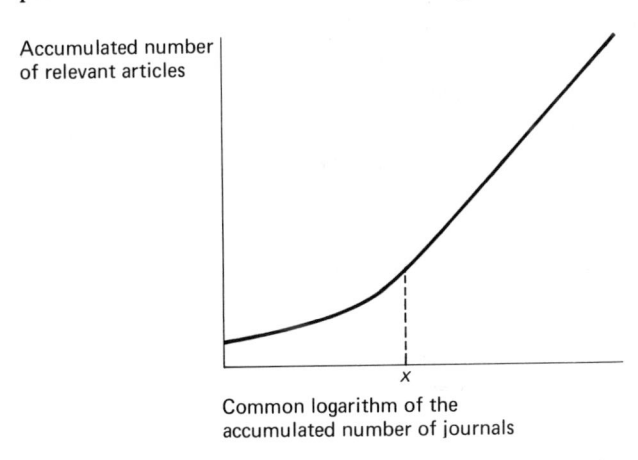

Figure 4.1. Accumulated number of relevant articles as a function of the common logarithm of the accumulated number of journals, when journals are arranged in descending order of productivity.

Bradford's law has been shown to be mathematically equivalent to empirical laws generally associated with George Kingsley Zipf. These empirical laws describe, with great regularity, a remarkably wide variety of phenomena covering almost all subject areas of the social sciences. For discussion in greater depth, see Zipf (1949), Rapaport (1957), Mandelbrot (1953; 1966), Simon (1955), Brookes (1968), Fairthorne (1969), and Naranan (1971).

2. Vickery (1948) recognized that Bradford, in his haste to emphasize the linear portion of his curve, presented a mathematical formulation that violated his law, as he himself stated it. Vickery corrected the mathematical formulation in order to reflect both the curved and linear portions of Figure 4.1.

If $R(n)$ is the cumulative total of relevant references found in the first n journals ranked 1, 2, 3, . . . in order of decreasing productivity, then Bradford's law requires

$$R(n) = R(n^2) - R(n) = R(n^3) - R(n^2) = \cdots \qquad (4.1)$$

for all integral values of n equal to or greater than one ($n \geq 1$). Vickery points out that Bradford's law applies to any number of zones.

3. Kendall (1960) applied Bradford's law to 1763 references in a bibliography of operations research published by the Operations Research Society of America in 1958. He found an identical graph to Bradford's (Figure 4.1): over a large part of the range, "the linearity is remarkable and in fact better than in Bradford's own examples." (P. 33.)

Kendall stated the Bradford-type situation in terms of a stochastic process described by Simon (1955). Let $f(i)$ be the frequency of journals containing i references.

(1) If p articles have appeared, the probability that a new $(p + 1)^{\text{th}}$ article will appear in a journal which already has i references is proportional to $i f(i)$, that is to the total number of references in journals containing i references each. . . .

(2) But there is also a probability that the $(p + 1)^{\text{th}}$ article may appear in a journal not hitherto having an article. This is a constant. . . .

(P. 35.)

4. Cole (1962), after ranking journals by decreasing order of useful references, plots the logarithm of the fraction x of the most productive journals

against the fraction $F(x)$ of all useful references found in these journals. The fit is very close to a straight line of form:

$$F(x) = 1 + K \log x. \tag{4.2}$$

He suggests that the slope K is a concise and useful measure of the extent of scattering of references, which may be characteristic of the subject field.

5. Leimkuhler (1967) shows that the $F(x)$ of Equation 4.2 is an approximation of Bradford's law, and that the exact form of the distribution function $F(x)$ of references in each fraction of the most productive journals, derived from Bradford's law, is

$$F(x) = \frac{\log_e (1 + Bx)}{\log_e (1 + B)} = \frac{\log_{10} (1 + Bx)}{\log_{10} (1 + B)}, \tag{4.3}$$

where B is a constant related to both the subject field and comprehensiveness of the collection.[7] Leimkuhler calls Equation 4.3 the Bradford distribution. From Figure 4.2, it can be seen that a small fraction of the most productive journals accounts for a high proportion of useful references.

6. Groos (1967) plotted more than 20,000 journal entries in physics according to the Bradford format. He found an excellent fit for highly and

[7]. $e = 2.71828$. The logarithm to the base e of a number, called the natural logarithm, is the power to which e has to be raised to equal the number. In other words, the natural logarithm of a number N, written $\log_e N$, is the power x that satisfies $e^x = N$. As for common logarithms, there are standard tables that are used to determine the natural logarithm of a number.

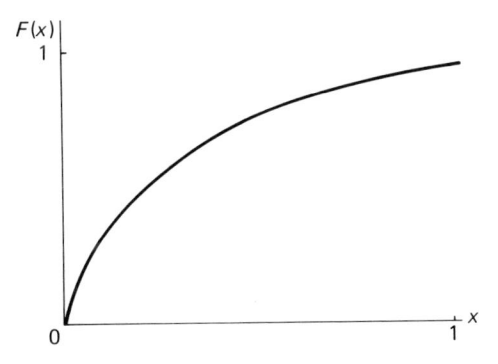

Figure 4.2. The Bradford distribution relating x, a given fraction of the most productive journals, and $F(x)$, the fraction of all useful references included in these journals.

moderately productive journals. However, in what has been termed by Brookes (1968) the "Groos droop," he noted that the data suggest that at some point in the cumulative sum of titles the true curve falls away from Bradford's linear law. See Figure 4.3.

7. Brookes (1968) notes that if new journals are found containing relevant papers, then the Groos droop decreases. Therefore, he suggests that the droop may merely reflect the result of an incomplete search.

Brookes also clarifies a number of different aspects of the Bradford distribution. He utilizes Equation 4.1, reproduced here,

$$R(n) = R(n^2) - R(n) = R(n^3) - R(n^2) = \cdots \qquad (4.1)$$

for $n \geq 1$, where $R(n)$ is the cumulative total of relevant papers found in the first n journals when all journals are ranked in order of decreasing productivity. Letting $r(n) = R(n) - R(n-1)$ be the number of references in the nth journal, Brookes recognizes that $r(n) \geq 1$, since journals admitted to the count must contain at least one relevant paper. This recognition leads to the following very useful result, presented in this form in Brookes (1968, *J. of Documentation*) and Brookes (1969, *Nature*):

$$R(n) = \alpha n^\beta \text{ for } 1 \leq n \leq c \qquad (4.4a)$$

$$R(n) = N \log_e(n/s) \text{ for } c < n \leq N, \qquad (4.4b)$$

where α is the number of relevant papers published in the most productive

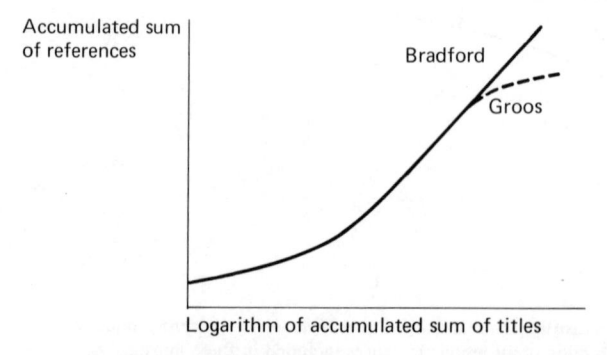

Figure 4.3. The suggested Groos refinement of Bradford's law.

journal, β is a constant less than 1, N is the total number of journals estimated to contain articles relevant to the subject of the search, s is the intersect at the abscissa of the straight-line portion of Bradford's law ($s \geq 1$, very close to 1 for the most specific subjects and higher for more general subjects), and c is the point at the abscissa where the linear portion of the curve begins (see Figure 4.4).

The estimated total number of references, regardless of how many are found, is

$$R(N) = N \log_e(N/s). \tag{4.5}$$

These results enable one to estimate, from an admittedly incomplete search, the total number of journals containing relevant articles and the total number of relevant articles. That is, if enough data are collected to ensure that the straight line is reached, the end of the line can be predicted. Equation 4.5 enables us to estimate the proportion of all relevant papers covered by any given number of the most productive journals.

Brookes states:

It cannot of course be proved that this law is universally valid, but all empirical evidence so far analyzed corroborates the law without exception.

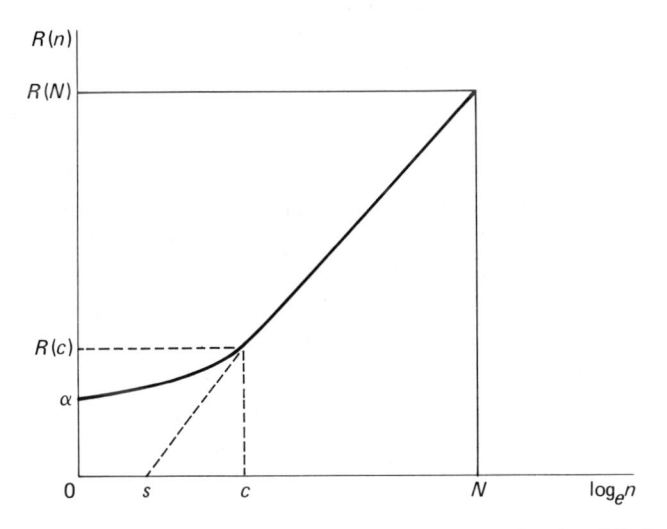

Figure 4.4. Cumulative number of relevant articles as a function of the logarithm of the cumulative number of journals, when journals are arranged in descending order of productivity.

And where the law has not been fully satisfied there have always been plausible explanations for the discrepancies. The practical value of the "bibliograph" is that it need be plotted only until the linearity has been convincingly attained. The end of the line, i.e., the value of N, the total number of periodicals contributing to the subject and the total of relevant papers they contribute, $R(N)$, can both be easily estimated. Thus, the values of N and of s can be estimated with adequate exactitude by examining only a fraction, and the best known, most productive and most accessible fraction of the relevant literature—sometimes examination of seven or eight periodicals suffices. (1970, *Information Storage and Retrieval*, pp. 131–132).

To explain the initial curved portion of Figure 4.4, Brookes hypothesizes an underlying stochastic mechanism similar to that of Simon (1955) and Kendall (1960).

In bibliographic terms the Bradford law implies that when the first papers on a new subject are written they are submitted to a small selection of appropriate periodicals and are accepted. The periodicals initially selected attract more and more papers as the subject develops but, at the same time, other periodicals begin to publish their first papers on the subject. If the subject continues to grow, however, there eventually emerges a Bradford "nucleus" of periodicals which are the most productive of papers on the subject. As this occurs, the pressure of the thrusting new subject on the space of these periodicals increases until restrictions are imposed by limitations of space and by editorial decisions to maintain a balance of scientific interest among all the papers published. (1969, *Nature*, p. 954.)

Hence, the c journals in the nucleus represent saturated journals that do not follow the linearity of unsaturated journals.

Brookes expresses a need to standardize the presentation of Bradford-type data to ensure comparability of estimates. He suggests that there be a three-year search span and that the minimum productivity for a journal to be included should be an average of one relevant paper per year.

If one defines the number of potentially contributory journals as those having $\frac{1}{2} \leq r(n) < 1$, then Brookes shows that the number of journals in this category is also N. That is, if there are N contributory journals, there are also N potentially contributory journals.

8. *Summary*. In this section, we have presented one of the most useful quantitative findings in library science and documentation. Although particularly relevant to journal selection, it has been utilized to aid library managerial decision making in a number of other areas: the extent of decentralization of library units, monograph title selection, journal binding,

indexing, shelf arrangement, photoduplication versus purchase, and journal weeding. According to Brookes, the Bradford law

... seems to offer the only means discernible at present of reducing the present quantitative untidiness of scientific documentation, information systems and library services to a more orderly state of affairs capable of being rationally and economically planned and organized. (1969, *Nature*, p. 956.)

Journal Selection

1. Goffman and Morris (1970) present empirical evidence that the circulation of journals does indeed follow Bradford's law in the same manner as references to journals. They then utilize Bradford's law in a rather curious way in order to develop a "so-called" library journal acquisition policy.

Bradford had divided journals into an arbitrarily chosen number of zones (three), and then called the zone of greatest productivity, containing a small number of the most productive journals, the "nucleus" zone. The number of journals in the nucleus is arbitrary because it depends on the number of zones chosen to effect the division: the greater the number of zones, the smaller the number of journals in the nucleus. As the divisions increase, eventually the nucleus would consist of only the one most productive journal. However, Goffman and Warren (1969) point out that unless the number of articles in the most productive journal is greater than half the total number of journals, if the nucleus consists of one journal, then the last two zones would have the same number of journals, contrary to Bradford's law of strictly decreasing numbers of journals in successive zones. They note that for Bradford's law to be strictly followed there is a maximum subdivision of journals into zones where the first zone must have a number of articles which is at least half the total number of journals. The maximum subdivision defines a "minimum nucleus."

The recommended library acquisitions policy of Goffman and Warren is to hold all journals in the minimum nucleus. This policy seems both trivial and arbitrary. A better procedure is to consider journal usage and costs over time, and perhaps alternative allocations of funds.

2. Cole (1963) makes an excellent initial effort at developing a journal selection policy. He utilizes his approximation of Bradford's law, Equation 4.2, and another very important empirical finding, the exponential nature of the use of journals over time. If x represents years since publication and

$f(x)$ represents the fraction of useful references x years or older, then $f(x)$ is related to x as in the following formula, which is represented in Figure 4.5,

$$f(x) = e^{-\lambda x}, \tag{4.6}$$

where λ is a subject constant and $e = 2.71828$.

Bradford's law indicates that the more journals the library carries in a subject area, the greater the number of circulation demands satisfied, but each additional journal satisfies a decreasing number of demands. The exponential law of journal usage (obsolescence) demonstrates that the longer journals are held, the more demands satisfied, but also at a decreasing rate. Cole represents unsatisfied demand as a function of the number of journals held (N) and the number of years they are retained (x). For a given space constraint on the number of journal volumes a library can hold, Cole determines the values of N and x that minimize unsatisfied demand.

3. In addition to the development of models for numbers of copies of monographs, Buckland, Hindle, Mackenzie, and Woodburn (1970) also present models pertaining to journal purchasing, discarding, binding, and interlibrary loans. They are developed in detail in Buckland and Woodburn (May 1968).

The authors utilize and extend the work of Cole (1963). They use maximization of the number of useful references in the library collection per dollar input as a performance measure for journal policies. Relating this performance measure with the two stated laws, they analyze a wide variety of library policies. Under the assumption that all titles are retained the same length of time, they analyze the effect of the choice of number of

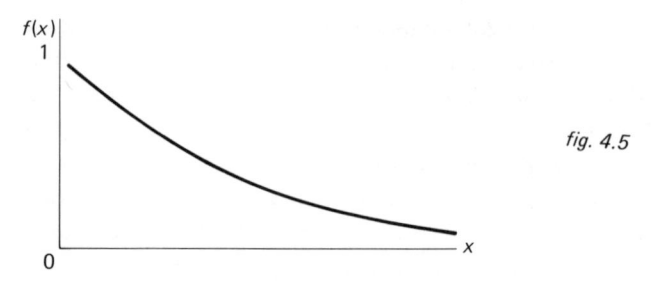

Figure 4.5. Exponential law of obsolescence.

journals and discarding time with and without budget limitations, and they allocate a limited budget between acquisition and storage.

The performance measure and the use of simple calculus enables the analyst to evaluate all possible strategies. The greater the number of titles, the more demand is satisfied, although each incremental number of satisfactions per additional title is successively smaller, and each title entails a purchase cost and storage cost. Also, the longer the titles are held, the more demand is satisfied, although each year the incremental satisfaction is successively smaller and the storage cost increases. The model indicates the strategy that attains the greatest number of useful references (demand satisfaction) per purchase and storage dollar.

They define a volume as one year of a journal title. Under the assumption that titles are retained for different lengths of time, they develop a method for determining the M most useful volumes to be held. It is seen that the best solution is to discard a title when its marginal utility of retention declines to a certain specific minimum level.

Extended model development is undertaken to determine the minimum library size for a new library that would satisfy a given percentage of demand, and to establish a coordinated policy for purchasing, discarding, and obtaining interlibrary loans based on a comparison of costs and effectiveness of each activity. In all the analyses, the following restricting assumptions are made: there is only one subject field of interest; the budget restriction applies only to funds allocated for journals; the cost of discarding is negligible; the journal titles do not differ significantly with respect to obsolescence rates, purchase price, size, and cost of binding; binding policies are the same for all journals; and journals can be placed in order of utility.

4. Williams, Bryant, Wiederkehr, Palmour, and Siehler (1968) and Palmour and Wiederkehr (1970) examine four university research libraries in order to develop a methodology for comparing serial borrowing costs with costs of acquisition, cataloging, processing, maintenance, storage, weeding, and circulation. They provide mathematical models to determine the frequency of use of a serial title at which it becomes less expensive to acquire a photocopy of an article from another library when needed than to subscribe to and maintain a file of the title. An implicit assumption is that borrowing a photocopy results in the same level of service as having the journal immediately available on the shelf. The models refer to decisions

similar to those of Buckland and Woodburn (May 1968), described above, but are less sophisticated. An interesting empirical finding is that use per serial volume decreases approximately 7 percent each year.

5. Brookes (Mackenzie and Stuart, 1969) also shows how one could determine, in a simple one period case, the number of periodical sets to purchase and the number of relevant periodicals for which photocopies are to be purchased. The number of relevant papers in any given number of ranked periodicals is expressed by the Bradford law. The total cost of buying the complete bibliography is expressed as the expected cost of purchasing periodical sets and the expected costs of purchasing photocopies in the periodicals not purchased. The optimal number of periodical sets to purchase is highly dependent on the ratio of photocopy cost to periodical cost.

6. In a manner similar to Cole (1963) and Buckland and Woodburn (May 1968), Brookes (1970, *Information, Storage and Retrieval*; 1971, *Nature*) utilizes the Bradford law of scatter and the negative exponential law of obsolescence to find the selection of periodicals that accomplishes any specified percentage of the total periodical coverage of a given scientific field. For convenience, Brookes describes obsolescence in terms of a geometric distribution, the discrete form of the negative exponential, where each year's use is a given fraction of the use of the prior year.

Brookes relates three solution techniques for determining P percent of the total 100 percent coverage:

(1) The Bradford-cut method. Ignoring the obsolescence factor, select the M periodicals ranked 1 to M which cover P percent of the total references in the subject area.

(2) The cross-cut method. Buy all periodicals and keep them t years, where t is chosen so that the average useful life of all the periodicals is P percent of the total useful life.

(3) The contour-cut method. Determine a critical discard level of current utility for each volume (year of periodical), below which the volume either is discarded or not purchased, such that the volumes held account for P percent of total use. In this manner, the most productive periodicals will be held for a long time, the lesser productive ones will be represented only by the most recent volumes, and it is very likely that many marginal periodicals will not be purchased at all. For use of this technique, Brookes describes some easy-to-follow graphical tools.

The last of the three methods is clearly superior. However, it does not consider costs and constraints in acquisitions and storage, it does not show how to choose the P percent of uses to be met, and it is a static model that does not deal with the effect of present decisions on future periods.

7. Kraft and Hill (1970) deal directly with the problem of selecting journals for acquisition over time. They begin with data on the expected usage of issues of journals in the year of issue. They utilize the Morse model of Markov probabilistic obsolescence, originally proposed for books, to describe the decrease in demand for journals over time. The objective is the investment of a limited budget in the journal issues that would meet the greatest amount of demand. It is implicitly assumed that a single copy of an issue meets all the demand. Here there is no consideration of queuing problems or multiple copies, not an intolerable omission considering the emphasis on journal titles and issue selection. A constraint is included to ensure that the sum of the costs of initially adding issues to the collection, the periodic storage and recurring costs, the costs for expected uses, and the subscription costs do not exceed a limited budget for each of several periods in the planning horizon. The formulation is one of linear programming, where the decision variables of whether or not to purchase a given issue of a journal are restrained to be either one (purchase) or zero (no purchase).

Although this "zero-one" linear programming formulation is theoretically sound, the authors recognize that because a typical problem would contain a great many decision variables it could not be solved by conventional methods. Therefore, they develop a dynamic programming approach[8] to break the problem down into subproblems, thereby making it manageable.

The model deals with one period (year) at a time. For each given period, a state variable is calculated, which is the amount of the budget left over for acquisition of new journals after paying for the storage and use of former acquisitions. Then, new purchase decision variables for the given period are determined in order to maximize present and future demand satisfied, subject to present and future budget constraints. For the next period, a new state variable is calculated, dependent on all past purchase decisions. The model continues recursively through all the periods of the

8. In many problems, it is not clear that the best decision, looking at each period individually, is best overall. It might be the case that some sacrifice in one period may mean that we are in a better position for the next period. Dynamic programming is a method for investigating such possibilities.

planning horizon. It generates a feasible solution, if one exists, satisfying all budget constraints. Although the feasible solution is guaranteed to be one of the best possible feasible solutions, the solution is optimal only in certain special cases.

8. Glover and Klingman (1972) indicate a mathematical formulation that is similar to that of Kraft and Hill but is more amenable to efficient solution techniques. Under certain assumptions, this new formulation permits the problem to be transformed into a linear programming transportation problem, for which there exist highly efficient techniques for obtaining the optimal solution.

In the general case, an approach is proposed for obtaining solutions, which, although suboptimal, are closer to the optimal solutions and are obtained more efficiently than in the Kraft and Hill solution technique. The approach combines dynamic programming with a surrogate-constraint strategy, which is a technique for reducing the number of constraints by combining them. If an optimal solution to the surrogate problem, with combined constraints, is feasible for the original problem, then it is also optimal for the original problem. If the solution is not feasible for the original problem, then heuristic procedures are presented to make the solution feasible and, at the same time, near optimal.

It is noted how some additional considerations may be incorporated into the original mathematical formulation. For instance, journals may be eliminated from future purchase or weeded from the library in order to provide money or space for other journals. Also, the size of future budgets may be made dependent on the degree to which budgets of prior periods are expended.

This formulation and the solution technique are theoretically sound and may prove to be of great utility. The main problems would be acquiring the necessary data on demand for journals in the year of publication, and estimating the parameters of change in demand over time needed for the Morse model of obsolescence.

There is an extensive literature on models of the obsolescence rate of journals. Most of the work is related to journal weeding policies. Therefore, a number of these articles are referred to in the later section of this chapter, which deals with the library function of maintenance and weeding of documents.

9. Summary. In this section, the models presented are cumulative in nature: each model incorporates the best features of the prior one and adds

some new features. The last formulation presented, that of Glover and Klingman (1972), based heavily on Kraft and Hill, has great potential as a practical tool for the planning of journal selection and weeding over time.

Selection Effort

1. Empirical findings about selection are presented in Evans (1970). In four academic institutions, he finds statistically significant differences in use among monographs selected by different methods. Librarians selected more useful titles than did faculty members, and faculty members selected more useful titles than did book jobbers.

2. Raffel and Shishko (1969) make a first, rudimentary, attempt at modeling selection principles (pp. 43–44). They aggregate all costs of ordering, purchasing, cataloging, and storing new acquisitions for a given period of time, for instance 15 years, into one single average cost per acquisition. Selection cost is independent of the number of acquisitions. The model minimizes total costs, which are linearly related to the number of acquisitions and to selection effort, subject to a given level of library use. Library use is considered to be a function of the number of acquisitions and the selection cost. Equating marginal benefits per dollar, the optimal strategy is shown to consist of purchasing the number of acquisitions and engaging in the selection effort that will make the ratio of the marginal use per acquisition to the marginal use per selection dollar equal to the cost per acquisition. It is assumed that the library use function in terms of acquisitions and selection effort can be obtained, but no attempt is made to do so.

Acquisition of Documents

Mullick, in Mullick (1966) and Johns Hopkins University (1965), has formulated a nonlinear programming model to determine the optimum number of employees for acquisition and cataloging. For these functions, fixed costs (costs independent of the number of documents processed) are higher than variable costs (costs dependent on documents processed), and fixed costs increase nonlinearly when staff or space is needed. Acquisitions are of three priority types: (1) rush order; (2) faculty and staff requests; and (3) *Publisher's Weekly* requests by assistant librarians. A Poisson probability distribution describes acquisition rates for each priority, and a negative exponential distribution describes service rates. The system is nonpreemptive, in that once a service has begun, it is continued. Given the maximum allowable waiting time for each priority, costs of delay, and parameters for both the arrival and service probability distributions, the model determines the optimal number of employees to minimize total costs.

Processing of Documents

Processing Work Flow

1. Buckland, Hindle, Mackenzie, and Woodburn (1970) develop a technical process model that applies to ordering, accessioning, cataloging, producing catalog cards, processing, and binding. It is a computer simulation that treats the particular technical process as an unknown "black box" and analyzes the work flow and backlogs from process to process. For each process, inputs are input rate (items per time period), labor allocation (man-hours per time period), work rate (items per man-hour), and processing capacity (items per time period). Outputs for each process are output rate (items per time period), backlog (items), and delay until arrears are cleaned up (time periods). The model determines the outputs for any given set of inputs, allowing the manager to evaluate various input alternatives. For instance, he may explore the effects of various allocations of man-hours to the processes. However, as the authors admit, the model ignores qualitative aspects of technical process output, such as the usefulness of the library catalog.

2. A more rudimentary approach is in Heinritz (1969). He explains that backlogs and overall processing time will be reduced if the average processing times within all functional subunits are equal. He presents an algebraic procedure for determining the allocation of full-time equivalent employees and the resultant costs in each department which yield equal average processing times.

Binding of Serials

Buckland and Woodburn (May 1968) develop an interesting procedure for determining optimal serial binding policies. They assume that all titles are to be bound at the same age with the same binding time and are discarded at the same age.

The usefulness, or the objective function, of the journal collection is expressed by the previously explained laws of obsolescence and diminishing returns. It is the number of references satisfied between acquisition and binding plus the number satisfied between binding and discarding. For a given purchase, binding, and storage budget, the objective function is maximized with respect to the age at which journals are bound and the age at which they are discarded. In addition, alternate policies are evaluated in which faster binding time can be purchased at higher binding costs.

Classification and Cataloging of Documents

Indexing

1. Rosenberg (1971) develops a statistical measure to be used in the situation where a document has been given one index term, and the problem is to find the most effective way of associating other index terms from a restricted vocabulary. It is assumed that there is a data base of previously indexed documents and the frequencies of occurrence and cooccurrence of all possible index terms are known.

Sixteen statistical measures are tested with respect to real data. The best measure is the conditional probability of a term being relevant, given the initial term. It is the frequency of cooccurrence of the two terms divided by the frequency of occurrence of the initial term. Since the denominator is the same for all potential second terms, the best procedure is to choose the term that has the highest frequency of cooccurrence with the given term.

The author points out that this procedure could be used in a manual system to eliminate errors of omission and yet retain flexibility, or it could be the first step toward a computerized indexing system. Also, in an information retrieval system, it could suggest additional index terms to the user who has an initial index term.

2. Cooper (1970) emphasizes the use of what he calls "design equations" to evaluate indexing. Analogous to an objective function in operations research terminology, a design equation relates a performance measure with design considerations, expressed in other circles as controllable variables.

The performance measure incorporated into the design equations is the expected search length, which is the average number of irrelevant documents retrieved before the relevant document (if only one) or one of the relevant documents (if more than one) is retrieved. Three situations are analyzed in which one document is needed which may be indexed by any number of terms. In the first one, one term is tried at a time. In the second, any number of terms may be tried at a time. In the third, terms may by cojoined in a request by the connectives "and," "or," or "not."

In each case, the expected search length is a function of the "imbalance" of the set of index terms. The application of a set of index terms to a set of documents has the effect of subdividing the documents into subsets that are uniquely defined by specific index terms. There is no "imbalance" if each of these subsets contains the same number of documents. The greater the disparities in subset size, the higher the "imbalance."

3. Schultz (1970) emphasizes the need to consider indexing costs in an indexing performance measure. She illustrates use of a cost-effectiveness measure as a guide for indexing medical documents.

4. A major work in revealing some of the unusual, basic underlying mathematical relationships in this area is Resnikoff and Dolby (1971). The authors describe libraries and information systems in terms of levels of access of information.

Initially, four levels are investigated for a given book: the title, the table of contents, the back-of-book index, and the full text. A large random sample of books from a medium-sized university library is investigated. The size, as expressed by the number of characters, is determined for each level for each book. For each level, the cumulative frequencies of size are plotted on lognormal probability paper. In each case, the plot is very close to a straight line, indicating that the size of each level has a lognormal probability distribution, or equivalently, the logarithm of the size is normally distributed. Since the lines are very close to being parallel, the lognormal distributions have the same (or almost the same) standard deviation.[9] The distinctions among the distributions may be described by their respective means.

A fascinating observation is made concerning the means of the level sizes. Plotting the logarithm to the base 10 of the means against the numbers 1 = title, 2 = table of contents, 3 = index, and 4 = text, it is seen that the plot is almost exactly on a straight line going through the origin. Letting n = the index number for level, $s(n)$ = size of nth level, and b = fitted constant, then $s(n) = 10^{bn}$. The constant b is determined to be 1.47247, and, therefore $s(n) = 10^{1.47247n} = (29.68)^n \approx (4e^2)^n$. The astounding result is that the average size of each level is slightly less than 30 times the size of the prior level. A zero level, $(29.68)^0 = 1$ character, may be thought of as the size of the initial letter of the Library of Congress classi-

---

9. The standard deviation is a measure of the amount of dispersion expected in the random variable of the probability distribution. If the probability distribution is such that the random variable is very likely to be very close to its mean value, then the standard deviation is low. On the other hand, if the random variable is quite likely to be very much above or below its mean value, then the standard deviation is high.

fication. The average title size is $(29.68)^1 \approx 30$ characters; the average table of contents size is $(29.68)^2 \approx 874$ characters; the average book index size is $(29.68)^3 \approx 25,822$ characters; and the average text size is $(29.68)^4 \approx 763,203$ characters.

Samples of two-year college libraries and university libraries were taken to determine their sizes. The cumulative frequency distributions of size were again lognormal with the same standard deviations as for prior levels. The mean sizes were respectively very close to $(29.68)^7$ and $(29.68)^8$ characters. The authors conjecture that bibliographic unit levels 5 and 6 may be encyclopedias and personal collections.

The authors show that these results are a general case of the Zipf power law principle of least effort (mathematically equivalent to the Bradford law). They claim that the lognormal distribution of the size of informational units is a mathematical consequence of certain reasonable assumptions concerning "effort" or "cost" of using an item in an access system if the complete system maximizes the output or informational per unit effort expended. Many examples are presented showing that the 30 to 1 ratio and lognormal distribution apply to all access levels of human communication: serial paper titles, abstracts, and texts; Library of Congress titles and subject headings; computer language hierarchies; and word and sentence length.

Back-of-book indexes are analyzed as possible aids toward new automated indexing systems and evaluative techniques. The average number of index entries per index is shown to be 836, with little variation among Library of Congress letter classes, and the distribution again is lognormal. The number of text references per index term in shown to be a power function, which is claimed to be a degenerate form of the lognormal distribution. There is a direct relationship between LC subject headings, monograph titles, and multiple reference index terms.

5. Summary. This section is not meant to be inclusive of all quantitative analyses regarding indexing. We have included four recent, diverse studies as representative of some of the work done in the area.

Original versus Temporary Cataloging

If a book is received by a library without a Library of Congress card, the library may temporarily catalog the book until the card arrives, originally catalog the book in which case the receipt of the LC card does not change the cataloging, or hold the book off the shelf until receipt of the LC card. Raffel and Shishko (1969) compare the costs of original cataloging with the costs of a temporary cataloging scheme, including temporary cataloging, retrieving, LC cataloging, and original cataloging costs.

Dewey and Library of Congress (LC) Correlation

Reynolds, Taylor, Meier, Miller, Stanfield, and Scholz (1971) analyze 59,000 MARC records in cases where both Library of Congress and Dewey classifications are available. They obtain two correlation matrices:
1. Between LC single letters and Dewey hundreds;[10] and
2. Between LC double letters and Dewey tens.[11]

If part of a document collection is classified by LC and another part by Dewey, the correlations may be used to place all documents in subject categories based on one of the two systems. In this manner, holdings and use may be delineated by subject.

Cataloging at the Library of Congress

Kochen and Segur (1970) describe a model that they use to determine the proportion of cataloging to be done at the Library of Congress as opposed to local libraries. The model is based on the assumption that the Library of Congress is able to choose the most popular titles to catalog and distribute the catalog records to all libraries that have acquired the titles. The remaining titles are cataloged upon acquisition by local libraries.

The total national cataloging costs consist of LC setup costs per title, LC marginal costs per local library supplied with a catalog record of a title, and local library cataloging costs. A general expression is obtained for the optimal number of titles to be cataloged at LC. Even using the most contrary numerical estimates for the variables involved, it is shown that the least total national cataloging cost decision is for *all* titles to be cataloged at LC.

If all 820 titles per day are cataloged at LC, instead of only 328 per day (40 percent) as is currently done, total cataloging costs could be reduced

---

10. The Library of Congress classification uses notation beginning with capital letters that correspond to 26 subject divisions. The Dewey Decimal classification uses numbers for notation. Therefore, the ten numbers 0–9 are used for an initial division into ten subject categories, but because the decimal point is placed after the third digit these are technically hundreds: 000–009; 100–199; and so on.

11. In the first case, each pair of LC letter and Dewey hundred has a space in a matrix of numbers. The number in the space is the correlation between the LC letter and Dewey hundred. This number indicates whether the two are directly related, that is if a document has one it has a tendency to have the other, or whether the two are inversely related, that is if a document has one it has a tendency not to have the other. The correlation number also indicates the extent of the relationship ranging from a complete lack of relationship (0) to a perfect direct relationship (+1) or a perfect inverse relationship (−1).

from $1.07 million per day to $.88 million per day. It is suggested that this potential saving could easily justify use of a computer system necessary for the increased LC volume.

Catalog Use

Lipetz (*1972*) conducted an extensive study, covering more than 2000 interviews and lasting one year, of use of the main catalog at Yale University Library. Data were obtained on initial search objectives, starting clues, intended approaches, and successes and failures. It is hoped that eventually such data will be a guide for library managers in determining the timing and method for conversion of a card catalog to a computerized catalog.

Control of Location and Use of Documents

Selection of Materials for Compact Storage

1. A pioneering work aimed at separating books into two sets for slow and quick access storage is presented in Fussler and Simon (1969), which was originally published in 1961. The authors investigate circulation use in various subject areas at the University of Chicago and other universities as a function of publication date, accession date, language, use in past five years, years since last use, and various combinations of these. For libraries possessing no record of past use, slow access storage of 25 percent of the economics collection using decision rules based upon language and publication date inconveniences only 3 percent of the total number of borrowers. If a library possesses circulation records for five years, storage of 25 percent of the economics collection based upon five-year use affects only 2 percent of the total circulation. Finally, if records for circulation use for 20 or more years are available, only 1 percent of the total circulation is affected by storing 25 percent of the economics collection based upon decision rules utilizing time since last circulation. Further details of the method of using time since last circulation as a means for reducing a library's on-line holdings are in Trueswell (1965, 1966; and 1969). Trueswell puts forth an 80/20 rule: 80 percent of a library's circulation is of 20 percent of a library's holdings.

Fussler and Simon provide insights into subject areas, different institutions, obsolescence, and browsing. They find great differences in use between subject areas, in that some subject areas need storage more than others. In addition to the University of Chicago, the authors sampled book use at Yale, Northwestern, and California at Berkeley. Their findings are that although the various holdings are quite different the pattern of use is quite similar. Past use at one institution is a good predictor of future use at another institution, and use of the various decision rules for storage yielded, for the different institutions, a very similar percentage of total use from storage.

They also conclude that obsolescence rates over time are fairly constant for natural sciences, corroborating the fit of Morse's Markov model with M.I.T. Science Library data, and decrease for social sciences and humanities. Popular books decline in use more rapidly than less popular books.

An extensive study of nonrecorded use reveals that it is three to nine times as great as recorded use, if a nonrecorded use and a circulation are given equal weight. However, for low use books that are candidates for storage, the available evidence suggests that browsing use is proportional to recorded use. Therefore, storage according to recorded use only is sufficient.

2. Leimkuhler (1966) makes a contribution to the analysis of selection of books by age for compact storage. He suggests that empirical results have indicated constant geometric growth in the size of library collections and constant geometric decrease in circulation rates of documents over time. By combining the growth and obsolescence models, he determines the proportion of circulation attributed to books d years or older, given the constant growth and obsolescence rates. A storage policy by age may be evaluated in this manner.

3. The results by both Fussler and Simon and Leimkuhler became the foundation and inspiration for Lister (1967) to present an excellent analysis of decision rules for compact storage of library materials using both age and usage criteria. Models are developed to describe all relevant costs of storage as a function of the age or as a function of intercirculation time. The costs considered in detail include compact storage and working collection building costs, maintenance and operating costs, circulation costs, and the cost of relocating books from the working collection to the compact storage collection.

The optimal age for storage, if the age policy is used, and the optimal intercirculation time, if the usage policy is used, are shown to be functions of two terms. One represents the compact storage relative advantage with respect to building costs, and maintenance and operating costs (less relocation costs). The other represents the relative advantage of the working collection in terms of circulation costs, including the costs of user delay. Although the author tests the models on three branch libraries of Purdue University, he is very quick to recognize the great difficulty in estimating a number of the parameters. Therefore, he undertakes a great amount of sensitivity analysis to determine the extent to which the decision rules, the savings attributed to storage, and the size of the storage and working collections are sensitive to the parameter estimates. In general, he finds that there is a great sensitivity to the difference in circulation costs. For low building costs, the model is sensitive to error, but it is relatively insensitive to error with high building costs. It is also sensitive to the overall length of the planning horizon for short horizons, but for longer horizons of from 10 to 25 years it is not sensitive to horizon length.

The basic model determines an optimum age or intercirculation time for storage. The model is also extended to the determination of different decision rules for each relatively homogeneous subset of library materials and to the case in which a different decision rule is made each year in order to maintain a constant annual rate of transfers to storage.

At first, it is hypothesized that the distribution of usage rates over the collection is needed in order to determine the optimal usage rate for storage. However, it is shown that the optimal rate is dependent only on cost, growth, and horizon parameters and is independent of the actual distribution of usage rates. In addition, the storage and working collection sizes are dependent only on the proportion of books having an intercirculation time that is lower than the optimal time used for the decision rule, and not on the entire distribution.

There is a detailed comparison of the two selection policies. The age policy has the advantage in being somewhat easier for the library to implement and somewhat easier for the user to locate books. But the age policy results in storing some old books that are used frequently and in not storing some fairly new books that are used infrequently. Therefore, the age policy incurs higher capacity-related costs, which are only somewhat offset by a decrease in circulation costs. The models for the two policies, along with the distribution of usage for books of a given age, are used to determine the differences in costs. The conclusion of the author is that, on balance, the usage policy is preferable for monographs and, because of the importance of continuity of time, the age policy is preferable for serials. A summary of Lister's work appears in Andrews (1968).

4. The model of constant geometric decrease in circulation rates over time used by Leimkuhler and by Lister is only one of a number of models

describing book use. In the context of determining which books to place in a slow access storage area by usage policy, Jain (1968) presents an extensive analysis of book circulation use studies and models.

Four classes of book-use models that predict expected future circulations are discussed, and an additional one is proposed. The four classes are the exponential class (for example, the Leimkuhler model), the logarithmic model (containing a logarithmic term), the square root class (containing a square root term), and Morse's Markov model, which is discussed under the book selection function and again later and is in a class by itself. Jain criticizes Morse's use of the Poisson probability distribution to predict demand for books, in that it underestimates the probability of exactly zero demands in a given year for a given book. He proposes a "P_n model," which employs a truncated Poisson distribution, having a separate higher probability for the event of no annual demand. Further details of the P_n model are presented in Jain, Leimkuhler, and Anderson (1969).

In his thesis, Jain further documents his estimation, sampling, and data collection procedures, which also appear in Jain (1969). In addition, he includes a bibliography of 569 different library use studies, each containing empirical findings with or without mathematical models.

5. In Morse (1968) and Morse (1972), the Markov model of book use, described earlier under selection of documents, is applied to decisions regarding book retirement to compact storage. Two policies are evaluated for the M.I.T. Science Library: retiring the oldest books in the collection (age policy) or retiring the oldest books of those that did not circulate in the past year. The evaluation is undertaken with respect to the number of circulations expected from compact storage each year in the next ten and the proportion of books that will regain popularity (four or more annual circulations) after their retirement.

6. Thus far, all the models designed to aid in selecting materials for compact storage have focused on the circulation rates of the resultant storage and working collections. A different, and very interesting, aspect is investigated in Morse (1970). Morse utilizes search theory developed in World War II for maximizing the probability of successfully locating enemy submarines in order to develop a mathematical model of library browsing behavior. The model shows that the proportion of the potentially helpful books in a section of the collection which are found by a browser depends on the search effort and on the total number of books in the section. If one or more sections have a higher proportion of books of potential interest,

that is, a higher "interest potential," then the browser can concentrate more search effort on these sections and thereby make his search more efficient.

The librarian aids the browser by arranging books on shelves, not alphabetically or at random, but by "subject class," so if the user knows the Dewey or LC code of interest he can quickly find the sections of high interest potential. Morse points out that a problem arises when the collection becomes very large, so that the interest potential for a subject class is diluted by old and highly specialized books that are seldom used. At this point compact storage not only enables a part of the collection to be stored in a less expensive location, but also it enables the working collection to regain its browsing effectiveness; for a given search time, more potentially useful books are found. However, if too many books are put into compact storage, then the working collection will be oversearched and many potentially useful books that are in compact storage either will be passed up or found only after a very high search time.

From an assumption that the average interest potential is proportional to the average circulation, models are developed to express the expected search success as a function of the proportion of books remaining in the working collection as a result of selection by usage and by age. The optimal proportions of books to be retired by each of the two methods of selection are determined in order to maximize the success rate. The results for different collection sizes and average ages are explored.

7. Summary. The models in this section evaluate decision rules for selecting materials for compact storage based on the criteria of age or usage. The main emphasis is to determine the usage rates of the working collection and the storage collection for any given decision rule. Fussler and Simon supplied the foundation for analysis in this area with an early, extensive study of empirical usage rates that would occur upon the adoption of a variety of decision rules. Leimkuhler took an important step toward systematic analysis of selection of materials by utilizing growth and obsolescence models to determine the proportion of use attributed to books of a given age or older. Lister incorporated Leimkuhler's models with a thorough analysis of costs to determine least-cost decision rules for both age and use storage policies. It is a fine analysis, which unfortunately remains in the relative obscurity of a Ph.D thesis. Jain and Morse evaluated storage decision rules by means of their respective P_n and Markov models of book use. Finally, we discussed an unusual formulation by Morse,

evaluating both age and use storage decision rules in terms of expected search success, which is expressed as a function of average interest potential of the working collection. A combination of the Lister and Morse models would appear to have particularly promising possibilities.

Storage of Library Materials

1. Cox (1964) investigates the physical considerations of compact storage in order to minimize shelving space. Five different storage models are presented, each based on a distinct set of assumptions.

The first model, which also is presented in Leimkuhler and Cox (1964), is based on the assumption that a collection of books of a known size distribution is to be placed on shelves which have given, equal widths. The heights of the shelves, however, are adjustable. If all books are placed on shelves which are of one given height, that of the tallest book, then there is a great deal of wasted space. On the other hand, there is no wasted space if every book is put on a shelf of its exact height. The initial alternative is a waste of space and the latter alternative is impractical. A middle range of alternatives is to have a certain specific number of different shelf heights and place each book on the shelf which has the lowest height at which the book fits. For any given number of shelf heights, the model explores these alternatives by determining the specific heights and the number of linear feet of books stored at each height that minimizes total shelf area. Also, it analyzes the decrease in wasted space as the number of height classes of shelves increases. The wasted space is shown to be a function of the mean and maximum book height. For both discrete and continuous distributions of book heights, computational algorithms are developed to assign book heights to shelf heights in order to minimize shelf area.

The second model of Cox considers book width in addition to book height. Shelf heights and widths are chosen for a collection of books with a known distribution of height and width in order to minimize total shelf volume. The additional consideration of width makes the model three-dimensional, but, by using shelf and area to replace book height, the formulations and solutions are similar to the two-dimensional case. For both models, it is seen that there is very little additional space saving in having more than three shelf height (or width) dimensions.

In the next three models, the constraints of stack construction and book classification are considered. In each case, shelf heights are chosen that minimize the number of stack units.

The third model, the within shelf storage model, assumes that the method of book retrieval is to ascertain the shelf size class and then follow that size shelf height throughout the stacks according to the book classification system. Each stack unit is set up identically with the same number and placement of shelves of the same height. The model considers both the case where the total height of the stack is fixed and the case where the top could be removed to provide additional space. The model is used to determine the number of shelf height classes and the heights of the shelves in order to minimize the number of stack units.

The fourth model, the within stack storage model, assumes that each stack is made up of shelves of one, and only one, height, and therefore, for each shelf height class, there is a corresponding set of one or more stack units with shelves of that height. This model also is used to determine the number of shelf heights and the corresponding values of these heights, such that the total number of stack units is minimized.

The fifth model, the random shelf storage model, assumes that no attempt is made to place books into size classifications. Books are selected at random with respect to height. They are placed in the stack unit by first fitting the bottom shelf, then placing the next shelf at the height of the tallest book on the prior shelf, then fitting the new shelf, continuing until a book is to be shelved which does not fit into the stack unit, and then beginning a new unit to be filled in the same manner. A computer simulation is performed to accomplish the random shelf storage and to determine the expected number of stack units required.

Throughout, Cox points out that storage models are analogous in many ways to classical inventory problems, and very interesting geometrical interpretations are made. The models are tested on data obtained from both the Purdue and Auburn University libraries.

2. Raffel and Shishko (1969) utilize work by Metcalf (1965) to determine the area required per section of stacks, the number of volumes per section, and the amount of unusable area for the M.I.T. Libraries. In addition, they obtain maintenance, building, land, and storage equipment costs to evaluate various storage alternatives: open versus closed access, conventional versus compact storage, on- versus off-campus retrieval systems, and microform storage.

3. Booth (1969) analyzes the effectiveness of a variety of different configurations of library stacks. The average distance traveled by a user or a mechanical access operator is determined. It is assumed, with some empirical evidence, that the ranking of usage of a library item times its frequency

of use is the same constant for all items. Evaluated in this manner are linear, radial, circular, bicircular, concentric circular, and spiral stacks with a number of different modes of access.

4. Leimkuhler (1968, *American Documentation*) applies search theory to an overly simplified situation of a person looking for one item in a library or in any information system without the aid of a classification or indexing system. In this situation, Leimkuhler investigates a trade-off between library file effort of ordering items so that users will be able to identify items with a high probability of success and search effort of the user.

At one extreme, the library files all its items in a decreasing order of probability that an item will yield the information sought, thereby reducing search effort to a minimum, given no classification or indexing system. At the other extreme, the library files its items randomly, thereby minimizing its file effort at the expense of the user. Alternatives between the extremes are to identify m zones of decreasing likelihood of use and put each item into one of these zones: the user searches the zones sequentially and searches the items within a zone randomly. If $m = 2$, the division could represent a working collection and compact storage.

Leimkuhler develops a model that determines the expected number of items searched before success for each of the stated alternatives. For any given number of zones, the model identifies the proportion of items to be placed in each zone. The model is first presented with a generalized function of use of the ordered items. Then, Leimkuhler uses his Bradford distribution formulation of Equation 4.3, which identifies the proportion of productivity in each given fraction of the most productive items. Each increase in the number of zones reduces the expected number of items searched, but the reduction decreases very rapidly as the number of zones is increased. In terms of the problem as stated, with best estimates of parameters, the model shows that the first zone of a two-zone system should contain a little less than 20 percent of the collection and yet would satisfy about two-thirds of the searches.

5. Summary. The Cox models appear to be of greatest utility for the planning of library material storage. Shelf heights of stack units may be adjusted to store the library materials in a manner that minimizes shelf area, shelf volume, or the number of stack units. Raffel and Shishko and Metcalf may be useful for estimating the floor area and costs of various storage alternatives. The Booth models of user accessibility for different

stack configurations are an interesting initial attempt but are in an early stage of model development. The Leimkuhler models of placement of items into zones of ease of access are more theoretical in nature than the aforementioned models.

Loan Period

An individual borrower prefers a very long loan period because he can keep the book as long as he wishes without the bother of renewals, overdue notices, and fines. Other potential borrowers prefer the book to have a shorter loan period in order to get it back on the shelf.

For any given level of demand or popularity of a given title, a library can either increase the number of copies or shorten the loan period in order to increase the level of satisfied demand (but not necessarily the level of satisfaction). In both cases, it is more likely that a copy of the title is on the shelf when sought by an individual user. Of course, if the demand is very low, there is a very high likelihood of finding the title on the shelf, regardless of the number of copies or loan period. On the other hand, many copies or a very short loan period may be needed to result in a fairly high probability of finding a very popular book on the shelf.

1. Previously, we have described models for the selection of library materials and the determination of the number of copies which also can be utilized to evaluate the length of the loan period. Morse (1968) develops analytical models based on queuing theory. These models enable the analyst to compute the expected fraction of time titles are off the shelf and the expected number of unsatisfied persons seeking titles, given past circulation rates, number of copies, use time, and loan period. In this manner, the effects of changes in loan period for all books or merely for high circulation books are evaluated.

2. Another model described previously is that of Buckland, Hindle, Mackenzie, and Woodburn (1970). In this case, Monte Carlo simulation is used to trace repeatedly, via computer, the logical flow of the borrowing process. The effect on user satisfaction level is computed for any given loan period, amount of in-library use, number of copies, and proportion of times unsatisfied users ask for titles to be reserved. Buckland (1972) reports that the result of analysis of various alternative combinations was to establish a one-week loan period for the 10 percent most used books, the rest subject to four return dates per year. This policy increased the proportion of immediate search success for a specific title and increased the propensity

toward browsing without a specific title in mind. The effect at the University of Lancaster has been an unexpectedly great increase in the level of library use.

3. With respect to periodicals, Goyal (1970) uses the equilibrium results of queuing theory to express the probability of finding a title on the shelf and the expected waiting time as functions of the period. Then, overall customer satisfaction is expressed as a linear function of three variables: the loan period, the probability of finding a title on the shelf, and the expected waiting time. An expression is derived for the optimal loan period, which maximizes customer satisfaction, provided that the demand rate and coefficients of satisfaction for the three variables are given.

In-Library Use

1. McGrath (1971) presents the results of correlation studies of circulation and in-library use at the University of Southwest Louisiana. For both the cases where 39 university departments and 141 major LC and Dewey Decimal categories are used as units of association, the number of books circulated and the number of books left on tables by users are very highly correlated (correlation coefficients of .86 and .84). McGrath concludes that use of circulation records to show overall library use is substantiated.

2. For 39 subject areas, Bommer (1971) substantiates this result at the Lippincott Library of the University of Pennsylvania (correlation coefficient of .92). Also, a linear relationship between circulation and in-library use is established, with almost one in-library use for each circulation.

Security Guards

Morse (1968) determines the number of stolen books and periodicals per year and the resultant number of lost user-hours. He compares these losses with the annual cost of a security guard.

Return of Circulated Library Materials

The efforts of a group of student engineers working on a part-time basis at the University of Michigan Library are presented in Burkhalter (1968). They had conducted approximately forty operations research studies of the library and reported as a staff unit to the assistant director. An arrangement of this type shows interesting promise for aid in university library decision making.

Although the emphasis is on determining appropriate costs, there is some discussion of benefits of various alternatives. A number of articles explore various aspects of the return of circulated library materials: renewals and overdues, exterior book return, and reshelving.

1. In the initial study, Burkhalter and Race (1968), an extensive analysis is made of the frequency and costs of renewals and overdues, resulting in a change in the overdue notice process, and of the relationship between the number of days a book is in use and the number of days a book is kept out before its return. More than half of the books circulated are used for at least ten days, and a considerable number of students wait until the due date to return books regardless of completion of use.

2. Drott and Hoag (1968) evaluate a number of possible exterior book return collection systems for the University of Michigan Library in terms of annual cost, costs of conversion, customer acceptance and utilization, and the effect on other library functions. The costs and savings of each system are heavily dependent on the percentage of books returned to the outside depository.

3. Benford, Burkhalter, Ehrnstrum, and Hoag (1968) is a study to reduce the time and cost of getting books back on the shelf. Proposed corrective action consists of more efficient trips to the drop box collection, faster removal from the hold area, better layout of shelves in the sorting area, and longer stack personnel work periods.

Summary

We have discussed models and empirical findings for a variety of decisions within the function "control of location and use of documents." The first two sections relate to the control of document location, emphasizing the selection process and the actual placement of documents in storage. The models could yield information answering such questions as the following:

1. If we wish to place 50 percent of the collection in compact storage, and we select materials by age, what is the cutoff age and what proportion of uses would then be from compact storage?
2. If we wish to place 50 percent of the collection in compact storage, and we select materials by time since last circulation, what is the cutoff intercirculation time, and what proportion of uses would then be from compact storage?
3. For the age selection and intercirculation time (use) policies, what cutoff points and percentages of materials stored would result in the lowest overall library cost?
4. How should shelf heights of stack units be arranged in order to store a collection most efficiently?

With respect to the control of document use, we discussed models for loan period, in-library use, security guards, and the return of circulated

materials. These models can be used to provide managerial insight into the following questions:
1. How would an increase or decrease in loan period affect the number and proportion of users who are able to find library materials?
2. How does the pattern of in-library use compare to the pattern of circulation use?
3. How does the cost of a security guard compare to the cost of stolen materials in terms of lost user-hours or replacement dollars?
4. What are the benefits and costs involved in alternative systems for handling renewals and overdues, exterior book returns, and reshelving?

Facilitation of Use of Documents

Photoduplication

1. Brookes (March 1970, *J. of Documentation*) investigates the situation in which a library has the choice of subscribing to a periodical or obtaining photocopies of articles in the periodical, requested by users, from a photocopying service. He utilizes the Bradford-Zipf distribution of articles in periodicals, subscription costs, and photocopying costs (1) to identify the periodicals that he recommends the library to subscribe to and (2) to estimate the cost savings in this procedure, as opposed to subscribing to all periodicals having one or more relevant articles. The estimating procedure is graphical and is presented in a very simple and practical manner.

2. Beck, Benford, and Deardorff (1968) and Beck and Drott (1968) analyze accounting systems for photoduplication. Systems are developed for cash collection and for crediting the appropriate university department or outside business firm.

3. Raffel and Shishko (1969) study the costs and user preferences of a variety of alternative systems for providing reserve materials at M.I.T. One of the alternatives is to photocopy all articles and parts of books required in a course and distribute them to the students enrolled in the course. Another alternative is to lower photocopy prices to the local commercial level.

Microfiche

The cost of microfiche systems for providing reserve materials also has been evaluated by Raffel and Shishko (1969). Proposed systems involve placing on microfiche all course-required articles and parts of books and distributing them to students. Each student would be given a portable microfiche reader, or readers would be placed in dormitories and libraries. These alternatives were considered to be too expensive for the benefits achieved.

Maintenance and Weeding of Documents

Book Relabeling
Beck (1968) investigates the book relabeling system for the divisional libraries at the University of Michigan. He concludes that decentralized relabeling at the divisional libraries results in comparable quality to the centralized relabeling at lower cost. Also, one type of label is found to be more economical than another.

Book Weeding
Selection of materials for discarding entails similar considerations to the selection of materials for compact storage. Therefore, the earlier discussion of the latter is applicable here.

1. Cooper (1968) is a survey of the various criteria suggested for weeding: least used materials, language, date of publication, number of copies in library, number of libraries holding items, subject area, status, and expert judgment. The results of a systematic weeding project at Columbia University are presented. It is concluded that criteria ought to be selected on the basis of goals of the institution, the nature of each subject discipline, and the needs and patterns of the users.

2. Leimkuhler (1969) expresses the costs associated with a given book as the sum of a fixed acquisition cost, a holding cost dependent on the time the book is held, and a use cost dependent on the number of uses of the book. The holding cost is a linear function of time, and the use cost is a linear function of use, which is an exponentially decreasing function of time.

Leimkuhler suggests that, in the absence of a quantification of library benefits, a close to optimal library policy is to minimize average cost per use. Considering the acquisition, holding, and use costs, it is shown that in the first unit of time the average cost is high because of the high acquisition cost. Initially, each unit of time reduces the average cost because the acquisition costs are averaged over more periods. However, as time goes by, the use rate diminishes, and therefore holding cost increases for each use. At some point, the average cost reaches a minimum and then begins to increase. Leimkuhler determines the holding time that corresponds to the minimum average cost. It is seen that this holding time is a function only of acquisition and holding cost parameters, not on use cost, and that it is very similar to the economic lot-size formula of inventory theory. It indicates the holding time before weeding for which average cost per use is a minimum.

3. Sinha (1971) develops a comprehensive collection control model for acquisition and weeding decisions. It is described on page 90.

Journal Weeding

A good journal selection policy, with direct or indirect consideration of storage constraints, should determine retention time for journals. A number of the methodologies discussed in the journal selection section of the selection of documents function include, as part of a final product, a journal weeding policy. They are equally relevant to journal weeding and journal selection. A particularly outstanding technique is that proposed by Glover and Klingman (1972).

An essential element of each journal selection and weeding technique is a model of the obsolescence of journals, that is, the decline in use over time. We include here a discussion of a number of efforts to model obsolescence in journals, particularly scientific journals.

1. A good deal of the discussion of obsolescence of journals has been in terms of a concept of "half-life" of radioactive substances borrowed from the physical scientist. The half-life is the time required for disintegration of half the atoms of a sample of a radioactive substance. The rate of disintegration is such that at any given time the half-life of the remaining material is the same as the half-life of the original mass.

An analogy with scientific journals was expressed at the 1958 International Conference on Scientific Information. In a paper published as part of the proceedings of the Conference, Bernal (1959) described the half-life of a particular piece of scientific information as the period during which half of all remaining uses (references or enquiries) will be made or, counting back from a given date, the period during which half of all uses have occurred.

2. Burton and Kebler (1960) note the difficulties involved in a direct analogy. "Unfortunately, . . . obsolescence time cannot be precisely measured. Unlike a radioactive substance, which becomes something entirely different on disintegration, literature simply becomes unused, but *not* unusable. It is obsolescent, but not 'disintegrated.' " (P. 19.)

They revise the definition to be "the time during which one-half of all the currently active literature was published." Using this definition, they studied data based on citation counts in current selected source journals in nine engineering and scientific fields. For each field, the most recent period that accounts for 50 percent of all citations is presented in Table 4.1.

As seen, there is great disparity of half-lives. Burton and Kebler suggest that a short half-life reflects rapidly changing problems, techniques, and interests. Also, they suggest that each subject field is composed of both
(1) Classical literature, with a long half-life
(2) Ephemeral literature, with a short half-life
The differences among subjects may reflect different proportions of these two types of articles.

3. As discussed earlier under journal selection, Cole (1963) expresses the negative exponential functional relationship of journal usage over time. Equation 4.6 and Figure 4.5 on page 102 show this relationship.

$$f(x) = e^{-\lambda x}, \tag{4.6}$$

where x is the number of years since publication, $f(x)$ is the fraction of useful references x years or older, and λ is a subject constant.

An alternative, convenient form of Equation 4.6 is

$$\log_{10}(100 f(x)) = 2 - Kx, \tag{4.7}$$

where $K = \lambda \log_{10}(e)$ is a constant and $100 f(x)$ is the percentage of references older than x years. If x is plotted against the left side of Equation 4.7

Table 4.1. Burton and Kebler Findings of Literature Half-Lives

Subject Field	Years
Metallurgical Engineering	3.9
Physics	4.6
Chemical Engineering	4.8
Mechanical Engineering	5.2
Physiology	7.2
Chemistry	8.1
Botany	10.0
Mathematics	10.5
Geology	11.8

or x is plotted against $f(x)$ on semilog paper,[12] the plot is a straight line with slope $-K$ (Figure 4.6).[13] Four different sets of data are used to confirm this distribution pattern.

The half-life is equivalent to the median age of current references. Cole shows that the median $x(\frac{1}{2})$ can easily be calculated as follows:

$$x(\tfrac{1}{2}) = (2 - \log_{10} 50)/K = .301/K. \tag{4.8}$$

Cole points out that not only are half the references older than the median age but one-quarter of them are older than twice the median age, one-eighth are older than three times the median age, and so on.

An immediate consequence of the preceding analysis is to calculate the fraction of usage covered by any given retention period. Cole extends this analysis by utilizing Bradford's law to determine the number of journals and number of years they are to be retained in order to minimize unsatisfied demand subject to a space constraint. Unsatisfied demand includes demand for journal titles that are not held and demand for volumes that are older than those held.

4. Bourne (1965) assembled reported results of fifty different studies con-

---

12. Semilog paper is a special type of graph paper. One axis is ruled in the typical rectangular manner of equal spaces for equal numerical quantities. The other axis is ruled so that equal relative increases require equal distances. For instance, the distances between 1 and 3, 3 and 9, 9 and 27, and so on are all the same; similarly, for the distances between 20 and 40, 40 and 80, 80 and 160, and so on.
13. Slope reflects the number of units of vertical increase for every unit of horizontal increase. A slope of $-K$ means that for every unit of horizontal increase, the line *decreases* on the vertical scale by K units.

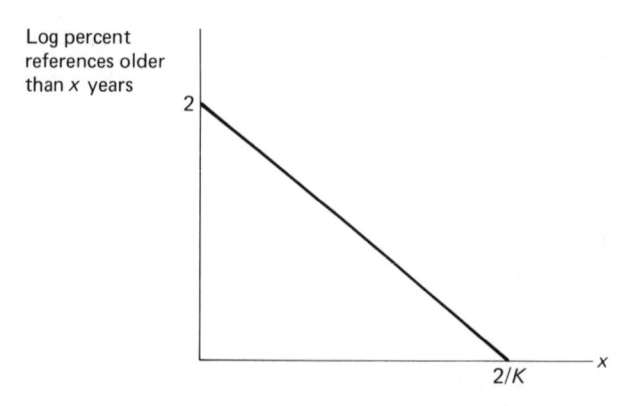

Figure 4.6. Semilog plot of the exponential law of obsolescence.

cerned with the use of literature as a function of age, including a wide variety of subject fields. For most of the studies, the author utilized a count of citations as a measure of use. In others, he counted circulations. Although one may expect to find a difference between the two methods because of the longer lag time between publication and citation than between publication and circulation, Bourne concludes that the data seem to support the view that there is no obvious difference in the two techniques. He also shows that different studies within a given subject field have measured widely different half-lives, thereby casting doubt on the use of the half-life concept beyond the individual study.

5. Brookes (1970, *ASIS*) analyzes a number of factors involved in the measurement of rates of obsolescence of periodicals which may account for discrepancies in published measures alluded to by Bourne (1965).

(1) Often, the journals comprising the literature of a wide subject area are not specified.

(2) Obsolescence may be confounded by the simultaneous operation of two different rates of decline, one relating to immediate scientific interest and the other to historic interest.

(3) If references date back far enough, there is lack of uniformity because of the effect of the two world wars, during which there was a decline in the rate of increase of scientific publications.

(4) Grouping references into integer-year intervals in effect places all references within an interval at one end of the interval, and is, thereby, a source of bias.

(5) Perhaps the greatest source of variation is "a blithe disregard of the limits to precision imposed by sampling, especially by the sampling of the negative exponential distribution that underlies all measures of obsolescence." (P. 320.) Brookes shows that for the sampling error to be within ± p percent of the correct half-life, with a probability of 95 percent, then the sample size n has to be at least

$$n = (235/p)^2. \tag{4.9}$$

For an estimate of the half-life that is correct to within 10 percent of its true value, $n = 552$ references. Brookes argues that if sample sizes are given for published measures of obsolescence, then we could determine the extent to which sampling variance accounts for discrepancies.

6. MacRae (1969) suggests that the age distribution of scientific cita-

tions is a result of two factors: citation behavior favoring recent literature and growth of the literature. He combines the two rates of decay and of growth into one exponential function to reflect the age distribution.

7. Line (1970) presents a technique for eliminating the growth element from the determination of half-life in order to obtain a half-life figure that reflects only the rate of decay of journals. He refers to the median citation age as apparent obsolescence. After identifying the yearly rate of growth of the literature in the subject field, which is assumed to be the same each year, Equation 4.10 may be used to transform the median citation age into the corrected half-life reflecting real obsolescence.

$$h = \log_{10}.5/[(1/m)(\log_{10}.5) + \log_{10}G], \tag{4.10}$$

where m is the median age, G is the growth factor, and h is the corrected half-life.

8. Brookes (December 1970, *J. of Documentation*) criticizes Line's technique of correcting the apparent obsolescence. He utilizes the discrete geometric probability distribution of Equation 4.11, which is an approximation of the continuous negative exponential distribution.

$$p(t) = (1 - a)(a^{t-1}) \text{ for } t = 1, 2, \cdots, \tag{4.11}$$

where a is the annual aging factor, $1 - a$ is the annual rate of obsolescence, and $p(t)$ is the probability that a given citation is t years old. Brookes shows that Line's assumption that the growth of the literature increases the apparent obsolescence may be reflected as follows:

$$(1 - a_t)/(1 - a_0) = e^{gt}, \tag{4.12}$$

where g is the annual rate of growth, $1 - a_0$ is the annual rate of obsolescence at time 0, and, $1 - a_t$ is the annual rate of obsolescence at time t. Implicit in Line's reasoning and in Equation 4.12 is that the increase in the number of references due to the growth of the literature is offset by a higher apparent obsolescence rate, resulting in a utility or lifetime expected usage that is constant from year to year.

Brookes introduces another factor, which he deems very important: the growth of the number of contributing scientists. He shows that

$$(1 - a_t)/(1 - a_0) = e^{(g-s)t}, \qquad (4.13)$$

where s is the annual rate of growth of the number of contributing scientists. A positive s tends to decrease the decline in use over time. The growth of the literature and the growth of the number of contributing scientists have opposite effects. If $g = s$, then the rate of obsolescence remains unchanged.

9. Oliver (1971) studies semiconductor physics literature for five years in order to evaluate Equation 4.13. She finds a literature growth rate g of 13.4 percent, a scientist growth rate s of 15 percent, and a constant obsolescence rate of about 79 percent. Her conclusion is to substantiate Equation 4.13 in that g and s have canceling effects that if close to equal can leave the obsolescence rate relatively unchanged.

10. Sandison (1971) criticizes the use of the following terms for library purposes: (1) the number of citations of journals of a given age, (2) the journal half-life, and (3) the journal aging factor. Instead, he suggests (1) the number of library uses per item of a given age, (2) a 50 percent consultation probability age, which is defined as the number of years required for the relative probabilities of consultation of individual items to fall by 50 percent, and (3) the item-consultation decay rate, which is the annual rate of decrease in observed relative probabilities that each available item will be consulted.

Sandison applies his measures to extensive data from the National Reference Library of Science and Invention in London. Item-consultation decay rates are obtained for different types of searches, readers, document types, and subjects.

11. A comprehensive theoretical modeling effort of the dynamic interactions of literature growth and citation behavior is presented by Krauze and Hillinger (1971). They incorporate the following assumptions based loosely on past empirical findings:
(1) The rate of citing earlier papers depends on the rate of increase in the number of papers and the probability of a given paper citing an earlier one.

$$R(t, x) = n(t - x)p(t, x), \qquad (4.14)$$

where $R(t, x)$ is the rate at which literature of time $t - x$ is cited at time t, $n(t - x)$ is the rate at which new articles appear at time $t - x$, and $p(t, x)$ is the probability that a given paper at time t will cite a paper x years old. (2) The literature is growing exponentially.

$$L(t) = Be^{\lambda t}, \qquad (4.15)$$

where $L(t)$ is the number of articles written up to time t, $\lambda > 0$ is the literature growth factor, and $B > 0$ is a constant. It follows that $n(t - x)$ is the change in $L(t - x)$ over time.

$$n(t - x) = \partial L(t - x)/\partial t = \lambda Be^{\lambda(t-x)}. \qquad (4.16)$$

(3) The probability that a given paper will cite another given paper is equal to the probability that the latter paper is read times the probability that it is cited given that it is read.

$$p(t, x) = p_r(t, x)p_c(x), \qquad (4.17)$$

where $p_r(t, x)$ is the probability that an article x years old will be read at time t and $p_c(x)$ is the probability that an article x years old will be cited given it is read.

(4) The probability that an article x years old is read at time t declines exponentially with x but is also both proportional to the effort devoted to searching the literature and inversely proportional to the size of the literature.

$$p_r(t, x) = [E/L(t)]e^{-\epsilon x}, \qquad (4.18)$$

where E is a measure of the effort devoted to searching the literature and $\epsilon > 0$ is the reading probability decay factor. In this expression, it appears that the factor of the number of contributing scientists suggested by Brookes (December 1970, *J. of Documentation*) is important but is conspicuously absent.

(5) The effort devoted to searching the literature increases with the size of the literature but less rapidly than the size of the literature.

$$E = FL(t)^{1-\alpha} \text{ or } E/L(t) = FL(t)^{-\alpha}, \qquad (4.19)$$

where $0 \leq 1 - \alpha \leq 1$ is the rate of decrease of search effort with increase in literature size and $F > 0$ is a constant. If $\alpha = 0$, a constant fraction of the literature always is read. If $\alpha = 1$, a constant effort is expended regardless of the size of the literature.

(6) The probability that an article is cited given it is read decreases exponentially with its age.

$$p_r(x) = De^{-\delta x}, \qquad (4.20)$$

where $\delta > 0$ is the citation decay factor and $D > 0$ is a constant.

Substituting Equations 4.15 through 4.20 into Equation 4.14 and integrating over all x result in an expression for the number of references at time t.

$$R(t) = [\lambda/(\lambda + \epsilon + \delta)]DF\, B^{1-\alpha}e^{(1-\alpha)\lambda t}. \qquad (4.21)$$

The same analysis yields an analogous expression for the number of citations in the future of a paper written at time t. It is shown that the number of times an average paper is cited is greater than the number of references it contains.

Summary

We briefly made reference to an analysis of whether book relabeling ought to be decentralized. With respect to book weeding, Leimkuhler has developed a useful model to determine the relationship between book retention times and costs of acquisition, storage, and use. It can answer the question of what holding time results in a minimum average cost per use. Models included in the earlier section on selection of materials for compact storage are also relevant to book weeding. Morse (1968) and Jain (1968), for instance, describe book use over time, and inform the library manager of the expected number of unsatisfied users resulting from any specific weeding policy.

In the section on journal weeding, we discussed mathematical analyses that describe obsolescence and growth of scientific journals. These functional descriptions are essential elements in any rational journal acquisition and weeding policy.

Aids for Location of Documents in Other Libraries

1. Raffel and Shishko (1969) determine costs of various schemes for the M.I.T. Library to locate documents in other library collections. The cost of microfilming and maintaining catalogs is seen to be quite expensive.

Eventually, on-line computerized catalogs or closed-circuit television might be feasible. An interesting alternative at relatively low cost is a telephone "hot line" between cooperating libraries.

2. Wood and Bower (1969) present results of a survey of sources of references for periodical use at the National Lending Library for Science and Technology in England. The data for the number of times for which abstracting or indexing publications are used suggest that the Bradford-Zipf law holds for bibliographic aids as well as for periodicals.

3. Brookes (1970, *Information Storage and Retrieval*) assumes that use of bibliographic aids conforms with the Bradford-Zipf law in order to determine the "viable" minimum number of bibliographic aids to be held by a local library. He assumes that there is a regional library having B bibliographic aids relevant to the subject, and there is a local library having $B' \leq B$ relevant bibliographic aids. If user cost for a search at the local library is c and his cost at the regional library is $ac \geq c$, then Brookes shows that the local library will only be used if the perceived probability of finding the bibliographic aid sought is greater than $1/a$. Utilization of the Bradford-Zipf law then yields the minimum number of aids for use of the local library, in terms of a, B, and the Bradford parameter s. (See Equation 4.4.)

Facilitation of Access to Other Libraries

Interlibrary Borrowing Decision Rules

Buckland and Woodburn (May 1968) and Buckland, Hindle, Mackenzie, and Woodburn (1970) investigate the trade-off between storage of journal volumes and interlibrary loans. They utilize the Bradford law of scattering and the Cole law of obsolescence to obtain decision rules for the retention time of a purchased title and for the cutoff point for purchasing ranked titles. A purchased title is retained until its use decreases to such an extent that the annual interlibrary borrowing cost to satisfy requests no longer exceeds the annual storage cost. A title is purchased if its expected use for the period during which it will be stored by the library is high enough so that the interlibrary borrowing costs to satisfy these requests are greater than the sum of the purchase cost and total storage cost.

The aforementioned policy satisfies all journal requests either from stock or from interlibrary loan at a minimum cost to the library. However, the authors recognize that since interlibrary loans have higher user delays than satisfaction from stock, a library may want to make an additional expenditure to increase the proportion of satisfactions from stock, thereby reducing the average delay. If costs could be attributed to delays, an overall optimal policy could be derived.

Retrieval Systems

Raffel and Shishko (1969) discuss the benefits and costs to M.I.T. of alternative systems for obtaining books for its users from other libraries. Included are a direct messenger service and the provision of transportation to its users to travel to other collections.

Networks

Networks give each library the potential of extending its reach well beyond its own resources, thereby enabling it to specialize in materials frequently used by its particular users.

1. Duggan (1969) identifies salient network components, transactions, and configurations. Two measures of library participation are suggested for borrowing and lending transactions:

(1) The extent of dependency of a library on the network is the ratio of its number of borrowing transactions to its total number of transactions with other libraries in the network.

(2) The extent of participation of a library in a network is the ratio of the number of transactions of the library to the number of transactions in the entire network.

2. Nance (1970) develops a mathematical model for the exchange of inquiries or messages regarding the availability or location of resources in a library network. The objective criterion of the model is the maximization of network "utility," which depends on the number of messages sent over each of the links or channels between libraries and the relative utility of the channels. The constraints are the capacities of the channels.

3. Korfhage, Bhat, and Nance (1972) apply basic concepts developed by network theorists to library networks that supply their members with both information and documents. A number of possible network configurations are presented and analyzed. A general network model is defined including the users, the information resources, the information centers, the channels of information transfer, and the channels of document transfer.

4. Reynolds, Taylor, Meier, Miller, Stanfield, and Scholz (1971) study the benefits and costs of three library network plans for interlibrary loans, technical services, and collection management in the state of Washington. Included is an interesting analysis of book overlap between libraries. It is seen that since no one library of the 33 libraries analyzed contains more

than 48 percent of the total number of titles in the group, there is a great potential in cooperation through networks.

Personal Assistance

Libraries provide a service of aiding users in identifying and locating documents and of satisfying user requests for information. Traditionally, this service has been called the "reference" or "information" service.

1. Terence Crowley, in a study reported in Crowley and Childers (1971), explores the use of a technique of unobtrusive measures in evaluating the effectiveness of the information service in medium-size public libraries. Of all public libraries in New Jersey with total expenditures between $100,000 and $750,000, he selected the six highest and six lowest on a combined ranking of total expenditures and per capita expenditures. He hired anonymous proxies to ask certain specific questions sometimes by telephone, but usually in person. Only 54 percent of the responses were judged correct.

He concludes that there is no significant difference in correctness of response between the high and low expenditure libraries. He finds the anonymous inquiry to be a highly valuable evaluative technique to determine what responses actually are given to users.

2. Thomas Childers undertook a similar, but more extensive study of information service, also reported in Crowley and Childers (1971). He chose a sample, stratified by total expenditure, of twenty-five New Jersey public libraries. Twenty-five questions were selected for telephone inquiry at the selected libraries. The responses were scaled in a number of alternative ways to indicate the degree of correctness. Correlation analysis was used (1) to investigate whether there exists any relationship among a number of published independent variables describing the financial support, personnel, materials, circulation, hours, valuation, and population served of the selected libraries, and (2) to investigate possible relationships between the independent variables and the dependent variable of correctness of response.

The percentage of correct responses is 55 percent or 64 percent, depending on whether a lack of an attempt to answer is included as an incorrect response or is discarded. The overall percentages and the fact that no relationship is found between expenditures per capita and correctness of responses corroborates the Crowley study. However, a definite relationship is found between the total expenditures and the correctness of responses. The difference between this finding and that of Crowley may be explained by the scaling procedures or by the fact that the Crowley libraries tended to be larger. Stepwise regression is used to create a predictive equation of seven independent variables, and this accounts for 90 percent of the variation in the correctness of responses.

3. Kochen (1971) describes a computer program designed to simulate a network of information referral consultants. The program assumes the existence of a directory that, for each type of request, informs each consultant of alternative documents which may provide the answer and of other consultants who may either provide the answer or to whom he may switch the inquiry.

The input to a single run of the model is a type of request to one particular consultant. The model traces the likely chain of referral consultants and documents until an answer is obtained. Given an input matrix of costs corresponding to each possible activity in the directory, the model calculates the cost of the run. Many runs may be used to determine average costs for consultants and types of requests. Different designs of networks and directories may be evaluated in this manner.

4. Kochen (1972) expands his analysis of networks of information and referral centers. He outlines formulations of a number of mathematical models of different aspects of the centers.

His first model is of the growth in usage of an information and referral center. It is based on the assumption that the probability of a satisfactory response increases until the rate of requests reaches 80 percent of capacity. An additional assumption is that frequency of use is based on this probability. The model traces changes in states, defined in terms of frequencies of use, over time for all potential or actual users. The output is the daily case load and the number of active users.

A second model extends the first in that it assumes a directory of a certain number of entries of information. Each query that is not included in the directory is incorporated into it in the next time period, thereby enabling the system to learn from failure and increase the probability of future success.

A third potential of model development is presented in a concept of "zoomability" of a directory of information. Kochen suggests that a directory ought to have a hierarchical classification scheme associated with it, and that it ought to have a capability built in for a consultant to see either the entire decision tree at one glance or any position of it, large or small.

Publications, Advertisements, and Exhibits

Jestes (1968) undertakes an analysis of use of a reference room in a large university library. An important detriment to the efficient use of the reference room is identified to be the present floor plan and the lack of a locator chart. There are penciled location instructions written on the catalog cards, but the terms used for location in general do not match those on the floor plan.

Jestes proposes a location chart and a new floor plan in which the terminology is consistent with the penciled locations on the catalog cards. By estimating the dollar value of time for undergraduates ($2/hour), graduates ($4), faculty ($10), and library staff ($4), and by estimating the numbers of each type of user, Jestes estimates the present costs of using the catalog, asking for a book at the desk, and looking for a book. The cost of using the new system is evaluated by assuming average time changes in catalog use and in looking for a book.

Jestes says he finds, but it appears that he assumes, that the new system will save the user two minutes per use. Installation cost is $152, maintenance is negligible, and annual user time savings is valued at over $2100.

Library Initiative Communication

University of Durham (1969, Chapter 7) contains a description and an evaluation of a current-awareness service for social science faculty members. As part of a "Project for Evaluating the Benefits of University Libraries" (PEBUL) at the University of Durham, an intensive service was set up on a trial basis. The service was run for two years for about thirty persons from economics, business, politics, and economic history departments.

Each faculty member involved in the service was interviewed to determine his research and teaching interests. He then received copies of tables of contents of new relevant journal issues as well as index cards of relevant journal articles and other recent publications.

At two different times, the participants were given detailed questionnaires to evaluate the service. The main finding is that there was a very wide range of opinions on the usefulness of the service. Although some derived little or no aid from the service, most found it extremely useful. Most clearly preferred the service over such other hypothetical alternative uses of the same amount of funds as additional book grants, paid visits to other libraries, and personal research assistants. Many expressed willingness to pay personally for at least part of the cost of the service.

Planning and Administration

Library Legislation

St. Angelo, Hartsfield, and Goldstein (1971) is a study of state library legislation. Its objectives are

1. To analyze current state library legislation in relation to demographic variables and governmental structure in order to determine patterns of state-level legislation
2. To correlate information about legislation (for example, expenditure levels)
3. To analyze the relationship between state support for libraries in the light of 1 and 2.

The study utilizes three principal statistical techniques: correlation analysis, factor analysis, and Guttman scaling from nominal to ordinal data. One enlightening result is that state library appropriations are unaffected by state resources; poor states are just as likely as rich states to have higher state library appropriations. Another interesting result is that a history of higher appropriations does not guarantee continued higher appropriations; lower appropriations in preceding years do not preclude higher current appropriations.

Library/User/Funder Analysis

Baker and Nance (1968, 1970) and Baker (1968) have outlined an overall model of the three-way interactions of a university library, its users, and its funders. The funders exercise control over the library by means of resource or operational constraints. The users influence the library by behaving in accordance with a reward-cost theory of generating and evaluating alternative need satisfactions in terms of expected rewards and costs.

Industrial dynamics is used to construct a computer simulation of five sectors of the library: ordering of material, book loan, periodical loan, man-hours of service, and space. Hypothetical interactions among the sectors, the funders, and the users are identified. Some attempt is made to

evaluate alternative policies of the Purdue University Physics Library, but the model as presented is in an early, preliminary state of development.
Participative Decision Making
Marchant (1970) notes that there has been increasing recognition in administrative theory of the benefits of participative management. He feels that better decisions are made in a group decision-making framework than in a bureaucratic decision-making framework and that they are carried out better. He investigates the hypothesis that the greater the amount of library staff participation, the better the library performance.

Data from a variety of published sources and from questionnaires are analyzed to test the participative decision-making hypothesis. Marchant identifies two indexes of the independent, controllable variable representing the degree of staff participation. Both indexes are derived from a Profile of Organizational Characteristics developed by Rensis Likert. The first index is derived from the results of questionnaires, issued to top management and professional staff of 22 participating libraries, on the decision-making process: the organizational level, the degree of awareness, and the extent of involvement. The second index is an overall profile index of the organization of the library, including not only the questionnaire results on the decision-making process but also results concerning leadership, motivation, communication, interaction and influence, goal setting or ordering, and control.

Five dependent, performance variables are identified. They are (1) faculty evaluation of library services, (2) circulation of materials for home use, (3) library long-range planning, (4) library staff uniformity in library evaluation, and (5) staff satisfaction. In addition, eleven control variables are identified that are considered to affect the relationship between the independent and dependent variables: (1) decentralization of library collection, (2) library autonomy, (3) library budget, (4) within-grade salary differential, (5) beginning librarian salary, (6) size of staff, (7) size and growth of collection, (8) number of doctoral degrees granted, (9) staff breadth of education, (10) length of service in library, and (11) perquisites granted to professional librarians. In addition to questionnaires sent to library top management and professional staff and to selected faculty of 22 university libraries, data relating to the dependent and control variables were obtained from the Office of Education's statistical report of college and university libraries, the Association of Research Libraries statistical report of member libraries, the Office of Education report of degrees granted by institutions of higher education, and the American Library Directory.

It was hypothesized that if the control variables are controlled, then each of the dependent variables would be directly and strongly correlated with the degree of staff participation in decision making. The results deny any strong correlation between participative decision making and four of the five dependent variables: long-range planning, uniformity of evaluation, circulation, and faculty evaluation. However, a strong correlation is shown between the degree of staff participation in decision making and staff satisfaction. It is concluded that participative decision making affects library performance through increasing staff satisfaction.

Data Processing
Hayes and Becker (1970) provide a comprehensive treatment of library data-processing management, technology, and subsystems. After reviewing library networks, representative mechanization projects, scientific management, and cost accounting, this book advises library managers in the planning, description, budgeting, evaluation, and implementation of a library data-processing system. Hardware and software computer technology for data input, machine language, processing, storage, display, output, and communication are presented.

Among the most useful aspects of the book are the data-processing descriptions and analyses concerning each of the major library subsystems: administrative, circulation control, ordering, catalog and index production, serial records, and information services. For each subsystem, functional requirements are described; criteria of evaluation are presented; relevant experiments and operational systems undertaken in libraries are reviewed; representative forms are presented; files are described in great detail; hypothetical sample computer systems are developed; and processing times and costs are estimated. It is emphasized that the capability of utilizing library models is dependent on the organization of the library data-processing system.

Projecting Library Growth
1. Hayes and Becker (1970; pp. 64–67) describe two types of models used to project library growth: exponential growth models and program-related growth models. Exponential growth models based on a constant percentage of annual growth have been fitted to historical data of library

collection size. These models either have not explained library growth or have attributed it to the growth in publication rate.

Program-related growth models attribute library growth to growth in the educational institution that the library services. For instance, university library size is conceptualized as a function of numbers of students, faculty, and doctoral programs.

2. A recent program-related growth model has been developed by National Center for Higher Education Management Systems at WICHE (1971). The model is computer based and simulates the resources of manpower, money, and space needed to operate a college over a ten-year period. It is a general model for any institution to utilize by supplying its own individual parameters. It can be used to predict resource requirements for present programs and to experiment with requirements needed for hypothetical policy options.

Resource predictions of personnel, facilities, and dollars are made for 90 potential departments, disciplines, or student majors; 30 potential instructional, research, or public service activities; 22 potential space types; 7 potential student levels; 6 potential academic staff ranks; 4 potential types of instruction; 4 potential course levels; and 4 potential nonacademic staff ranks. The implications of change in university programs on library resources are part of the output of the model.

Overall University Library Resource Allocation

1. Mathematica (June 1967) presents aggregate multiplicative models of demand and supply for circulation. Demand for circulation, per time period, is directly related to population, income per capita, and the number of dollars it costs to supply an extra unit of circulation at demand-supply equilibrium. Supply for circulation, per time period, is directly related to book stock, labor services, and processing equipment. Given a total revenue constraint, equilibrium circulation is determined in terms of the other variables.

2. University of Durham (1969) presents a linear programming model for overall university library resource allocation. Generally, a linear programming model identifies a set of activities (variables which are the end products of the organization) and a set of resources to be utilized in the activities. Each additional unit of each activity requires a specific combination of resources and yields a specific quantitative (usually monetary) benefit to the organization. Since the resources are scarce, each resource

constitutes a constraint, and the overall objective is to use the resources for activities in such a way as to maximize the total return to the organization.

In the University of Durham model, seven activities are identified: increasing the bookstock, obtaining interlibrary loans, providing library materials for consultation in the library, issuing items on long loan, issuing items on short loan, senior librarians giving advice to users, and junior librarians helping users. These activities are considered the final outputs of the library. Seven resources are identified: senior librarians, junior librarians, clerical staff, porters, book budget, seats, and shelving. Each resource constitutes a constraint in that the sum of the products of the number of activities times the per unit resource amount is less than or equal to the amount of the resource available. In addition, three demand constraints are imposed, in that users require a minimum number of long loans, short loans, and library material in the library.

The remaining problem, and the one emphasized in the University of Durham report, is that there is no price structure to determine the benefit to the organization of an additional unit of each activity. It is proposed that the marginal costs of the activities be used as a first approximation of the weights in the objective function. Then the weights are adjusted to yield the actual blend of activities in the period for which the data apply. The resulting weights are the implicit relative benefits for the activities, as determined by how the library actually operated.

The resulting objective function and set of constraints are then used to analyze the implications for changes in technology and for changes in resource constraints. A change in technology means that the combination of resources necessary for an activity changes, and resource constraint analysis suggests which resources of the library should be increased if expansion is necessary.

Overall Public Library Resource Allocation

As an illustration of an overall public library resource allocation model, we now discuss a framework formulated for a doctoral dissertation entitled "A Model to Aid Large Public Libraries in Allocating Operating Funds to Programs," which is in the process of being written partially under sponsorship of the same research project as the present volume. It is a general model for large city public libraries and is formulated with respect to the specifics of The Free Library of Philadelphia.

Although The Free Library makes some attempt to consider a wide variety of factors in allocating document resource funds, as is true of most large municipal public libraries, it relies primarily on past circulation. Branches with higher circulation receive more document resource funds, in addition to more and better personnel and services. Since high circulation is, to a great extent, the result of higher education, the system tends to allocate more funds for the gifted segments of the population and less funds for the disadvantaged. In any case, there is no current analytical model being used for the provision of library services.

The model that we are formulating is an attempt to provide guidance in relating decision making with an overall library objective. By means of a mathematical programming technique, it converts certain managerial assumptions and preferences into an optimal allocation of funds. This allocation is not meant to be a mandatory one. Rather, it represents a managerial tool aimed at giving the director a broader perspective. He may change his assumptions, or he may use the model to evaluate alternative allocations.

Wallace (1967) has suggested that it may be desirable to measure public library use in terms of better and more libraries, better labor relations, better workers, broadened and continuing education, greater social understanding, and increased civic awareness. However, as we have concluded in Chapter 2, until the day that these ambitious measurements are made operational, a more productive course for measuring public library use is to consider its output in terms of direct or indirect exposure of individuals to documents of recorded human experience.

As noted in Chapter 2, an aggregate amount of document exposure is a less meaningful measure of output than the exposure per capita of the population of potential users. A relatively high amount of document exposure merely may be the result of a relatively large population of potential users, in which case there may be a relatively low exposure per capita. Similarly, a relatively low aggregate amount of document exposure may be associated with a high exposure per capita. Therefore, we define output for each library unit (and for each population group) on a per capita basis.

We break down library use by adults and by children into circulation use, in-library use, and telephone use. In order to avoid working with a multidimensional output of public library use, we prefer a common unit of measurement for the three exposure types. Our choice is hours of document exposure. An improvement on this choice might be to include weights for the relative value of an hour of each type of circulation use, of in-library use, and of telephone use, perhaps for different types of users. However, these evaluations prove unnecessarily burdensome since the assumption of equal relative value of all hours of document exposure is not an unreasonable one, at least in an initial analysis.

For circulation use, relevant library unit circulation counts are recorded by adult nonfiction, adult fiction, and juvenile. The number of hours of document exposure per circulation count (by the borrower or anyone else) has been estimated from a questionnaire given to a sample of borrowers.

In-library use has been determined by adult and children annual library unit attendance, time spent per visit, and the proportion of in-library time devoted to document exposure. The best way of estimating attendance for the library units that do not maintain attendance records is to take small samples, to estimate for each library unit, or for each of a few relatively homogeneous groups of library units, the average circulation per adult or per juvenile visit. Attendance then is determined by dividing total circulation counts by circulation per visit.

Time spent in a library unit per visit has been obtained by giving users time-recorded cards upon entering the building, collecting them upon departure, and recording the difference between time of entrance and departure. The proportion of in-library time devoted to document exposure has been determined by observing samples of users.

The remaining element of library use is telephone use. Because it reflects a relatively small number of use hours, it has been eliminated without great effect. However, it could have been included by determining the annual number of adult and child telephone services per library unit and the average document exposure time per telephone service.

The allocation model is formulated in order to maximize total annual library use in terms of document exposure time. Since funds generally are more efficient in producing library use in high-education population segments, this allocation may result in almost all of the library's limited funds going to library units serving these segments. It is generally acknowledged that a metropolitan library should reach out to the disadvantaged. (See, for example, Martin 1967, pp. 39–52.) Therefore, we establish constraints so that sufficient funds are channeled to library units serving the disadvantaged in order to raise use rates in all subsections to at least a certain minimum level.

By far, the most important method of document exposure is reading. In order to explain and predict document exposure, it is necessary to have some understanding of the difference between "readers" and "nonreaders." There has been very little research on this difference. An important exception is Martin (1967, pp. 25–38).

Martin arranged hour-long interviews with 1913 randomly selected households in the Baltimore area, covering 6314 adults and children. These interviews obtained detailed information about background, socioeconomic status, activities, and reading. Martin summarizes his detailed findings in a rather facetious "easy" three-step prescription to produce book readers.

(1) As a first step, simply see to it that infants are born into families that are already made up of readers. . . .
(2) As a second ingredient, education and more education is needed to make a reader. . . .
(3) If you want a reader—that is, a continuing book reader through life— you must have an adult who participates. (Pp. 25–26.)

The first point is that the study found a positive relationship between readers and the presence of books in their homes when they were young, their being read to, and their early contact with the public library. The factors both expose the child to reading and help establish the idea that reading is a valuable experience.

The third point is a rejection of the popular conception of the reader as a recluse. The study found a positive relationship between reading and all forms of participation: the more extensive and intensive the participation, the greater the relationship. The participation may be in cultural activities (plays, art, concerts, reading clubs, exhibits), civic and community activities (P.T.A., women's clubs, election campaigns, writing a letter to a congressman), vocational associations (business organizations, labor unions), or church groups.

The majority of people read books in response to stimulation, not in response to boredom. If really empty time confronts the individual, he is more likely to turn the television knob than to seek out a book. Book reading may appear to be a retreat, but actually it is more a regrouping of forces, a consideration of new intelligence, and a moment of refreshment before returning to the fray. (P. 26.)

Martin considers the second point about education as the most important. "Education is overwhelmingly the factor most closely associated with reading." (P. 25.) "[The data show] the clearest social relationship, the association of reading and education." (P. 29.)

We use educational grade level as an important independent, uncontrollable variable to explain library use. Because they are positively related to education, other socioeconomic variables presented in the United States Census, such as income or percent professional and managerial, also are highly correlated with library use and could be independent variables. However, since education is most directly related to reading, we use it alone, in the form it is presented in the United States Census, "median school years completed by persons 25 years old or over." This variable is an important one in explaining both adult and juvenile library use. An additional educational variable computed from census data that may be helpful in predicting adult library use is the proportion of adults in high school or college.

The first factor presented by Martin, home exposure to books, is highly correlated with education. It is merely a suggestion that reading and library use perpetuate reading and library use.

The third factor presented by Martin, social participation, is one that is susceptible to measurement. However, measurement would entail counts of social participation activities in each group of census tracts. It would necessitate an operational definition of a social participation activity and a means for combining these activities into one measure. Although we feel that this variable is relevant, we feel the increase in library use prediction is not sufficient to justify the added effort involved in including it.

The educational variables used to explain and predict library unit document exposure are the average educational grade level of adults attributed to the library unit and the average educational grade level of the parents of children attributed to the library unit.

In a national sample of 1549 adults, Mendelsohn and Wingerd (1967) state: "The three manifestations of 'fair to poor' service expressed by persons critical of their local libraries are of the following ranking according to frequency of mentions:
1. Poor selection of books
2. Overcrowded; inadequate facilities
3. Poor personnel and service"

In addition to using the uncontrollable variable of educational grade level to explain and predict document exposure, we identify three major controllable variables of library managers that correspond to these three manifestations: (1) physical facilities, (2) document resources, and (3) service effort to bring individuals and documents together.

Provision of physical facilities is essential for library use: both to store document resources and to promote document exposure. The quality of physical facilities influences the number of library visits and the length of stay per library visit. The quality of a library unit, defined on a "per capita" basis, is measured by area available, annual hours open, and a utility index. The utility index includes such factors as age of building, time since last major improvement or addition, location relative to the residence of the population, and design.

Although physical facility quality is a controllable variable, it is treated in the proposed allocation model as a given, uncontrollable variable. The discontinuity inherent in changing physical facilities and its long planning horizon would cause special problems if it were treated as controllable. In addition, it would increase the complexity of the allocation considerably.

Since the overall objective is to encourage document exposure, primarily by means of library ownership of documents and their accessibility to the public (as opposed to emphasis on interlibrary loan), the quality of the document resources of a library unit is an important determinant of library use. Consistently, in user surveys, the reasons stated most often for dissatisfaction with public libraries are that books are out or selections are limited, and the reason stated most often for satisfaction is the provision of a variety of good materials.

At the Free Library, annual counts of additions, withdrawals, and net stock are kept for each library unit, for the following document forms: adult nonfiction book; adult fiction book; children's book; periodical; newspaper; unbound document; photo, picture, or print; pamphlet; microcard or microprint; map; talking book; sound recording; tape recording; manuscript; microfiche; educational firm; microfilm; and slide. We define a set of accession periods of at least annual lengths. Assuming that withdrawals are made half on a FIFO (first in, first out) basis, and half on a basis proportional to the number of documents held from each accession period, we have used the annual data of additions and withdrawals to estimate the current number of adult and juvenile documents of each form which was acquired in each accession period at each library unit. In order to combine the various document types acquired in various accession periods into one measure of the quality of document resources, we utilize a subjective evaluative variable of the current value to a library unit of a typical adult or juvenile document of a given form and accession period.

We define "service effort" to include the following activities:

1. Personal assistance for document identification and location and for conveying information
2. Publications, advertisements, and exhibits
3. Personal communication at the initiative of the library with members of the population being served

In the allocation, we assume that funds are already allocated to all categories of library expenditures except for this service effort and the variable costs of documents.

Librarians often regard the in-library reference service as the sine qua non of library service. In addition, they agree that major effort at community involvement is necessary to encourage library use for persons of limited education. (See, for example, Martin 1967, pp. 39–52, and Mendelsohn and Wingerd 1967, pp. III 14–15.)

Service effort usually is provided by employees of the library, but also may result from contracted services such as for a publicity campaign. Also, service effort may have some cumulative effect. That is, service effort last year may have motivated individuals to become library users or extended their use of the library. For this reason, we take into consideration service effort for the prior year, in addition to the year for which allocation is to be made.

Records about salary and funds for contracted service effort are readily available. In addition, staff members (or perhaps divisional heads) will be questioned as to the proportion of time spent on service effort, inside or outside library facilities, and as to the library unit or units benefiting from this effort. In many cases, for programs involving more than one library unit or both adults and children, expenditures have to be apportioned to the units and population subsets involved.

For each population subset (adults and children) and library unit, we have suggested one output variable for library use, one uncontrollable variable for education, one controllable variable for physical facilities that is treated as uncontrollable, and two controllable variables for document resources and service effort that are treated as controllable. We formulate a model for adults and children to explain library use as a function of education, physical facilities, document resources, and service effort.

The model is of the type referred to in operations research as a "mathematical programming model" suggesting an optimum allocation of funds between current expenditures for document resources and service effort, between adults and children, and among library units in order to maximize total document exposure, subject to the constraints that per capita document exposure is at least a certain minimum amount for all areas in the city. The form of the model is a result of a combination of theoretical reasoning, practical considerations, and careful scrutiny of the available data.

Conclusion

The results of almost all of the aforementioned model-building attempts have been published since 1968. It is obvious that library model building to aid library managers is in its infancy. We have noted some of the shortcomings inherent in these initial attempts. This exciting endeavor to coordinate what is known about libraries in order to facilitate decision making should obviously be continued and strengthened.

Let us reemphasize here the relationship between models and data. In a library, as in any organization, the number of possible activities one could observe and the number of possible ways of recording these observations are infinite. The collection of these data usually is expensive and results in a confusing complex of so-called "information." The data are useless unless they are filtered and organized in order to aid a manager in making decisions. Organization of data by relating them to decision alternatives and performance entails establishing decision models. Therefore, decision models are required to provide criteria for determining what data are needed to make decisions, and to inform us on how these data are to be used.

In commenting on library automation, Morse (1968) states:

It is the author's belief, based on discouraging experience, that neither the computer experts nor the librarian (for different reasons) really know what data would be useful for the librarian to have collected, analyzed, and displayed so he can make decisions with some knowledge of what the decision implies. What is needed *before* the computer designs are frozen is for models, of the sort developed in this book, to be played with, to see which of them could be useful and to see what data are needed and in what form, in order that both models and computers can be used most effectively by the librarian. (Pp. 141–142.)

5

DEVELOPMENT OF A MANAGEMENT INFORMATION SYSTEM FOR LIBRARIES

Introduction

We have presented various aspects of library managerial decision making. In Chapter 2, we began with statements of library objectives, and we suggested various measures of document exposure to represent overall library performance. In Chapter 3, we suggested a Planning-Programming-Budgeting System (PPBS) approach to library managerial decision making. This approach to planning and the development of library programs leads to consistent and economical library performance, and it provides useful guidance in the librarian's choice of programs and courses of action. This approach includes long-range strategic planning based on library functions and also on population subsets, document subsets, library units, and geographical areas; analysis of costs and benefits by library program structure; and a rational organization for decision making and budgeting. In Chapter 4, we emphasized the importance of library decision models in understanding the complex interrelationships that exist in large libraries, and in providing the library administrator with appropriate tools to make predictions and evaluations of library programs.

In this chapter, we discuss the need for an information system to support library management planning and decision making. This information system is the cement that binds together the various elements of a library's organization with one another and with the library's objective of serving its clientele. This system provides data necessary for the daily operations of a library as well as for the formulation, validation, and implementation of models. Ideally, it also provides information about the effectiveness of library services and operations, about the population of users and the population of nonusers, about the library-user interaction, and about other relevant factors. As mentioned previously, the design of an information system includes a specification of a number of possible observable activities. The number of possible ways of recording these observations is infinite.

Characteristics of an Information System

Library managers easily can be overwhelmed by an overabundance of data, which are not necessarily useful for any particular management decision. Beer and Ackoff (1969, p. 529) state:

According to a management joke of venerable vintage a manager was one who had no time for the facts; he was too busy making decisions. To update this quip for today we would have to say that a manager is one who has no time for decisions; he is too busy assimilating the facts.

A fantastically impressive stream of bits assails this planet from radio stars in outer space: theoretically this is information, but obviously it will never even constitute data unless something, some day, can be inferred from it.

Therefore, a major undertaking in designing an information system is to evaluate the utility in decision making (benefits) and the effort necessary to collect (costs) data elements under consideration for inclusion in the information system.

The following discussion has been adapted for library management information systems from a more general treatment in James C. Emery (1969, *Organizational Planning and Control Systems*, passim). There are several characteristics of an information system which need to be considered in order to assess a particular system's benefits and costs. These characteristics include: specific content of the information input, selectivity of the data, time lags, accuracy, reliability, generality, and flexibility. We shall briefly discuss these factors in relation to their effects on the benefits and costs of an information system for a library.

Specific Content of the Information Input

This is the broadest characteristic to be considered, and there are two facets that deserve attention: the choice of data elements to include in the system and the informational content of these elements.

Data elements that are chosen for collection and inclusion in the information system are representations of reality. The greater degree of detail in the data element, the more the information system will reflect reality. Decisions that rely on these information sources may be better because of the greater realism, but the costs of a more detailed data system are much larger than for a less detailed system.

Aggregation of data elements will lower the storage and processing costs of the information system, and will result in a diminished degree of realism. The reduced costs may justify appropriate levels of aggregation. In addition, aggregation may highlight patterns or trends that would be overlooked in unaggregated data. The length of retention of data in an information system is a further consideration. It may be important to retain certain data on a daily basis (for example, attendance counts); other data might just as profitably be stored on a weekly or monthly basis (for example, book transactions within subject categories). The level of aggregation and length of retention are important considerations in the design of an information system.

With respect to the quality of information in an information system, clearly a system that consists of useless random noise cannot provide a decision maker with anything of value. An input into the data system can have very low informational content or very high informational content for the library manager or may lie at any point between these two extremes. An example may help to clarify this concept of informational content. The number of windows in the library carries very little information with it, while the number of patrons entering the library but not checking out any books has a great deal of informational content. The quality of response that can be expected from any information system can only be as good as the wealth (or lack of wealth) of information of the system's inputs. Low-quality inputs cannot produce high-quality outputs; nonetheless, the converse of this statement is not necessarily true since high-quality output depends not only on high-quality input but also on factors such as asking the proper questions, time lags between data capture and system output, and so on. Further discussion of the specific content of a library information system is deferred to the last two sections of this chapter.

Selectivity of the Data

Data can be presented to a decision maker in a number of ways. Unless a great deal of care is taken, the decision maker easily can become inundated with only marginally relevant facts. Important information may be buried in a massive report containing many other bits of information that are not as important, and hence it is necessary to choose carefully those facts to be presented to the decision maker. The exception principle can be most helpful in this regard. Management by exception requires the establishment of tolerance limits for critical decision variables. Any variation from week to week within these preset limits is not reported to the manager. However, if these limits are exceeded for any given week, a report of this occurrence would be sent to the manager as a warning that something unusual has happened. This principle restricts the flow of information that the manager must assimilate by filtering out common or normal occurrences. Naturally, the actual values of these tolerance limits are subject to managerial discretion. Too narrow limits may not filter out sufficiently "unusual" occurrences; limits that are too wide may not warn the manager early enough to react to the unusual circumstance. Although some trial and error may be required to set adequate tolerance limits, management by exception can be a useful principle to follow. It increases programming costs to some extent, but it filters out a great deal of unnecessary information and increases the value of any single report.

Time Lags
There are two types of time lags that need to be considered in order to estimate the benefits and costs of an information system. The first is the time lag between an event and its appearance as an element in the data base. For example, the time lag between the placement of an order for a new book and the insertion of a copy of the order into a "books-on-order" file may only be a few hours. However, the time lag between a report of a lost book and the expunction of all catalog entries referring to this book may be weeks or even months. The second type of time lag is the information retrieval time of the information system. Quick retrieval time is definitely an asset, while slow retrieval time can be both bothersome and costly.

Costs vary inversely with both update time and response time. If a very short update time is required, many more hours of labor would be needed to capture the relevant information and enter it into the information system. Similarly, if a very short response time is required, the storage mode and processing machinery necessary to meet this requirement are more costly than would be the case otherwise.

Accuracy
Accuracy is another characteristic of an information system with benefit and cost implications. Very few decisions require 100 percent accuracy, and such a requirement would be very costly indeed. Nevertheless, a high degree of accuracy is valuable in that it improves the quality of the information required in decision making. Operating decisions, like processing a book from the acquisitions department to open circulation, usually require greater accuracy than higher-level decisions. The reason for this is that higher-level decisions are normally less sensitive to minor errors. For example, the decision to open a new branch library will not depend on whether there are exactly 10,050 or 12,066 residents in a certain area. The decision would likely be the same for either case, provided of course that

sufficient funds are available.

The cost of increasing the accuracy of an information system depends on the implementation of error-control procedures, error-detection routines, and error correction. More stringent accuracy requirements are naturally more expensive. Often a statistical sample can be substituted for a population census in order to estimate relevant decision variables, but at a calculated loss of accuracy.

Reliability

Reliability in an information system means freedom from failure and the provision of continuous, consistent service. This characteristic is most commonly applied to computer-based information systems, but it can also be used to describe manual systems. How accessible are the data files, and how easily can they be consulted in order to obtain desired information? Computer systems are fast, but certain types of equipment and data-processing procedures are more subject to failure and error than others. The value of a reliable system lies in its ability to remain in operation when it is needed and to have relatively few periods of downtime. The costs of any particular information system will vary. Normally the cost of a system increases in proportion to its increase in reliability. Since libraries for the most part have not adopted computer-based on-line information systems, this characteristic is relatively less important; however, university libraries in particular are beginning to adopt such systems.

Generality

This system characteristic refers to the ability of the system to respond and be useful in a multitude of ways. Certain data elements, for example, may be valuable in more than one decision process. Similarly, an information system designed to support the financial activities of a library may be modified slightly in order to serve the personnel and operations activities as well. Functions and decisions overlap, and the greater the generality an information system possesses, the more valuable it will be to the organization.

Flexibility

Over a period of time many changes can occur in the operations of any organization. Perhaps the most significant are a change in management and a change in the scale of operation. Either of these changes can have a significant effect on a management information system. New management may desire different reporting procedures, more frequent reports, specialized information studies, and so on. Will the present information system be able to satisfy the demands of a new management team? In addition, if the library expands its book collection at an annual rate of 10 percent, will the present information system be able to handle the increased load and will it still operate efficiently? These types of questions should be asked during the design stage of an information system. The value of the system increases if it is flexible and can incorporate change. The cost implications of these systems should also be considered.

Library Information System Structures

For purposes of classification and design, a general library information system can be conceptually broken down into a number of separate subsystems. Each subsystem can then be considered separately. It is often easier to design an information subsystem for a separate function, such as circulation control, than to try to design one information system for the entire library. However, interdependencies between the subsystems will exist, and these need to be taken into account in a total system design.

Two alternative breakdowns of a general library information system are given. Figure 5.1 depicts an information system hierarchy based on a design by Robert M. Hayes and Joseph Becker (1970).[1] They identify six major subsystems, each of which is composed of a number of separate files.

Figure 5.2 depicts an information system design based on the program structure presented in Chapter 3. It differs from the Hayes-Becker design in fundamental ways. It identifies four sources of library data: the population to be served, library service and operations, user-library interaction, and the rest of society. Without recommending any particular system design for all libraries, we will present a crosswalk between the Hayes-Becker information system and the alternate system based on the program structure of Chapter 3. Then we will discuss in further detail the characteristics and content of these alternative system designs.

The purpose of a crosswalk between the two information system designs is to indicate how library personnel might translate any data file from one system into the other system. Table 5.1 depicts the crosswalk from the list of seventeen functions to the six Hayes-Becker subsystems. A "?" indicates that there is no clear correspondence or else no counterpart in the other

---

1. The description of the Hayes-Becker system is based on Chapters 14 through 18 of the referenced volume.

Library Information System Structures

system. Table 5.2 depicts the crosswalk from the Hayes-Becker subsystems to the list of function numbers.

The content of the Hayes-Becker system design is outlined now. The six information subsystems are decomposed into files, and the files can be further subdivided into accounts, records, and data elements. Their system design is organized in the following way:

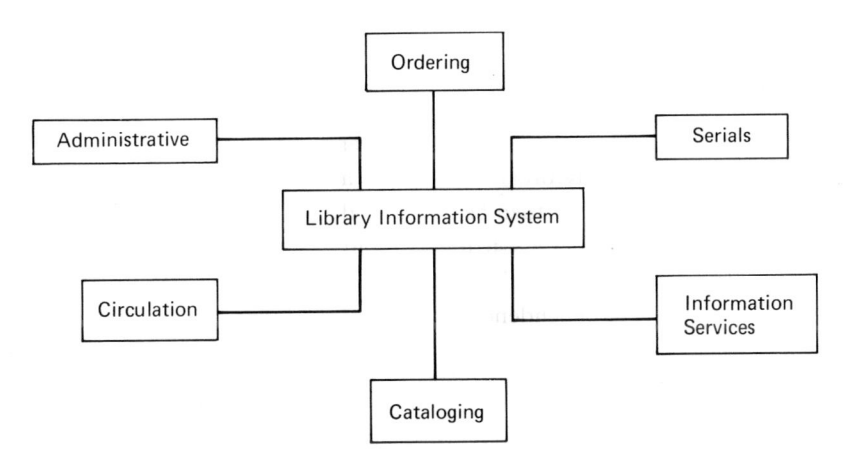

Figure 5.1. Hayes-Becker library information system.

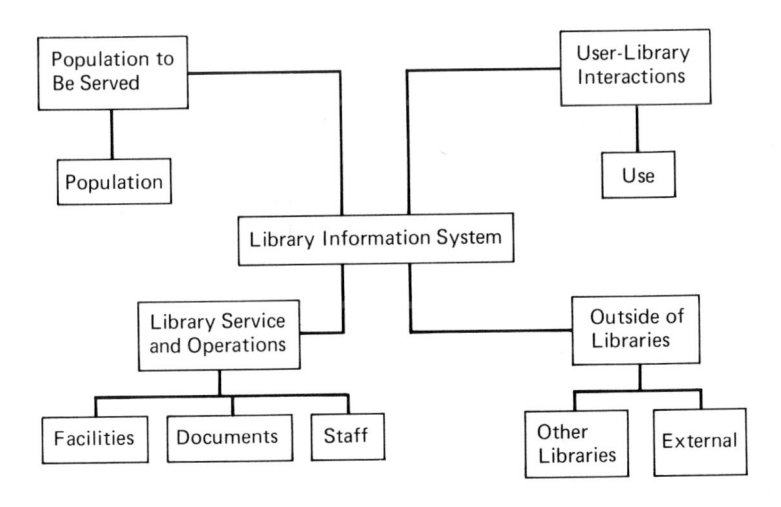

Figure 5.2. Alternative library information system design.

Table 5.1. Crosswalk between Seventeen Functions and Hayes-Becker Subsystems

Function	Hayes and Becker Subsystem
Providing Physical Facilities	
1. Provision of building area	Administrative
2. Provision of user furnishings	Administrative
3. Maintenance of facilities	?
Providing Access to Documents and Indexes within the Library	
4. Selection	Ordering; Serials
5. Acquisition	Ordering; Serials
6. Processing	Ordering; Serials
7. Classification and cataloging	Cataloging; Serials
8. Control of location and use	Circulation; Serials
9. Facilitation of use	Circulation; Serials
10. Maintenance and weeding	?; Serials
Providing Access to Documents in Other Libraries	
11. Provision of aids primarily to locate documents in other libraries	?
12. Facilitation of access to documents in other libraries	?
Promoting Library Use	
13. Personal assistance for document identification and location and for conveying information	Information Services
14. Publications, advertisements, and exhibits	?
15. Personal communication at the initiative of the library with members of the population being served	?
Planning, Administration, and Support	
16. Planning and administration	Administrative
17. Support	Administrative

Table 5.2. Crosswalk between Hayes-Becker Subsystems and Appropriate Function Numbers*

Hayes and Becker Subsystem	Function Numbers
Administrative	1, 2, 16, 17
Circulation	8, 9
Ordering	4, 5, 6
Cataloging	7
Serials	4, 5, 6, 7, 8, 9, 10
Information Service	13
?	3, 10, 11, 12, 14, 15

* See Table 5.1 for functions associated with each function number.

I. *Administrative Subsystem*
   A. Financial files
      1. Balance sheet accounts file (by account number within department)
         a. Salary-related accounts (Salary; Payroll taxes; Pension fund; Insurance; Social Security)
         b. Supplies accounts (Office supplies; Book preparation supplies; Automotive supplies; Building maintenance supplies)
         c. Printing and reproduction accounts (Office copying equipment; Printed forms; Reports)
         d. Office expense accounts (Postage; Telephone and communication; Office services; Office equipment, purchase; Office equipment, rental)
         e. Facility accounts (Rent; Utilities; Construction materials; Motor vehicles)
         f. Book accounts
         g. Financial accounts (Cash; Accounts payable; Accounts receivable; Depreciation)
      2. Purchase Order file (by purchase order number)
      3. Accounts payable file (by vendor number)
   B. Personnel Files
      1. Personnel file (by employee number) (Application forms; Interviews and references; Appointments, transfers, and promotions; Performance ratings)
      2. Payroll records file (by employee number) (Time records; Checks issued to employees; Payroll change records)
   C. Management Files-Cost Accounting
      1. Direct cost accounts (by process and job) (Historical costs; Standard costs; Time, Amount of work performed; Material used; Administrative unit; Level of complexity)
      2. Overhead cost accounts (by type of expense)
II. *Circulation Subsystem*
      1. Transaction file (by call number) (Documents charged to borrower-user or other library; Documents charged to internal library function; Documents returned but not purged)
      2. Call card file (by transaction number) (when book card or borrower card is missing)
      3. Hold call card file (by call number)
      4. Borrower registration file (by borrower identification number)
      5. Scheduling file (by call number) (deliveries and pickups)

6. Security file (by call number) (for military classified records)
7. Overdue file (by call number)
8. History file (by call number) (analysis of prior circulation records)

III. *Ordering Subsystem*
1. In process file (by author and title) (shows vendor and order status-edited; purchase order written; I.D. card written; encumbered; order received; invoice received; order paid; overdue; back ordered; partial order received; wrong material; defective material; canceled; waiting to be cataloged; clear from in-process file; copied to standing order file)
2. Order file (by order number) (shows vendor and documents of outstanding orders, without bibliographic information)
3. Vendor file (by vendor number) (shows orders)
4. Fund file (by fund code number) (status of each fund)
5. Invoice file (by invoice number within vendor number) (for each invoice received, shows items received, canceled, and outstanding)

IV. *Cataloging Subsystem*
1. The catalog or index (by author, title, and subject) (for bibliographic description, intellectual access, intellectual organization, physical access, alerting, and administration)

V. *Serials Subsystem*
1. Master serial records file (by serial identification number) Cataloging Data—name changes; alternative titles; analytic entries for separately titled issues; a unique identifier; a limited set of subject headings; reference to abstracting and indexing journals by which the serial is or is likely to be covered

    Ordering Data—renewal dates; names and addresses of publisher, society, or association; vendor number; fund number; reference to associated publications

    Receiving Data—frequency of publication; volume and issue numbering practice; expected irregularities; check-in points; claiming criteria

    Binding Data—style and color; number of issues per binding volume; binding dates; special instructions for binding

    Holdings Data—bound volumes and separate issues; gaps and missing issues; wants; locations of holdups

    Distribution Data—names and addresses of individuals and organizations, and locations for distribution

2. Receiving file (by serial, by receipt, or by issue expected)

VI. *Information Services Subsystem*
1. Data base for users (by subject key word)

The Hayes-Becker library information system design not only specifies the content of the system in an extensive fashion, but it also indicates the type of reports and analyses that the system facilitates. The following list indicates the major reports that result from their system. No special-purpose programs are required to obtain these reports for the most part. Analyses that do require special programs are indicated in parentheses.

I. *Administrative Subsystem*
  A. Financial
    1. Expenditure reports
    2. Analyses of variances
    3. Budgetary plan
    4. Reports by vendor
    5. Checks to vendors
    6. Cash status reports
    7. History (bookkeeping; vendors)
  B. Personnel
    1. Service reports
    2. Performance evaluations
    3. Checks to employees
    4. Payroll reports
  C. Management-Cost Accounting
    1. Labor efficiency reports
    2. Labor distribution reports
    3. Actual versus standard comparisons
  D. Management-Production Control
    1. Production schedules
    2. Future work-load forecasts

II. *Circulation Subsystem*
    1. Recall notices
    2. Overdue notices
    3. Long-term circulation list
    4. Hold list
    5. Replacement borrower cards
    6. Replacement book cards
    7. Registered borrower list
    8. Fines
    9. Document distribution schedule

(10. Analysis of document use by user)
(11. Analysis of document use by document)
(12. Analysis of document use by user and document)

III. *Ordering Subsystem*
   1. Status of items on order by author/title
   2. Estimates of cataloging work loads
   3. Notices to requesters
   4. Claims notices
   5. Orders printed
   6. State of library funds, including danger signals
   7. Invoice payment authorization
   8. List of canceled and out-of-print items
   9. Vendor report of number of items ordered; average delivery time, and number canceled due to inefficiency

IV. *Cataloging Subsystem*
   1. Frequency of use of material
   2. Frequency of assignment of subject terms and of co-occurrence

V. *Serials Subsystem*
   1. Expected arrival list
   2. Current information list
   3. Invoice charges approved and disapproved for payment
   4. Bindery control list
   5. Claims and renewal requests
   6. Error list
   7. New acquisitions list
   8. Current expenditure characteristics
   9. Subject heading list
   10. Master shelf list
   11. Routing lists
   12. Membership lists

VI. *Information Services Subsystem*
   1. Information retrieval

We shall now discuss in greater detail the characteristics and content of the information system based on the program structure of Chapter 3. With respect to the specific content of this information system, we mentioned previously that important design considerations are degree of detail and level of aggregation. Library data elements may be defined according to one or more of the following eight categories:

(1) Time Period

If time period is not indicated for a data element, we assume that it is associated with a year and is aggregated not more frequently than annually. Time period is indicated if less than annual subtotals, by hour, day, week, month, season, semester, and so forth, appear to be relevant. For instance, time period is indicated for attendance, which may be tabulated with respect to any time frame.

(2) Population Subset

For public libraries, the population to be served may be subdivided into population subsets with respect to age, reading or educational level, occupation, geographical area, or other special characteristics. For university libraries, they may be defined with respect to status (undergraduate, graduate-master's, graduate-Ph.D, faculty, staff, other) and subject area of interest. They are described in detail in Chapter 3, where it is emphasized that they may be very broad in scope or very narrow. For example, for the number of persons in the population served by the library, it may be useful to tabulate by population subset. The term "per capita" is used to refer to each person in the population to be served or to each person in a population subset; actually, it indicates a division by the appropriate number of persons.

(3) Document Subset

Document subsets may be defined with respect to form, subject matter, and other characteristics, as described in Chapter 3 and Appendix II. An example of a data element for which document subset subtotals may be relevant is number of documents added.

(4) Library Unit

Each separate physical location of a library may be considered a different library unit. Also, larger units may be segmented even further; for example, departmental libraries or subject departments in the same building. An example of a data element for which library unit subtotals may be relevant is the number of microform readers.

(5) Exposure Type

In Chapter 2, we discussed various types of document exposure, including circulation, direct in-library exposure, indirect exposure (where a library employee communicates to an individual as a substitute for direct exposure), photocopy use, and interlibrary loans. An example of a data element for which exposure-type subtotals may be useful is the number of document exposures.

(6) Staff Type

The library staff may be delineated by extent and type of education and experience. This delineation may be accomplished with respect to degree attained or primary function performed. Ordinarily, there is a distinction between professional and nonprofessional personnel, with possible additional categories of semiprofessional and student assistant. Staff Type is a useful tabulation for full-time equivalent personnel, particularly if delineated further into library functions. Alternatively, separate counts may be made of full-time and part-time staff.

(7) Storage Locations

Documents are stored in various library units and, within library units, in various locations. Each relatively distinct location may be identified for certain data. For example, it may be helpful to delineate the number of linear feet of shelving by storage location.

(8) Use Period

In addition to being placed in a storage location, every library document is assigned a specific use period. The period may range from a one-hour, in-library reserve charge to an unlimited circulation use. An example of a data element for which use period subtotals may be beneficial is the mean time between the withdrawal and return of a document.

The eight dimensions just listed are the major categories for defining most library data elements. However, for a particular decision, there may be other dimensions that might also be relevant. Significant indicators of input, output, and performance of each library function are formulated by taking ratios of appropriate data elements. The ratios of quantitative data elements must be examined in conjunction with whatever descriptive or qualitative information may be available to a library decision maker. Analysis of descriptive information may yield additional relevant quantitative data elements. For purposes of illustration, a list of selected quantitative data elements and examples of appropriate ratios pertaining to the function, provision of aids to locate documents within the library, are presented below in the section dealing with data for program indicators.

Benefit and Cost Criteria for Management Information System Elements

In the preceding section the methodology for defining the data elements relevant to the various decision areas of the library is presented. Since a major effort is required to design and implement an information system to collect, store, and utilize all of these data, in this section we discuss criteria for assessing the benefits and costs of data elements to be included in a library management information system (MIS). In a later section we will indicate which data elements in general we believe possess the highest priority for inclusion into the information system.

Information has value only if it is used in the decision-making and planning process. Not only must information be used in order to have value, but it must have a certain amount of surprise content. Information that tells us something we already know or very strongly suspect has very little value. Furthermore, if information has value, then the content of the information must cause the decision maker to reach a different decision than he would have reached in the absence of the information. Finally, the result of this "improved" decision must be evident in the attainment of a higher level on some payoff or objective function. James C. Emery, in an unpublished paper, "Cost/Benefit Analysis of Information Systems," stated that *"In short, the value we attribute to information is the incremental effect it has on achieving some desired benefit."* (1971, p. 2.)

The benefits of an item of information may often be difficult to estimate, but two questions may help to highlight the pertinent considerations:
1. How will this information help to reduce costs?
2. How will this information lead to an improvement in service?

There may be intangible issues involved in both of these questions (for example, increase in client goodwill). However the answer to these questions will at least identify the factors contributing to the usefulness of an item of information.

In order to clarify further the concept of the value of information, the following type of analysis can be carried out by the library administrator when he is deciding whether to include a certain data element in a MIS. The usefulness or value of a particular data element can be evaluated in terms of
1. Its contribution to the decision that is to be made

2. The contribution of the decision, when carried out, to the performance of the library
3. The sensitivity of the decision as a function of the data
4. The sensitivity of the contribution of the decision, when effected, to the performance of the library
5. Multiple uses of the data in other decision areas

For example, in evaluating the data element, number of circulation uses of documents in a particular document subset, as applied to the decision of determining the optimal amount of funds to be allocated to that document subset for the purchase of additional documents, the following statements regarding usefulness would seem relevant. This data element should play a major role in deciding the amount of funds to be allocated to the area for the purchase of additional documents. The decision regarding the amount of funds to be allocated to the document subsets probably has a major effect upon a document exposure performance measure. The amount of funds allocated in a given document subset probably should be quite sensitive to varying circulation rates. On a short-term basis, probably document exposure would not be highly sensitive to the amount of funds allocated for document purchase within a given document subset. Finally, this data element is useful in other decision areas.

The difficulty or cost of collecting data for a particular data element can be evaluated in terms of

1. Its availability in the desired form as a by-product of library operations or from other sources
2. Its availability in raw form requiring sampling or other techniques to obtain the data in desired form
3. Requirements to collect and synthesize the data, often utilizing sampling techniques

An example of data that are by-products of normal library operation is circulation use. A count of the number of titles in a particular document subset obtained from the shelf list represents an example of the second type. Finally, an example of a data element requiring both collection and synthesis is the average length of time a user consults a document within the library. Furthermore, in each of the three cases there is sometimes an additional cost associated with the implementation of the data collection activity. For example, to obtain circulation use data per document subset, certain procedures must be developed if the data are to be collated manually and certain programs must be written and debugged if the data are to be collated on a computer.

In some cases desired data that are difficult to collect can be estimated as a function of a more readily available data element. For example, in-library use of books appears to be a function of circulation use. Hence, once this relationship has been determined (often by performing a special study), estimates of in-library use can be made as related to circulation use data.

Once the usefulness and the difficulty or cost of obtaining the data have been ascertained, a benefit-cost analysis can be performed to determine the priority of inclusion in the MIS. For example, data of marginal usefulness and requiring a high cost for collection would be assigned a low priority for inclusion into the MIS. On the other hand, data that are exceedingly useful and readily available, would be assigned a high priority for inclusion. Other data elements at neither of these extremes must be evaluated from a benefit-cost point of view to determine their priority for inclusion.

Finally some data are required by higher funding agencies or are requested by organizations of which a library might be a part. If the form of the data requested is incongruent with information the library is collecting, steps must be taken to determine how the data in the proper form might best be obtained. In other cases, data are requested that are not currently being collected in any form. If the library deems it necessary to collect these data, means must be devised to obtain the data even though they are not part of the library's management information system.

Evaluation of Data Elements

General

At one extreme, a management information system (MIS) is composed of *all* data that are relevant to the decision-making and planning process. Here we assume that only data which potentially affect a decision or plan would be included in this system. At the other extreme, no data would be collected or used in the planning and decision-making process. The design, implementation, and operation of a management information system to collect data for *all* the relevant data elements entails a major commitment and undertaking that can be very costly. On the other hand, collection of no data whatsoever results in inadequate planning and ineffective decision making. Hence, the composition of the ideal management information system for a particular library obviously lies somewhere between these extremes. In the preceding section we outlined criteria for including a specific data element in the system based upon usefulness and cost of collection and synthesis.

We do not imply that the determination of the optimal composition of an individual library's MIS is an easy task. In fact, this is an extremely difficult task. Not only is it difficult to estimate the utility of including an individual autonomous data element in the MIS, but it is even more difficult to estimate this quantity if it is dependent upon which other data elements are included. Furthermore, in some instances, data for a particular data element can be estimated as a function of another data element with a fair degree of accuracy. If it is less costly to pursue this course of action, it is important to ascertain the trade-off between accuracy of the estimate and the cost savings. Hence, the process of selecting the data elements to be included in the MIS requires some rather intensive and difficult evaluation. To date, the analytical models which have been developed to assist in this task are rather sparse.

Discussion up to now has centered upon the selection of the optimal set of data elements to comprise the MIS of a particular library, when the optimization is conducted at the individual, autonomous library level. Using this procedure, one library might collect data for 50 different data elements while another library might collect data for 500 data elements.

Considerations of the data needs for library systems, higher funding agencies, and so on, have not been discussed. It may be noted that the data required by other agencies may be more exhaustive or differ from the data deemed optimal for an individual library. In this situation, if there is no mandatory requirement to supply the figures, the individual library must decide whether to provide the data and, if so, how it can best be done.

Because of the prohibitive costs associated with collecting complete data for certain data elements, the employment of sampling techniques is recommended to obtain data for these elements. At this time we offer a few suggestions and cautions when using sampling techniques. For estimating a total on the basis of a sample, the variance of the estimate is usually less if the estimate is made as a function of another related data element for which complete data exist or if the estimate is made utilizing seasonal indexes. For example, it might be desired to estimate the total number of in-library document uses over a one-year period. One method is to obtain complete in-library use data for a "typical week" and multiply this by 52. A better estimate can be obtained, if it is known, for example, that there are three in-library uses for each circulation use, by multiplying the total number of circulations by three. Of course, even in this case, at periodic intervals complete in-library use must be obtained for a specified period of time to verify or modify the in-library use to circulation-use ratio. Another possibility is to utilize seasonal indexes. These indexes might be available from past data or obtained from a library that might be expected to experience similar user demand patterns. For example, if the seasonal index for a particular week is known to be .90 and 270 in-library uses were observed, the best estimate of the total number of yearly in-library uses is $(270/.90)(52) = 15,600$.

No attempt is made in this report to cover in detail any specific sampling plan because of the uniqueness of each situation at different libraries. Unfortunately, there are innumerable examples of inaccurate estimates based upon the results of improperly designed samples. The best procedure is to seek the advice of a statistician who can design a plan to fit the peculiarities of a specific situation to yield valid estimates at a minimum cost of data collection.

In the remainder of this chapter, we make no attempt to specify the time period for the collection of data for each data element. For example, should circulation data be collected on a per hour, per day, per week, per month, or per year basis or should users be sampled to determine the average length of time spent with a document on a weekly, monthly, yearly, or even four-year basis? These sorts of decisions depend upon many factors such as the use made of the data, required accuracy of the data, higher agency requirements for data, and so on.

In addition, virtually all the data elements enumerated in this chapter are required on a library unit, as well as overall library basis. For example, for decision-making purposes it is about as important to know the number of circulations at a particular branch library as it is to know the number of circulations for the entire library. Hence, data for data elements specified in this chapter should be collected on a per library unit as well as overall library basis.

Finally, as part of the development of any automated library system, whether it be a circulation system, acquisition system, or any other system, programs should be included that provide relevant management information in the desired format as a by-product of the operation of the system. Up until now, this has rarely been a consideration in the installation of a new system.

In the remainder of this section, we discuss some of the more important data elements based upon the usefulness criterion. In addition, we indicate the relative degree of difficulty of obtaining these data. These data elements are discussed as they relate to library performance measures, cost data, program performance measures, and program inputs and outputs.

Data for Library Performance Measures

In Chapter 2, we stressed the importance of constructing performance measures to evaluate the effectiveness of the library in attaining its objectives. It was indicated that number of document exposures, item-use-days, and document exposure time represent possible library performance measures. In addition, document retrieval time and the proportion of satisfied demands were presented as indicators that measure a particular aspect of library performance. In this section, we discuss the data elements required in the construction of some of these measures and indicate the relative degree of difficulty in obtaining the data.

Before proceeding with this analysis, we wish to indicate that in the construction of each of these measures library administrators are interested in measuring performance on both a population subset and a document subset basis. This is because certain decisions and programs have a direct effect upon a document subset performance measure while other decisions and programs have a direct effect upon a population subset performance measure. An example of the former is selection of documents within a given document subset while an example of the latter is promotion of library use within a particular population subset. In addition, often library administrators are interested in per capita measures. Hence, for the three document exposure measures, measures of document exposure per capita per population subset per time period and document exposure per document per document subset per time period are of interest.

For purposes of exposition, we shall define various data elements that will be collected either periodically or continuously at several degrees of detail. We will specify three major levels of aggregation: document subset, population subset, and time period. For example, we may collect data on total book use by noting at the moment of checkout the document subset to which the book belongs, the population subset associated with the user, and the time period during which the transaction occurred. If we let U

represent the variable "book use," then U_{dpt} represents the occurrence of a book use within document subset d by an individual from population subset p during time period t. Document subsets can be specified in any manner convenient to library management. Chapter 3 provides examples of various document subsets. In an analogous fashion, population subsets can be defined (see Chapter 3 for many possible examples) as well as time period covered.

The advantage of this notation is the ease with which various levels of aggregation can be presented. If we wish to disregard document subsets, we merely have to add U_{dpt} across all values of d. We can preserve the order of the subscripts by placing a dot in place of the aggregated dimension, so that book use by individuals in population subset p during time period t (disregarding the particular document subset) would be represented by

$$U_{.pt} = \sum_{d} U_{dpt} \qquad (5.1)$$

Similarly total book use in time period t, disregarding both document and population subsets, would be represented by

$$U_{..t} = \sum_{d}\sum_{p} U_{dpt} = \sum_{p} U_{.pt} \qquad (5.2)$$

We can now define the following variables:
A = Attendance Count
U = Circulation Use
T = Number of Document Loans to Other Libraries
F = Number of Document Loans from Other Libraries
B = In-Library Use
R = Indirect Library Use
D = Average Number of Days a Circulated Document Is Consulted
E = Average Exposure Time of Circulated Documents
O = Average Exposure Time of Documents Borrowed from Other Libraries
I = Average Exposure Time for In-Library Document Use
H = Average Exposure Time for Indirect Document Use

Each of these variables can conceivably be defined according to the three dimensions: document subsets, population subsets, and time period. We will assume that this is the case, and we will now indicate how each data element required to construct performance measures might be reasonably collected.

We will discuss the data needed to construct the three performance measures discussed in Chapter 2. The first six variables listed, A, U, T, F, B, and R, are needed to construct a measure of the number of document exposures. The addition of the variable D allows one to construct the measure item-use-days. If information is collected on the variables E, O, I, and H, then one can construct the more complex measure of document exposure time. We will discuss methods of collecting the data needed to construct these measures in increasing order of complexity, beginning with components of the measure, number of document exposures.

Number of Document Exposures

To compute the number of exposures, essentially four items of data are necessary on a document subset and population subset basis. They are number of circulations, number of in-library uses, number of indirect uses, and number of interlibrary loan uses. Recall that an indirect use occurs when a librarian conveys information to a user without the user contacting the document.

The number of circulations per document subset emerges as a by-product of normal activity to control the whereabouts of a particular document. In this case a procedure can be established whereby a count is made of the number of circulations per document subset per time period. Of course, to accomplish this, document subsets must be explicitly defined to include specification of relevant call numbers. Some work has been accomplished on this problem by McGrath and Durand (1969) and by this research project.[2] To measure circulations on a per document basis, a count of the number of documents per document subset must be known. To obtain this, a count is required of the documents within the document subset. After this initial "inventory" is accomplished, the count can be easily updated utilizing acquisition and weeding activity data and information on missing documents. Certain economies can be achieved by estimating the number of documents per document subset by sampling to determine the average number of documents per inch of cards and multiplying by the number of inches of cards in the document subset.

The number of circulations per population subset per time period, in

2. At the University of Pennsylvania, D.D. and L.C. classification numbers have been identified with the subject areas within those subject categories pertaining to the broad category of Business.

general, can be rather easily obtained as a by-product of the circulation system provided relevant population characteristics are recorded at the time a user withdraws a document. These characteristics could be solicited from the user at the time of each withdrawal or included in the user's registration or "I.D." card. However, for circulation systems that are not automated, obtaining these data would require considerable effort. As a practical expedient, a sampling technique could be employed to estimate the number of circulations per population subset. Of course, the foregoing assumes that population subsets are defined and can be identified by population characteristics. Finally, if it is desired to determine circulations per person per population subset per time period, it is necessary to ascertain the population count for each population subset. The difficulty experienced in gathering these data depends upon the desired precision of the population subsets and the availability of the data from extralibrary sources (for example, municipal and census data for the public library and university data for the university library).

In some instances, in-library use of documents is recorded as part of an activity designed to control documents. For example, in university libraries, often the use of documents on reserve, the use of recent periodicals, and sometimes even stack uses are recorded. For the purpose of this discussion, let us consider the extreme case in which no data for in-library use evolves as a by-product of library activities. Collection of data describing in-library use of documents per document subset can be accomplished in two different ways. One is to record the call number of documents that are left out on desks and tables by users. The other is to obtain these data from the user via questionnaires or interviewing. If the technique of counting documents left out is used, care must be taken to obtain an estimate of the proportion reshelved by users. Use of the questionnaire or the interviewing technique introduces a bias caused when users refuse to cooperate or provide information inconsistent with their behavior. Furthermore, both the counting technique and questionnaire and interviewing techniques require considerable effort for data collection. For this reason it would be useful to estimate in-library use of documents as a function of other data, if possible. In particular, for documents permitted to circulate, there are indications that in-library use can be described as a function of circulation use, as was done by Fussler and Simon (1969, p. 115). For documents not permitted to circulate, no comparable recorded document use data are available. One possibility for these document subsets in which the documents are not permitted to circulate is to relate in-library use with attendance count. This would seem to be a good possibility for the public library but would have to be approached with caution in the university library because of the tendency of students to use the library as a study hall, especially during examination periods. In any case, it would seem that in-library use of documents per document subset could be estimated as a function of circulation per document subset and attendance count after determining the relevant relationships as a result of sampling in-library use data directly. Finally, given that the number of documents per document subset is known, in-library use of documents on a per document basis could also be estimated.

Obtaining in-library document use per population subset can be accomplished directly only by employing the interview or questionnaire technique. Because of the high cost associated with these techniques, it is advisable to employ one of them on a sampling basis in an attempt to relate in-library document use per population subset to circulation use and attendance. Once these relationships are established, estimates of in-library use can be made, with questionnaires or interviews administered on a periodic basis to update or verify the parameters of the relationship. If these data are desired on a per capita basis, it is necessary to divide the in-library use per document subset measure by the number of persons within the population subset.

In order to compute a measure of the number of exposures, a count of the number of indirect document uses is required. For this purpose, the call numbers of documents that are used in providing information to a user may be recorded. It would be a fairly easy matter to obtain the number of indirect uses per population subset. To obtain this count, the librarian would query the user regarding relevant population characteristic information. If it is believed to be too much of a burden to ask librarians to jot down call numbers of documents consulted and to query users to obtain population characteristics, attempts can be made to relate these data to attendance counts, requiring periodic sampling to update and verify the relationship.

Finally, it would seem desirable to compute a measure of the number of documents obtained from other libraries on a per document subset and per population subset basis. This measure is of interest by itself, in addition to being of interest as part of the overall document exposure measure. Since these uses are recorded by the library, the number of uses per document subset could be provided on a continuous basis. In general, to obtain these data on a per population subset basis would require additional information from the user. Sampling techniques could be employed here to estimate these data if provision of complete information is infeasible.

Document loans to other libraries per document subset per time period is a useful performance measure, but it should not necessarily be aggregated with the overall document exposure measure. Obviously, it makes little sense to compute a measure of this use per population subset. Further aggregation of this measure with other measures will provide a picture of overall document use, but it should be kept separately to provide a measure of particular aspects of library operation.

In summary, it would seem inconceivable that a library could and would collect complete data for all the data elements required to compute this performance measure for the number of exposures per document subset, per population subset, and per capita per population subset. Hence, it would seem prudent to employ sampling techniques to estimate certain data. At this point we indicate how each data element required to construct this measure might be reasonably collected.

$A_{..t}$ = *Attendance Count per Time Period*

If possible, data for this element should be collected on a continuous basis. If the installation and maintenance of turnstiles is too costly, attendance data should be secured from comparable libraries, and seasonal indexes should be computed. Then estimates of attendance may be made with some degree of accuracy based upon these seasonal indexes and periodic samplings.

U_{dpt} = *Circulation Use per Document Subset per Population Subset per Time Period*

If possible, data for this element should be collected on a continuous basis. If this is not possible for cost or other reasons, estimates can be made based upon periodic samples of circulation data and of users via questionnaires or interviews. Derived from this data element will be two other bits of information:

Circulation Use per Population Subset per Time Period

$$U_{.pt} = \sum_d U_{dpt} \qquad (5.3)$$

and

Circulation Use per Document Subset per Time Period

$$U_{d.t} = \sum_p U_{dpt} \qquad (5.4)$$

$T_{d.t}$ = Document Loans to Other Libraries per Document Subset per Time Period

Since document loans to other libraries result in recorded uses for the purpose of control, it is relatively easy to obtain these data on a continuous basis. If it seems infeasible to obtain these data, a sampling procedure could be employed to estimate how document loans are apportioned to various document subsets given the total count on a per time period basis.

F_{dpt} = Use of Documents from Other Libraries per Document Subset per Population Subset per Time Period

Data concerning document subsets are normally easy to obtain, as they are recorded in order to control the documents while in use, prior to returning them to the library from which they were obtained. If this is deemed infeasible, samples can be obtained to estimate the distribution of total document uses of this type within the various document subsets.

Unless population characteristics are solicited as part of the procedure for a user to obtain a document from another library, special data collection efforts are required. Solicitation of population characteristics could take the form of an imprint on an "I.D." or registration card or a requirement to provide such data as part of the procedure for requesting the document. If neither of these techniques is employed, sample data can be obtained to estimate the apportionment of these uses to the various population subsets.

Two derived bits of information easily obtainable from F_{dpt} are

Use of Documents from Other Libraries per Population Subset per Time Period

$$F_{.pt} = \sum_d F_{dpt} \qquad (5.5)$$

and

Use of Documents from Other Libraries per Document Subset per Time Period

$$F_{d.t} = \sum_p F_{dpt} \tag{5.6}$$

B_{dpt} = In-Library Use per Document Subset per Population Subset per Time Period

Except where these data are recorded as part of a process to control documents, it would be impractical to collect this information on a continuous basis. However, it is necessary to take periodic samples to obtain data by either counting documents left out on tables or by administering questionnaires or interviews to users. Estimates of this use can then be made as a function of circulation use per population subset and attendance.

Two relevant subtotals of this data element are important:

In-Library Use per Population Subset per Time Period

$$B_{.pt} = \sum_d B_{dpt} \tag{5.7}$$

and

In-Library Use per Document Subset per Time Period

$$B_{d.t} = \sum_p B_{dpt} \tag{5.8}$$

R_{dpt} = Indirect Document Use per Document Subset per Population Subset per Time Period

Data for this data element can be collected without much difficulty by having librarians record the call numbers of documents used to convey information to users and query the user to collect the relevant population characteristics. If this seems to be impractical or burdensome, periodic samples could be taken to relate indirect library use with circulation use per population subset and attendance counts.

Two relevant levels of aggregation of this data element are

Indirect Document Use per Population Subset per Time Period

$$R_{.pt} = \sum_d R_{dpt} \tag{5.9}$$

and

Indirect Document Use per Document Subset per Time Period

$$R_{d.t} = \sum_p R_{dpt} \tag{5.10}$$

Other Data Requirements

For the construction of several performance measures, certain other information should be available to the librarian on a periodic basis. This information relates to the population of potential library users and the number of documents per document subset in the library's collection. Thus, the following statements concerning these data are relevant.

PERSONS PER POPULATION SUBSET. For large city public libraries, the number of persons per population subset should be determined on a periodic basis. Sources for this include census and municipal data. For the university library, the number of persons per population subset should be determined on a semester basis. This presupposes that population subsets have been defined and specified in terms of population characteristics.

NUMBER OF DOCUMENTS PER DOCUMENT SUBSET. If the library lacks an exact count of the number of documents per document subset, estimates can be made on the basis of sampling the shelf list. To accomplish this, samples are taken to estimate the number of cards per inch which, when multiplied by the number of inches of cards, yields an estimate of the number of documents per document subset. This estimate should be periodically updated on the basis of new documents acquired and old documents weeded. All of this presupposes that document subsets have been defined and identified according to Dewey Decimal or Library of Congress call numbers.

Item-Use-Days

We indicated in Chapter 2 that the item-use-day performance measure is a slightly more accurate measure of performance than the number of exposures. The only difference in the measures is that circulations are weighted according to the average number of days a user consults the document in the item-use-day measure. Hence, the same data are required for this measure in addition to data describing the average number of days a document is consulted while out on loan on a per population subset and a per document subset basis. These data must be obtained by querying users by questionnaire or interview upon return of documents that have been borrowed. The item-use-day measure can be computed on a per document subset, per document per document subset, per population subset, and a per capita per population subset basis. Specifically, the additional data necessary to construct this measure may be summarized as follows.

$D_{dp.}$ = Average Number of Days a Circulated Document Is Consulted per Document Subset per Population Subset[3]

For this data element, users would be asked to indicate the actual number of days the document was consulted during the loan period for documents circulated in each document subset. At the same time, they could be asked questions to determine the relevant population characteristics.

The two related bits of data derived from this information are

Average Number of Days a Circulated Document Is Consulted per Population Subset

$$D_{.p.} = \sum_d D_{dp.} \qquad (5.11)$$

and

Average Number of Days a Circulated Document Is Consulted per Document Subset

$$D_{d..} = \sum_p D_{dp.} \qquad (5.12)$$

Document Exposure Time

As indicated in Chapter 2, this performance measure provides a more complete and truer picture of library output than either number of document exposures or item-use-days. Likewise more data are required to compute this measure. As in the previous cases, measures on a per document subset, per population subset, and a per capita per population subset basis are desired.

Data required to construct this measure include all of the data required to construct the measure for the number of document exposures, in addi-

---

3. In this and subsequent equations, the variables have been averaged over time; hence, the subscript referring to time period has been replaced with a dot. However, the equations can be generalized if we realize that the variables may in fact change over time.

tion to average exposure time data, for each type of exposure on a per document subset and per population subset basis. Each of these additional required data elements will be discussed in turn.

$E_{dp.}$ = *Average Exposure Time of Circulated Documents per Document Subset per Population Subset*

$O_{dp.}$ = *Average Exposure Time of Documents Borrowed from Other Libraries per Document Subset per Population Subset*

Since it would entail a good deal of effort and funds to obtain complete information concerning both of these data elements, a sampling technique can be employed. This technique would involve querying users upon their returning of circulated documents to estimate the time spent consulting the document, in addition to population characteristics regarding the user and document identification data.

The four relevant subtotals are also important items of information:

Average Exposure Time of Circulated Documents per Population Subset

$$E_{.p.} = \sum_{d} E_{dp.} \tag{5.13}$$

Average Exposure Time of Circulated Documents per Document Subset

$$E_{d..} = \sum_{p} E_{dp.} \tag{5.14}$$

Average Exposure Time of Documents Borrowed from Other Libraries per Population Subset

$$O_{.p.} = \sum_{d} O_{dp.} \tag{5.15}$$

Average Exposure Time of Documents Borrowed from Other Libraries per Document Subset

$$O_{d..} = \sum_{p} O_{dp.} \tag{5.16}$$

$I_{dp.}$ = *Average Exposure Time for In-Library Document Use per Document Subset per Population Subset*

Data for this data element could be estimated as a result of questionnaires or interviews administered to a sample of library users requesting them to indicate which documents they used, how long they used them, and certain population characteristics.

The relevant subtotals are

Average Exposure Time for In-Library Document Use per Population Subset

$$I_{.p.} = \sum_{d} I_{dp.} \qquad (5.17)$$

Average Exposure Time for In-Library Document Use per Document Subset

$$I_{d..} = \sum_{p} I_{dp.} \qquad (5.18)$$

$H_{dp.}$ = *Average Exposure Time for Indirect Document Use per Document Subset per Population Subset*

Data for this data element can be secured on a sample basis by asking librarians to indicate which documents were used, how long they were used, and for whom the information was provided.

The relevant subtotals are

Average Exposure Time for Indirect Document Use per Population Subset

$$H_{.p.} = \sum_{d} H_{dp.} \qquad (5.19)$$

and

Average Exposure Time for Indirect Document Use per Document Subset

$$H_{d..} = \sum_{p} H_{dp.} \qquad (5.20)$$

This concludes enumeration of selected data elements required to construct various library performance measures and a discussion of how the data for the data elements might reasonably be collected. In a similar manner, data elements could be evaluated that are necessary to construct the document retrieval time and percent satisfaction rate performance measures. It is important to note that these latter measures, although not as inclusive in terms of the dimensions considered as the document exposure measures, are nonetheless valuable for evaluating certain specific activities. For example, determination of the document retrieval time and the percent of requests satisfied for documents requested by a library from other libraries would be valuable in the decision-making process.

Data for Program Indicators

GENERAL. In general, data elements necessary to construct program input indicators, program output indicators, and program performance measures possess a high degree of usefulness when evaluated in terms of the criteria. No attempt is made in this report to evaluate all the data elements required in the construction of the various program measures. However, to provide a flavor of how this might be accomplished, we indicate some of the thinking that is pertinent for this process for a particular program. For illustrative purposes, we select function eleven, the provision of aids to locate documents within the library, as the program.

In general, for each program there are inputs, outputs, and program performance measures. The program performance measures provide an indication of the output per unit input for the program. In addition, of vital concern is the relationship of the program output to the library performance measure. In a theoretical sense, we would expect the performance of the library to increase at a decreasing rate as the output of a program increases. This relationship is indicated in Figure 5.3.

Library performance can be evaluated in terms of a measure of document exposure. Of interest here is the effect upon document exposure as a program output is increased. Program output is, of course, a function of program input, which can be summarized in terms of expenditures of funds. Hence, ultimately what is sought is the determination of a benefit-cost ratio describing the increase in document exposures per dollar, so that

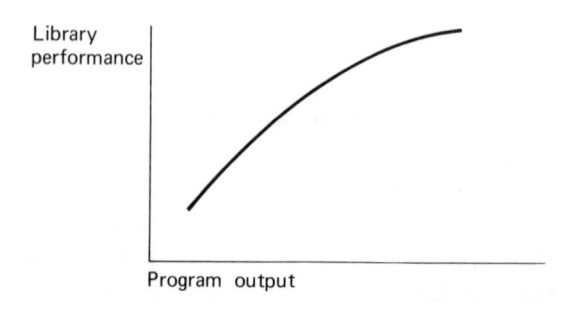

Figure 5.3. Relationship between library performance and program output.

alternative funding allocation schemes can be evaluated to maximize the library's performance.

In terms of the program (to provide aids to locate documents within the library), those outputs which can be quantified are
1. Number of documents that are originally classified
2. Number of documents that are added to the collection
3. Number of documents that are withdrawn or that are determined to be missing from the collection

Input to the program encompasses the personnel and other expenditures required as follows:
1. The number of man-years (and associated costs) to classify new documents
2. The number of man-years (and associated costs) to catalog new documents
3. The number of man-years (and associated costs) to purge catalog of entries for documents that are withdrawn from the collection

Program performance indicators include
1. Average number of man-hours (and cost) to classify a new document
2. Average number of man-hours (and cost) to catalog a new document
3. Average number of man-hours (and cost) to purge a catalog of entries for documents that are discarded

Other performance indicators for this program include
4. Average time duration between receipt of document and cataloging of document, if preclassified at time document is received
5. Average time duration between receipt of document and cataloging of document if not preclassified at time document is received

The first three program performance indicators are of the output per unit input variety. These can be used to evaluate the program operation and to predict the implications of increases or decreases in the number of documents added and withdrawn. An example of the usefulness of these types of indicators is presented at the end of this section. Indicators 4 and 5 relate the output of this program to the overall performance of the library. Obviously, the shorter the time period between the time of receipt of a document and the time at which it is cataloged, the greater the measure of document exposure. Of course, there is a price to bear when the average time duration is shortened. A simple example of how these indicators might relate to the document exposure measure and how alternative proposals can be evaluated in terms of benefit-cost ratios is presented at the end of this section.

SELECTED DATA. A listing of all the quantitative and descriptive data elements that potentially are relevant to the planning and management of an entire library is an enormous task. In this section, we present for illustrative purposes a listing of data elements for only one library function—provision of aids to locate documents within a library. We also indicate how these data elements might be collected. The following abbreviations are used in the list of data elements:

Ave. = Average
  D = Document(s)
  DS = Document Subset
  ST = Staff Type
  TA = Titles Added
  TW = Titles Withdrawn

Data Element

1. No. of D Acquired/DS
2. No. of TA to Catalog
3. No. of TW from Catalog
4. Percent of Preclassified D Acquired/DS
5. Percent of D Acquired Ultimately Classified by the Library of Congress/DS
6. No. of Man-years of Personnel/ST
7. Percent of D Uses Resulting from Consultation of a Subject Entry/DS
8. Percent of D Uses Resulting from Browsing/DS
9. Ave. No. of Man-hours to Catalog a New D
10. Ave. No. of Man-hours to Purge Catalog

Method of Collection

1. By-product of acquisitions process
2. Recorded by cataloging personnel
3. Recorded by cataloging personnel
4. Recorded as documents are received, or by sampling
5. By sampling documents that are, say, three years old
6. By having all personnel allocate their time to various activities
7. By sampling users

8. By sampling users

9. Recorded by cataloging personnel
10. Recorded by cataloging personnel

11. Time Lapse between Receipt of Preclassified D and Cataloging D
11. By sampling preclassified documents upon arrival

12. Time Lapse between Receipt of Not Preclassified D and Cataloging D
12. By sampling relevant documents

This concludes a brief treatment of the more important data elements relevant to construction of program input and output indicators and program and library performance measures. A few illustrative examples will now be given of how these measures might be used in the decision-making process.

Example 1
Suppose that the library anticipates purchasing 10,000 more documents next year than this year, of which 60 percent will be classified and cataloged by the Library of Congress. Suppose further that on the average a librarian can classify and catalog 1500 documents a year. This would necessitate classifying and cataloging $(.40)(10,000) = 4000$ additional documents that will require $4000/1500 = 2\frac{2}{3}$ additional full-time equivalent personnel in this area to accommodate this increase.

Example 2
Suppose that 60 percent of the 60,000 documents received by the library have a Library of Congress call number upon receipt. Let us consider two alternative strategies for classifying and cataloging the remaining 40 percent:
1. The library staff originally classifies and catalogs these documents as they are received at the library.
2. The library staff employs a temporary cataloging system for these documents for a one-year period while waiting for subsequent Library of Congress classification.

Let us assume that an additional 20 percent of the original set of documents will be classified and cataloged by the Library of Congress within a one-year period. Let us further assume that on the average one librarian can originally classify and catalog 1500 documents a year.

In the first alternative, the library will need originally to classify and catalog $(.40)(60,000) = 24,000$ documents. This process will require

24,000/1500 = 16 full-time equivalent personnel. If the average compensation (salary plus fringe benefits) for a classifier-cataloger is $10,000 per year, this alternative will cost the library (16)($10,000) = $160,000 per year. If on the average each document receives 2 exposures during its first year on the shelf, this set of documents will receive (2)(24,000) = 48,000 exposures.

The exposure-to-cost ratio for this alternative is computed to be

$$\frac{E}{C} = \frac{48,000}{\$160,000} = .30 \text{ exposures per dollar}$$

In the second alternative, documents received without a Library of Congress number are temporarily cataloged. This process might include the assignment of a temporary number to the document and placing the document acquisition form in the card catalog by author and title entries only. Let us assume that on the average documents that are temporarily cataloged will receive 1½ exposures during the first year on the shelf. We would expect this figure to be less than the 2 exposures per year figure, as these documents would not be listed in the card catalog under subject headings. In this alternative, the number of exposures experienced by this set of documents would be (24,000)(1½) = 36,000 exposures. If on the average one librarian can temporarily catalog 8000 documents per year, 24,000/8000 = 3 full-time equivalent personnel would be required for this process. In addition, the number of full-time equivalent personnel required for original classification and cataloging of the 20 percent of the documents that remain unclassified and uncataloged at year end by the Library of Congress is 12,000/1500 = 8 full-time equivalent personnel. The cost incurred by the library to pursue this strategy is (3 + 8) persons × $10,000 per person = $110,000. The exposure-to-cost ratio for adopting this strategy is calculated to be

$$\frac{E}{C} = \frac{36,000}{\$110,000} = .33 \text{ exposures per dollar}$$

In this manner the library can determine the preferable strategy for classifying and cataloging documents. In this case, the second strategy, employing the temporary cataloging system, is preferable since its exposure-to-cost ratio (.33) is greater than the exposure-to-cost ratio (.30) associated with the first alternative.

Example 3
Suppose that the Library of Congress decides to decrease its program of classifying and cataloging new documents to the extent that an estimated 10 percent fewer documents acquired by a library will be classified and cataloged by the Library of Congress. If a library acquires 60,000 new titles per year, an additional (60,000)(.10) = 6000 titles will require original classification and cataloging. Assume that on the average one librarian can classify and catalog 1500 documents per year at a cost of $10,000 (cost of salary and fringe benefits). Therefore, the additional cost to this particular library resulting from a cutback in the Library of Congress Program will be ($10,000) (4) = $40,000. If this cost is computed for all libraries and aggregated, the implications of the cost on a national level, as a result of this "cost economy," would be apparent.

Financial Data System

Introduction
Financial data are essential for the proper management of libraries, as they are for any organization. In this section, we evaluate presently or potentially collectable financial data in terms of use by management and methods of collection. We first discuss data related to funds received. Then we review data resulting from general library accounting of expenditures, relating to the performance of the entire library organization. More detailed cost data are then analyzed with respect to cost accounting and program budgeting. Finally we review various financial data elements of use to a single library but originating outside of that library.

Funds Received
In order to plan library programs, a manager must have information about the present and past levels of financial support and must be able to estimate future receipts. An essential annual data element is total funds received. Perhaps even more meaningful is the indicator obtained by dividing this data element by the population served: financial support per capita.

Total funds received, per capita funds received, and relative funds received by source are also useful and easily collectable data. Sources include

1. Financial support from units of local government: direct property tax

levy, direct school district tax levy, other direct tax levy, appropriation of county or township tax funds, appropriation of school district funds, tax funds for contractual services, school district funds for contractual services
2. Financial support from the state government: state aid as a local library, state aid as a district library, state funds for contractual services
3. Financial support from the federal government
4. Funds received from libraries and other agencies for contractual services
5. Fines, forfeitures, and charges: late documents, lost documents, photocopy service, rental book collections, sale of publications
6. Gifts and donations for the operating budget: Community Chests (United Fund), library patron groups, association membership dues, individual gifts and donations
7. Enterprise income: rent of buildings or parts of buildings owned by the library, interest or realized gain on investments and endowments
8. Miscellaneous receipts: interest on deposits, refunds
9. Income in kind: rent, utilities, personnel, gift subscriptions
10. Unexpended balance from previous year
11. Gifts and donations for the capital budget: building fund, investments, and endowments

General Accounting for Expenditures

Library accounting practice has not been designed primarily to supply meaningful information for management purposes. Expenditures are normally presented in a line item budget indicating the following typical objects of disbursements.
1. Personnel: library salaries, maintenance salaries, other costs
2. Library materials: book stock, periodicals collection, audiovisual materials, other nonbook materials
3. Binding and rebinding (including salaries of internal bindery)
4. Maintenance of plant
5. Fixed charges and debt service: rent, insurance, interest, amortization of long-term debts
6. Supplies and miscellaneous
7. Capital expenditures: sites, buildings, additions, furnishings, equipment

In Chapter 2, we emphasized the importance of an overall library performance measure in order to establish a criterion for choosing between alternative courses of action, including alternative investments of the limited resources of the library. The suggested overall performance measure consists in part of an output measure of document exposure, by one of several possible methods discussed in detail in the section of that chapter. We emphasized in Chapter 2 that the other essential element of a library performance measure consists of matching with the exposure occurring in any period of time the costs necessary to produce this exposure. In order to accomplish the matching, there must be an adjustment for payments that ordinarily influence document exposure in more than one year. If the prepayment is relatively long term, the adjustment may be most conveniently accomplished by an amortization procedure. However, typically since the library attempts no periodic matching of output and input, and does not attempt to measure true costs, prepayments are written off as current expenses instead of being amortized.

The incorporation of amortization or depreciation methods into library accounting would entail somewhat more accounting time. Also, some difficult questions about the items to be depreciated (particularly for donated buildings), the useful life, and the depreciation method would have to be answered.

However, the potential benefits of adopting an accrual method of accounting, along with a determination of document exposure, would appear to be very high. Such a revised accounting procedure would seem to represent an essential step in creating a criterion for management planning and decision. Also, the availability of an overall library performance measure enables the librarian to relate additional funds to the returns that they yield, thereby presenting to the public or the university a more convincing analytical argument for his needs.

Cost Accounting and Program Budgeting

In addition to an existing need for an overall library performance measure, there is perhaps even a more urgent managerial need for classifying, recording, presenting, interpreting, and controlling significant library costs of various aspects of library operations and service. However, current library accounting practice is designed primarily to account for funds received and expended rather than to supply the library administrator with the cost data to make managerial decisions. Both accounting and budgeting are usually performed in terms of emphasis on the objects of disbursements in a line item, rather than program, format.

"Cost accounting" is a term used to describe that part of the accounting procedure of an organization that determines, reports, analyzes, and controls costs of particular processes, jobs, service units, departments, and so on. Although cost determination studies may be undertaken on a special, nonrecurring basis, it is generally recognized as good accounting procedure that more meaningful and useful costs will result only if cost determination is part of the accounting routine.

If costs are analyzed in terms of the library programs established in a library's program structure (see Chapter 3 and Appendixes III and IV), then the library may be able to construct a library program budget rather than a line item budget. Termed "program budgeting," this construction represents in clearer terms what is intended to be accomplished.

Line item costs may be converted to program costs by means of a program crosswalk, whereby departmental line items are presented on the left side of a matrix and programs are presented at the top. The entries are allocations of line item costs to programs. Salaries represent perhaps the most difficult line item to be allocated in this manner. Raffel and Shishko (1969) and Baldwin and Marcus (1941) have allocated library salaries to programs by requesting employees to estimate and record time spent on programs and activities.

Costs of a unit of output are particularly useful for planning and controlling purposes. These costs generally comprise direct material costs and direct labor costs, internal or contracted, and may also include indirect costs of physical facilities, maintenance, administration, and support activities. Direct costs vary with the volume of output. Indirect costs vary over time, regardless of volume of output. A unit cost procedure that is gaining recognition is "direct costing," whereby unit costs are defined to include only direct costs.

Unit costs may be accumulated by two different methods: the job-order cost method and the process cost method. Job-order costing entails analysis of all costs necessary for one particular job: that is, the processing of one unit of output. Process costing involves accumulating costs for a process over a specific period of time and then dividing by the number of units of output during that period. If units of output are quite different, then job-order costing usually is preferable. If units of output are similar, then process costing usually is preferable. Both methods may be used by libraries. For instance, documents are the units of output of many library functions, such as ordering and preparing; process costing would yield cost per document without distinguishing type of document, and, if one process handles documents of different forms (such as books and films), job-order costing would yield separate unit costs for each document form.

Total, unit, and per capita costs may be used to establish input measures and to evaluate programs. Since programs may be formulated with respect to functions, library units, population subsets, and document subsets, costs may be useful for any or all of these dimensions. Table 5.3 presents some of the cost measures that may be useful for each library function. Since there are separate functions for the overhead costs of physical facilities, furnishings, maintenance, administration, and support activities, the resultant costs for the remaining functions are direct costs. Alternatively, the indirect costs could be allocated to the remaining functions. Each cost element in the table consists of expenditures for personnel, supplies and equipment, and contractual services. Unit costs are obtained by dividing by the unit of output. Per capita costs are obtained by dividing by population. Finally, relevant subtotals for total costs, unit costs, and per capita costs are indicated.

External Financial Data

A very important data element of use to a single library, but arising outside of the library, is an index of library materials prices. The only useful index of this kind is the Library Materials Price Index, sponsored by Council of National Library Associations (1969), a committee of the American Library Association, and published by the R. R. Bowker Company annually. It was criticized by Dan Lacy at a *National Conference on Library Statistics* (1967, pp. 19–20) as seriously misrepresenting the level and rise of prices paid for books by libraries. He states that it is distorted because it is an average of the present year's list prices of new hard-cover titles, regardless of extent of publication and discounts. Therefore, very expensive, limited editions are overrepresented and raise the index level artificially.

Conclusion

In this chapter the fundamental characteristics of a library management information system were presented. These characteristics describe, and are useful in designing, an effective information system for library decision making. To illustrate the relevant concepts of such systems, two alternate information system designs were described, the Hayes-Becker system and a

Table 5.3. Selected Cost Measures by Library Function

Function	Total Cost	Units of Output	Other Divisor	Data Element	Subtotals
1. Provision of building area	User area		Population	Cost of user area per capita	Library unit
	Staff area		Staff man-years	Cost of staff area per full-time staff member	Library unit
	Document storage area		Document volumes	Cost of document storage area per volume	Library unit, document form
	Function total	Square feet		Cost of providing building area per square foot	Library unit
2. Provision of user furnishings	Function total		Population	Cost of user furnishings per capita	Library unit
4. Selection of documents	Act of selecting	Titles selected		Selection cost per title selected	Document subset
	Act of selecting		Population	Selection cost per capita	Document subset
	Document expenditure	Volumes selected		Document expenditure per volume selected	Document subset
	Document expenditure		Population	Document expenditure per capita	Document subset
5. Acquisition of documents	Function total	Volumes added		Acquisition cost per volume added	
6. Processing of documents	All processing, except binding	Volumes added		Nonbinding processing cost per volume added	
	Binding of new documents	Volumes added needing binding		Binding cost per new volume bound	

Conclusion

7. Control of document location and use	Function total	Exposures	Cost of control of document location and use per exposure	Library unit
8. Facilitation of document use	Function total	Population	Cost for facilitating document use per capita	Library unit
9. Maintenance and weeding of documents	Binding	Volumes bound	Binding cost per old volume bound	Document form
	Weeding	Volumes weeded	Weeding cost per volume weeded	Library unit
10. Access to documents in other libraries	Incoming documents or photocopies	User requests satisfied from other libraries	Cost of obtaining documents per satisfied request	
	Outgoing documents or photocopies	Documents or photocopies sent to other libraries	Cost of satisfying requests by other libraries per outgoing document or photocopy	
11. Provision of aids to locate documents within the library of concern	Classification without preprinted card	Titles classified without preprinted card	Cost of classifying without preprinted cards per title	Document subset
	Classification with preprinted card	Titles classified with preprinted card	Cost of classifying with preprinted cards per title	
	Cataloging	Titles added	Cataloging cost per title added	
	Function total	Titles added	Cost of providing aids to locate documents within the library of concern per title added	Document subset
	Function total	Population	Cost of providing aids to locate documents within the library of concern per capita	

Table 5.3 (*Continued*)

Function	Total Cost	Units of Output	Other Divisor	Data Element	Subtotals
12. Provision of aids either to identify existing documents or to locate them in other libraries	Expenditure for indexes	Indexes added		Index expenditure per index added	Document subset
	Processing of indexes	Indexes added		Cost of index processing per index added	Document subset
	Function total		Population	Cost per capita of providing aids either to identify existing documents or to locate them in other libraries	
13. Personal assistance for document identification and for providing information	Function total	Questions answered		Cost of personal assistance per question answered	Library unit; Population subset
	Function total		Population	Cost of personal assistance per capita	Library unit; Population subset
14. Publications, advertising, and exhibits	Publications	Publications		Cost per publication	
	Advertising	Advertising campaigns		Cost per advertising campaign	
	Exhibits	Exhibits		Cost per exhibit	Library unit
	Function total		Population	Cost of publications, advertising, and exhibits per capita	Population subset
15. Personal communication with members of the population being served	Function total	Personal communication		Cost per personal communication	Population subset
	Function total		Population	Cost of personal communication per capita	Population subset
16. Planning and Administration	Function total		Population	Cost of planning and administration per capita	

Conclusion

	Function total		Population	Cost of support per capita	Library unit
17. Support					
ALL FUNCTIONS	Grand total	Exposure		Total cost per exposure	Library unit; Population subset
	Grand total	Visit		Total cost per visit	Library unit; Population subset
	Grand total		Population	Total cost per capita	Library unit; Population subset

system based on the program structure of Chapter 3. A crosswalk was developed indicating the relationship between the two designs for the purpose of demonstrating the opportunities for flexibility in the design of a management information system for a particular library. Then the basic unit of any information system was defined according to eight major dimensions. The choice between competing data elements depends on many factors, including the relative benefits and costs of the data elements, and a methodology was presented for assessing these factors. The usefulness of data elements in the construction of library performance measures was discussed, and three such measures were presented in detail. Data elements for program indicators, which are more narrowly defined than library performance measures, were also described and illustrated. Finally, the basic structure of an effective financial data system was formulated in such a manner as to make it useful for decision making.

6

HIGHER-LEVEL LIBRARY DECISION MAKING

We have examined various aspects of the planning and decision-making process in large public and university library environments. The problems are many, the solutions difficult, but the need for improvement in the management of libraries is great. Libraries can no longer continue to exist as passive institutions reacting to demands from society in traditional ways. The demands are new and challenging, and the traditional ways of meeting these demands may not be sufficient in the future. The basic societal pressures have often been cited: the knowledge explosion, the population explosion, the computer age, the education boom, the needs of the poor and disadvantaged, the movement to suburbia and the problems of the inner city. Can individual libraries acting alone meet these substantial challenges? Can the present trend toward cooperative arrangements among libraries meet these challenges any better? What should the role of the federal government be toward libraries and their problems? How about state governments and professional associations? How should these higher-level organizations and agencies coordinate their efforts to achieve their objectives? And are their objectives compatible (nonconflicting)?

These questions cover a vast range of problems for future library development. About the only simple statement to be made is that *no* library can afford to operate completely independently any more. As given in New York (State) Division of Evaluation, *Emerging Library Systems* (1967, p. 226), "If a single trend stands out most clearly as a development of present times, it is probably the condition which has been characterized as 'calculated independence.' No agency or individual operates alone or independently any longer. The keynote of social progress lies, in fact, in successfully relating individual efforts to mutual or overlapping interests." The American Library Association (*Standards for Library Functions at the State Level*, 1969) phrases these sentiments even more strongly:

The future of all library service lies in diminishing compartmentalization and in achieving greater coordination of resources and services for the benefit of the user. The individual more and more will expect and demand easy access to all libraries. Only those institutions flexible enough to respond to such demands will survive; others inevitably will be replaced by new structures designed to perform the needed functions. (P. 42.)

Library Systems

Cooperative arrangements among libraries can take an almost infinite variety of forms, depending upon the particular aspects of cooperation in which one has interest. Currently no one form of cooperation seems to have taken precedence over all other forms. If one were to study library systems or networks from the viewpoint of cooperation along the lines of the seventeen previously mentioned library functions, then there would be about 131,000 different possible combinations of library systems. That is, if libraries could agree to cooperate on any one function, or any set of two functions, and so on, then the total number of different possible combinations of library cooperative arrangements would be about 131,000. Of course there is nothing sacred about this list of seventeen functions and there are many other dimensions of possible library cooperation.

One dimension that has received attention is the type of governmental supporting unit of the public library system. The Nelson Associates, Inc. (1969) in a survey of public library systems across the nation used as the criterion for inclusion in their study "systems with more than one outlet open at least ten hours a week with paid staff and providing library service across political jurisdiction lines." (See Nelson Associates, Inc., *Public Libraries in the United States*, 1967, p. 19.)

The Nelson Associates found 491 multijurisdictional library systems satisfying this criterion. These systems followed five predominant patterns:
1. County library
2. Multicounty or regional library
3. Special district library
4. State supplementary library
5. Statewide, state-governed library

Each of these five basic patterns of library system development may have any one of five basic structural forms:
1. Consolidated unitary form
2. Contractual consolidation
3. Federation of whole library units
4. Cooperatives of individual libraries
5. Government by the state library

While certain patterns or forms of library systems may be more popular or more prevalent at this time, it is unlikely that any one particular pattern or form will become close to universally accepted. Similarly, in terms of financial arrangements among cooperating libraries and in terms of the number and type of services these libraries offer, there is a superabundance of different library systems. The inherent complexity of library cooperative arrangements presents a challenge for further study, but progress for future research must wait until a clear and useful definition is found for the concept "library system."

National Level

At the national level there is no single, unified decision-making body that both establishes national objectives and policies for library development and has broad responsibilities for carrying out these policies. Leach (1969, p. 346) wrote "The Federal Government is active in many ways in connection with libraries, but there is no detailed, comprehensive Federal library policy to date." Indeed, we must distinguish between policies for federal libraries per se—libraries whose clientele primarily consists of federal employees—and federal policies for all other types of libraries. The phrase "Federal library policy" as used here will refer to the latter meaning, policies formulated within the federal government relating to public, academic, or special libraries.

Generally there are three major centers for library decision making and library leadership within the federal government: the National Libraries, the Congress, and the Office of Education. Outside of government a number of national professional organizations exist for the promotion of library interests, for helping to establish national goals and policies, and for carrying out research into library problems. Some examples of organizations in this category are the American Library Association, The Council on Library Resources, and the Association of Research Libraries. All of these organizations and agencies can be considered to be national library leaders since library planning and decision making at the national level result from their collective efforts and influence. No one organization is dominant.

National Libraries

The National Libraries are the Library of Congress, the National Library of Medicine, and the National Agricultural Library. The Library of Congress is the most famous of the three, and it has become "recognized as the most important and the leading library in the country." (Leach, 1969, p. 349.) It performs most of the functions generally reserved for a national library, but it is not *the* National Library. It has taken a leadership role in book and library resource preservation, automation and cataloging, bibliographic services, and technical processes research. It is also the largest library in the country in terms of number of documents. However, it does not have a comprehensive national collection, and hence it must share the title of "National Library" with the other two libraries, the National Library of Medicine and the National Agricultural Library, whose function is to serve as national resource collections in the fields of medicine and agriculture, respectively.

Congress

The role of Congress in the national library picture has been rather unique. Ordinarily it would have been the duty of the executive branch of the government to propose new programs of federal aid for libraries. However, Knight and Nourse (1969) declared, "library-aid legislation has come about chiefly at the initiative of Congress, or perhaps better put, at the initiative of lobbyists active in behalf of libraries, rather than as part of any Executive program or drive." The principal piece of legislation that provided aid for public libraries was the Library Services Act of 1956, but the provisions of the law precluded aid to all but rural areas. In 1964 the program of aid for public libraries was broadened to include all libraries, whether rural or urban. At the present time federal aid under the 1970 Amendments to the Library Services and Construction Act (LSCA) is being used to provide library service (in areas inadequately served and in areas with a large percentage of disadvantaged persons), library construction, interlibrary cooperation, and service to the physically handicapped and institutionalized. Congress has enacted other library-aid legislation, in particular laws aimed at school libraries (Elementary and Secondary Education Act of 1965, Title II), college and university library resources (Higher Education Act of 1965, Title II-A), library research and training (Higher Education Act, Title II-B), medical libraries (Medical Library Assistance Act of 1965), libraries in depressed areas (Appalachian Regional Development Act of 1965), and several other types of library.

Office of Education

The Office of Education, an agency within the Department of Health, Education, and Welfare, is the third major organization on the federal library scene. In many respects the Office of Education is the most important organization, since it is responsible for the administration and implementation of the bulk of the various legislative programs pertaining to libraries which Congress has enacted. It also makes important contributions to the setting of national policies for libraries.

The Office of Education as a whole is responsible for programs involving the expenditure of over $4 billion; of this total, as reported in *The Bowker Annual*, about $2.4 billion was allocated for library-related programs in 1968 (Council of National Library Associations, 1968, pp. 184–185). The principal grant programs are covered by three laws: the Library Services and Construction Act of 1964 amended in 1966 and 1970, the Higher Education Act of 1965, and the Elementary and Secondary Education Act of 1965.

The goals of the Office of Education for carrying out its programs for library development are

1. To expand and extend library programs and services for the disadvantaged and handicapped
2. To provide greater equalization of state and local resources for library programs and services
3. To promote better utilization of library resources including cooperation and coordination among public, school, academic, special, and private libraries
4. To improve generally the quality of library programs

These goals have now become incorporated as statements of policy in recent library-aid legislation, but this does not ensure their fulfillment. The basic problem which the Office of Education faces in seeking to guide library development is that it has been granted very little discretionary authority over how the funds are spent. For example, the 1970 Amendments to the Library Services and Construction Act (LSCA) declare that "It is the purpose of this Act . . . to afford the States greater discretion in the allocation of funds . . . to meet specific State needs." Furthermore, "the determination of the best uses of the funds provided under this Act shall be reserved to the States and their local subdivisions." LSCA provides that each state shall submit a state plan for library development, that federal funds will be allocated to the states on the basis of each state's population, and that each state must provide matching funds on the basis of its per capita income. The federal share for library service and construction shall in no case be more than 66 percent nor less than 33 percent of the total funds. For interlibrary cooperation, the federal share is 100 percent.

The Office of Education's role in LSCA as well as in the other grant programs it administers is minimal. It is given little control in the use or allocation of federal funds, except in the broad sense that the state's expenditures must be consistent with the approved state plan.

The Office of Education performs many other functions with respect to library development besides administering the various grant-in-aid programs. One of its most important functions is to stimulate and support research efforts into library problems of all types. It also conducts in-house studies of important issues (such as forecasting the supply and demand for library manpower); surveys, collects, and publishes on a regular basis library statistical data through the National Center for Educational Statistics; publicizes and promotes the federal library programs; and provides for regional supervision and consultation with relevant state officials on problems or questions about the federal programs.

The lack of the essential element of control over allocations and expenditures distinguishes decision making within the Office of Education from normal, profit-oriented decision making. Of course, the Office of Education is certainly not unique within the public sector in this regard. In fact, many would argue that it is not the function of the federal bureaucracy to be concerned with individual local public investment projects since officials at the state level are in a better position to judge their worthiness in the light of local needs. Furthermore, state and local officials can be held more directly accountable for a particular program's success or failure than a federal official. The federal government, so the argument runs, should limit itself to functions it is better equipped to handle.

The precise role of the Office of Education is therefore somewhat nebulous, and in fact its function in the distribution of library-aid funds may be preempted entirely under recently introduced federal revenue sharing plans. The administration's proposal of April 6, 1971, states that "the federal government currently offers an array of programs designed to purchase specific educational materials or services. These programs range from the provision of textbooks and other library resources to the support of guidance and counseling services. Education Revenue Sharing would continue this aid but would pull together programs from at least fourteen separate statutory provisions into one flexible allocation under which States can decide how best to meet local education needs." (U.S. Congressional Record, 1971, p. 2471.)

Whatever may be the political fate of revenue sharing, decision making about library programs as well as education seems destined to be focused more and more at the state level. The trend at the federal level has been to distribute funds in some equitable fashion to the states, and then to give the states increasingly more control over the final distribution of these funds. It is therefore essential for state-level administrators to have a rational planning and decision-making framework by means of which they can efficiently allocate these scarce resources.

State Level

Although nomenclature from state to state may differ, the generic name given to the agency at the state level which deals with libraries is the state library agency. Sometimes there is no single agency; it may be separated into bureaus within the same overall department (typically the Education Department) or it may even be situated in different departments. Whatever the particular organizational structure, the state library agency has fairly well defined functions that it is called upon to perform.

The American Library Association's (ALA) *Standards for Library Functions at the State Level: Revision of the 1963 Edition* written in 1969 specifies the role of the state library agency. The ALA's version of library functions at the state level is partly descriptive of present practice and partly prescriptive of what direction present practice should take. Following are a few excerpts:

For statewide library development

1. The state library agency should exercise leadership and participate in the development of statewide plans involving all types of libraries at all levels within the state.

2. The state library agency should review continuously both federal and state legislation affecting library service . . . to ensure compatibility and to maintain a legal climate conducive to total library growth and development.

3. The state should gather, compile, interpret, publish, and disseminate annual statistics on all types of libraries in the state, including the state library agency. The state library agency should be a central information source concerning the libraries of the state.

4. The annual statistics gathered by the individual states should be designed to provide a common core of data among the states and for the nation.

5. It is the responsibility and obligation of the state library agency to initiate and encourage research.

6. . . . of first priority, every locality within the state should be encouraged to participate in a coordinated library system, so that every resident has access to the total library resources of the state.

7. A high-priority standard for library development is that of designating or developing a pattern of centers over the state so that everyone has access to more comprehensive resources and specialized staff.

8. The state library agency should make provision for reference, bibliographic, and interlibrary loan service to supplement community and regional libraries.

9. The state library agency must make provision for consultants . . . to stimulate all libraries to develop their full potential.

For state financing of library programs

1. State financial aid for libraries should equalize resources and services across the state by providing extra help for those least able to finance sound services and facilities.

2. Direct financial grants to local libraries should be conditional on the meeting of minimum standards of organization, qualifications of professional personnel, and financial effort for library support on the part of the governmental unit or appropriating body.

3. State financial assistance should be provided to help meet the substantial costs involved in organizing or reorganizing library units into adequate systems.

For statewide development of resources

1. An important component in statewide resources should be a general collection of sufficient size and scope to supplement and reenforce resources of other libraries.

2. Subject and reference resources should be available at regional centers within the state, at a distance which enables any serious reader to reach such facilities within a reasonable length of time.

For library resources to state government

1. Each state should maintain a complete collection of the documents of its own government and of current documents of comparable states, plus a strong collection of both local and federal documents.

2. Special information and reference service should be available to the legislative branch of government, and provided as part of or in close coordination with state library agencies.

For the organization of state library services

1. Every state should make administrative provision for the following major areas of state library service: providing, correlating, and serving print and non-print resources; giving direct service to state government; planning and coordinating total library service; and supervising state and federally funded programs.

2. The state library agency should function as a coordinating and service agency to expedite the cooperative programs of academic, special, school, and public libraries in the same community, region, state, and nation, to strengthen the total resources and services available to library

users, and to enable library support to achieve the maximum benefit through the coordinated effort of participating libraries.

For the organization of materials and communication

1. The state library agency has a responsibility to advance technical services through centralized facilities, to achieve economical, expeditious ordering and processing of materials, and to assure a consistent quality of bibliographic data to provide orderly and ready retrieval of information and materials.

2. "Efficient and rapid methods of storage, retrieval, and dissemination of information should be developed and utilized as part of state library service."

Library functions at the state level are a diverse conglomeration of traditional public library functions, special library functions, and functions related to library development and library finance. A useful sevenfold classification of state-level library functions is given by the American Library Association in *Library Statistics* (1966, p. 62):

1. General library services
2. Historical library services
3. Documents depository services
4. Law library services
5. Legislative reference services
6. Library development services
7. Others (for example, services to the handicapped, institutionalized)

The functions of the state library agency which deal with the provision of traditional public library and special library services pose challenging problems for library planners and researchers. However, the focus of our continuing interest lies in the formulation and development of a state-level management information system, which is a middle level in the hierarchy of building a management information system starting with individual library units and ending with a national system for library statistical data. This state-level management information system would logically be an essential part of the sixth function just listed, Library development services. The system would be used to assess statewide library development and to assist state administrators in the supervision and allocation of state and federal aid.

An effective management information system for libraries is important in another context. State tax revenues have not been keeping pace with the rising cost of current state programs and the demand for more state services. The squeeze on state budgets is severely felt by some programs, and support for libraries has sometimes suffered. State library administrators would be in a better position to justify their budget requests if they could marshal better evidence to support their cases. For example, if data from the management information system showed that a 5 percent cut in the library budget would reduce total library effectiveness by 10 percent, then the state library administrator would have a stronger argument for full funding than if he had no data at all.

Although many states have established substantial programs in support of their libraries and library systems, some states do not have a grant program at all. As summarized by Boaz in *Statistics of Public Libraries Serving Areas with at Least 20,000 Inhabitants—1968* (1970, p. 10), a total of eleven states reported that no state funds were contributed to public libraries' operating funds in 1968, and the 37 states that did report support of public libraries contribute amounts ranging from Maine's $600 to New York's $7 million. It should be pointed out that these data refer only to public libraries serving areas with at least 25,000 inhabitants. State support for libraries serving less-populated areas and for other statewide programs can often be substantial. For example, New York's support of its larger public libraries in 1968 is more than matched by its 1969 level of overall support for public libraries. In that year total state support amounted to $14.5 million for public libraries, excluding capital funds and monies for the state library and the division of library development. (New York State, 1970, p. 16.)

The trend toward cooperative arrangements among libraries and the development of library systems highlights the need for improved methods of funding and a wider basis of library support. The state is a natural boundary, the machinery already exists at the state level for raising tax revenues and distributing resources for local library support, and for other similar reasons it is clearly foreseen that the role of the state in additional funding of public library programs will increase.

The question that arises in this connection is "What is a fair share for State and Federal support of library programs?" This question has a long history of contradictory opinions.

In 1948, with Amy Winslow, (Carleton) Joeckel proposed a formula for public library support of 60% local, 25% state and 15% federal. At an Allerton Park Institute in 1961, Hannis Smith proposed a support formula of 40% local, 40% state and 20% federal. In 1964, Lowell Martin proposed as a reasonable ratio 50% local, 30% state and 20% federal. All of these proposals are in striking contrast to the actual pattern of support in 1964, which was 81.8% local, 8.6% state, 2.1% federal and 7.5% from library fines and endowments. (Nelson Associates, Inc., *American State Libraries and State Library Agencies*, 1967, p. 17.)

Obviously there is no consensus about what represents a "fair-share" formula, nor should there be. Any simplistic formula would overlook the important problem of equalization of resources. A relatively poor locality has greater need for state support than a relatively wealthy locality. The poorer locality would have a lower tax base, so that even if the two localities had the same population and the same tax rate, less revenue for library programs would be raised in the poorer community. Furthermore, if the two localities did in fact have the same tax rate, the level of tax revenues would represent more of a burden on the poorer community.

Local needs can vary just as much as local resources. A library serving a highly educated clientele will probably be called upon for more diverse or difficult demands than a library serving the less educated. Thus, not only should local *resources* be taken into account in any state grant program but local *needs* as well.

An interesting point of view in this regard was made by Nelson Associates. They argue that local funding of public library service is not sufficient, and

. . . if libraries are considered to have a social value, both state and federal governments must be prepared to share the operating costs of libraries. . . . Several formulas have been commonly discussed throughout the field but none have been argued systematically. The development and general acceptance of a "fair-share" formula is one of the important items of business on the library agenda. (Nelson Associates, Inc., *Public Libraries in the United States*, 1967, p. 64.)

However, it is not likely that any "fair-share" formula will be flexible enough to provide a state library administrator with the information or the tools to balance resources against needs in order to allocate state grants-in-aid in an optimal manner. A simplistic formula approach that is used to manage a state grant program is in the same category as using library standards to manage an individual public library. What the state-level library administrator needs is not a formula but rather a rational framework for deciding how best to allocate the state's scarce resources. This framework for decision making would have to be adaptable to allow for changing conditions, and yet the institutional setting in which decision making takes place must also be incorporated. For example, if a state had legal restrictions on the amount of state aid per capita it could allocate, the decision model must include this as a constraint. However, if the law could be changed, then this constraint could be relaxed and a new distribution of state aid might result. This kind of analysis can assist the decision maker in many ways: it can help him to reach a better decision regarding the distribution of state funds; it can supply him with information regarding the degree to which library resources will have to be reallocated in order to achieve the optimal mix; it will indicate how well or to what extent the state's objectives are fulfilled; it can be used to justify budgetary requests; and it can be used to indicate the consequences of either a budgetary increase or decrease.

These products of the state-level decision-making model rely upon the prior development of criteria on which to base the allocation and on the generation or collection of the data that are required for the model. The precise form and format of the data elements depend on the relationship between the importance of each particular data element and the cost of collection. For example, a sampling technique may cost less and provide sufficiently good information to justify its use instead of a survey instrument. Some types of data need to be collected more often than other types, and this factor influences cost. A state-level management information system should take all of these factors into consideration. The system will never replace the decision maker; it will be useful only to the extent that it will assist him to reach a better decision.

Another document growing out of this research project will deal more fully with the development of a management information system for state-level library decision making. (Whitfield, forthcoming.)

In the last section of this chapter, we discuss some future library trends and their implications for a library management information system.

Future Library Trends

Libraries are caught in the vortex of many crosscurrents of our modern technological society. Demands on library services will increase markedly in the future due to many causes: population growth; increase in the number of people continuing their education after higher school as well as on the postbaccalaureate level; exponential growth of new advances in science, technology, and the social sciences; and "information explosion" resulting in a proliferation of books, journals, government, business and professional group reports, manuals, abstracts, and catalogs. These changes have broadened man's horizons, widening old fields of endeavor and creating new ones too. Fragmentation of knowledge has led to intense specialization, and libraries have been severely challenged to meet present-day demands. The pressures put on library services portend new approaches to solve the libraries' problems. In the short run, these new approaches may consist of applications of computer technology and data-processing equipment, together with more extensive use of microform techniques, to existing library functions. In the long run, however, technological developments not even presently perceived may generate more radical changes in our current conceptions about libraries. While the basic functions of a library will remain the same, the methods of carrying out these functions in the future could conceivably involve only interactions between man and machine without the physical presence of a library.

Among the most promising future developments for libraries are applications of advanced computer technology. At the present time new areas of application are being developed in conjunction with the major library functions of acquisitions, circulation control, cataloging, serials management, and reference service. There are numerous plans and projects for the application of computer technology to library problems. For example, the cataloging function of libraries will probably change quite radically with the advent of computer technology. The Library of Congress Shared Cataloging Program is speeding the process along by extending its printed catalog card service to include material from many western European countries. In addition, its MARC Project will provide cataloging copy in advance of publication in machine-readable form. These events have made standardization in the cataloging process worthwhile for participating libraries, and large libraries in particular have found it advantageous to subscribe. Furthermore, quirks in cataloging can be overcome for computer applications by using standard book-numbering systems, which is another aspect of the Library of Congress service. These trends all point toward a fully automated catalog system, probably implying the replacement of the usual card catalog by the more portable book catalog, several copies of which could be made available throughout the library. By extension, a regional or national computerized union catalog published periodically and on a current basis would not be too farfetched, although whether such catalogs would be searchable by subject is a question whose answer lies in the more distant future. Regional bibliographic centers that provide on-line cataloging service to member libraries already exist, perhaps best exemplified by the Ohio College Library Center. Further advances in computer technology, such as virtual memory, will probably accelerate the adoption of new methods in automated library service. There are certainly some librarians who envisage a library user seated at a console (possibly remote) requesting information, say bibliographic references on a particular subject, specifying perhaps key words to retrieve all works written only in English after 1969, as described by Licklider (1965).

Much work has also been done on the procedural technology for storage and retrieval systems, automated indexing and classification, automated question-answering, and the like—and on related equipment and technology such as microform techniques and reprography. Developments along these lines will certainly continue. Microreduction of documents has been a significant buttress enabling libraries at relatively small cost to obtain out-of-print or otherwise large collections. Eventually, miniaturization techniques on a much more advanced level will be available in a wider variety of forms. These developments hold much promise for the future.

Another trend in library systems which is not independent of the technological developments just mentioned is the tendency for more cooperation between libraries and the centralization of certain library functions. These two trends are so closely tied together that it is often nearly impossible to disentangle them. For example, the compilation of current union catalogs would be impossible without the cooperation of individual libraries, but even with such cooperation the task of assembling and keeping the catalog current would be formidable indeed without the use of data-processing equipment.

The trend toward cooperation and centralization will take many forms. One principal avenue that libraries will probably follow is that of centralization of certain routine clerical and technical processes. The acquisitions function is a case in point, where a pooled computer system could economically prepare book orders, keep records of all outstanding orders, send reminders, record the receipt of books, provide for the allocation of funds, write the check for payments and, as a by-product, print out accession registers. Another avenue is that of centralizing certain technical processes, such as preparing books for circulation by printing catalog data on the binding and providing circulation cards, and so on. On the demand side, there will very likely be a strengthening of the concept of interlibrary loan, as it will become increasingly more difficult for libraries to acquire all the documents necessary to maintain a number of comprehensive collections. One of the major breakthroughs in this area may be the comprehensive acquisition of all published documents in specific fields of knowledge by one or several institutions, which would then become the suppliers upon request of these source materials. This development would eliminate a great deal of duplication in library holdings, but implementation of this idea requires fast and easy access to remote library holdings. Technological developments that would facilitate this arrangement would be the publication of national union lists or current bibliographies of those fields of knowledge covered by each designated institution (for example, X's holdings of law, Y's of medicine, Z's of economics) and the use of telefacsimile or slow-scan TV for the transmittal of information between libraries. A large-scale research effort is needed in this area directed toward the problems faced by cooperative library arrangements. In particular, it is important to examine what sorts of management information systems would be appropriate for their successful operation.

One more significant trend for the future development of libraries is the increasing awareness of the relevance and usefulness of library statistics for an effective management information system. To a large extent these statistics will be offshoots of the computerization of library functions. For example, a computerized circulation system will be able to provide for the automatic accumulation of document-use statistics that can be tabulated in any number of different ways, thereby assisting the librarian in his planning of the library's operation. Decisions, such as weeding of seldom used documents, may take place routinely on the basis of current and readily available circulation statistics. The librarian might decide that any document which has not been used for a certain period of time and published before 19XX be placed either in storage or onto microfilm. Various questions concerning circulation by students or faculty, or by broad subject area, or in-library versus take-home use will probably be readily available from an automated system, granting the librarian much more flexibility and assurance in his role as decision maker. Financial questions can also be easily handled under an automated acquisitions system. Summaries of costs of books already charged to each allocation, or to each vendor, or to various places of publication are statistics that would normally be gathered by a library, but an automated system provides these tabulations quickly and cheaply. Analysis of total and average book costs by subject or country of origin could also be made, so that librarians and administrators would be aware of these trends. These are only a few of the possibilities, but the point must be made that automation cannot substitute for a capable administrator. It is only effective as a management tool whose purpose is to furnish the decision maker with the information needed to make a decision. Although details of data collection and data forms will certainly vary from library to library—and no data system can be considered final or perfect—there are some aspects of any data system that have more lasting importance, notably the performance indicators relating final output to the amount of input used to produce this output. In the future, librarians will have more training as information specialists; thus, they will combine the skills of management science with the artistry usually associated with their profession.

APPENDIX I
UNIVERSITY LIBRARY
SUBJECT CATEGORIES AND AREAS

Subject/Department Categories	Subject Areas
Accounting	Financial Managerial
Anthropology	Ethnography Archaeology Physical Anthropology Cultural Anthropology–Culture Theory Linguistic Anthropology
Architecture	History-Theory Design-Construction
Astronomy	History Spherical-Practical Universe Studies–Cosmology
Biological Science	Cellular Molecular Organism-Development Evolution Ecology Behavior Biophysics Biochemistry
Chemical Engineering	Reaction Design Transport Processes
Chemistry	Physical Inorganic Organic Crystallography
City and Regional Planning	City Design–City Appearance Regional Planning-Studies and Approaches Regional Planning–Implementation Urban Management and Problems Social Policy Planning
Civil Engineering	Structural Mechanics Transportation Engineering Water Resources Engineering
Classical Archaeology	Classical Archaeology
Classical Language and Literature	Greek Latin
Communications	Media Communications Behavior

Subject/Department Categories	Subject Areas
Economics	Theory
	History
	Systems
	Growth, Development, and Planning
	Econometric Methods
	Economic and Social Data
	Fiscal Policy and Public Finance
	Fiscal and Monetary Theory and Institutions
	International Economics
	Agricultural Economics
	Industrial Organization and Public Policy
	Manpower and Labor
	Welfare Programs–Urban and Regional Economics
Education	Administration
	Elementary Instruction
	Elementary Curriculum
	Secondary Instruction
	Secondary Curriculum
	Social Foundations
	Psychological Foundations
	Psychological Services
Electrical Engineering	Power
	Circuit and Network Theory
	Control Theory
	Computer Design
	Electromagnetic Fields
	Electronics (Classical)
	Communications Theory
	Solid State Electronics
Engineering Mechanics	Dynamic and Vibration Analysis
	Stress Analysis
English	English Language
	Medieval English
	Renaissance
	Later seventeenth and eighteenth centuries
	Romantic
	Victorian
	Recent
	American to 1860
	1860–1915
	Recent
Finance	Business Finance
	Real Estate
	Trusts and Estate Planning

Subject/Department Categories	Subject Areas
Fine Arts	History of Art Painting-Sculpture-Graphics
Folklore	Folklore
General Reference Category	General Reference
Geography	Geography
Geology	Geology
Germanic Language and Literature	Germanic Philology German-Medieval to 1700 Eighteenth and nineteenth centuries Recent Scandinavian Dutch
History	Africa Ancient Medieval European Modern European Germany France Great Britain Russia Near East Asia United States Latin America
History of Science	History of Science
Industrial Management	Business Organization Operations Management
Industrial Relations	Labor Relations Personnel
Insurance	Property and Liability Life and Health Pensions and Employee Benefits Social Insurance
International	Marketing Operations
Law	Business Law
Library Science	Library Science
Linguistics	Linguistics

Subject/Department Categories	Subject Areas
Marketing	Consumer Behavior Distribution and Structure Promotion Marketing Research Marketing Management
Mathematics	Algebra Applied Mathematics Classical Analysis Functional Analysis Topology Geometry
Mechanical Engineering	Thermodynamics Fluid Dynamics Heat Transfer
Metallurgy and Materials Science	Physical Chemical Mechanical
Music	History-Theory Composition Scores
Operations Research	Problem Formulation Models
Oriental and South Asia Language and Literature	Ancient Near East (pre-Islamic–Egyptian) Modern Near East (Islamic Culture) Hebrew Arabic Persian Turkish South and South East Asia—Classical South and South East Asia—Modern East Asia—Chinese East Asia—Japanese
Philosophy	History and Problems—Ancient History and Problems—Medieval History and Problems—Modern Logic and Philosophy of Science Metaphysics Epistemology Philosophy of Religion and Psychology
Physics	Nuclear High Energy Solid State Gravitation and Astrophysics

Subject/Department Categories	Subject Areas
Political Science	Political Theory and Methodology American Government Comparative Government International Relations and Law Public Administration
Psychology	Learning and Motivation Sensation and Perception Personality and Psychopathology Physiological and Comparative Developmental Mathematical Psychology—Measurement
Public Utilities	Utilities Industry Public Regulation
Religion	Biblical Studies Christianity Judaism Other Religions Religion in America
Romance Language and Literature	Romance Philology French Language French Literature—Medieval Sixteenth–seventeenth centuries Eighteenth century Nineteenth century Recent Italian Language Italian Literature—Medieval Renaissance Modern Spanish Language Spanish Literature—Medieval Sixteenth–seventeenth centuries Eighteenth–twentieth centuries Latin American Literature
Slavic Language and Literature	Slavic Philology Russian Polish Serbo-Croatian Baltic
Sociology	Sociological Theory Social Organization Statistics and Methodology Demography Criminology Comparative Sociology

Subject/Department Categories	Subject Areas
Sociology (*Continued*)	Sociology of Health and Welfare Political Sociology Social Psychology
Statistics	Theory Applied
Transportation	Transportation Industry Traffic Management Public Regulation
	Total—218

APPENDIX II
DOCUMENT SUBJECT MATTER CATEGORIES

Number of Categories	Category	Source
3	The Humanities The Sciences: Physical, Biological, and Applied The Social Sciences	*Reference Books: A Brief Guide for Students and Other Users of the Library* (Enoch Pratt Free Library, Baltimore, Md., 1966)
3	Social Sciences Literature and Fine Arts Industry and Science	Dayton Public Library subject departments
3	Humanities Social Sciences Science and Technology	Bundy 1968
4	Reference Humanities Science Social and Behavioral Science	American Library Association, *Choice: Opening Day Collection* 1967
5	Business and Technology Literature and Language History and Travel Sociology and Religion Art and Music	South Bend Public Library subject departments
6	Science and Industry Local History and Geneology Literature and History Community Living Family Living Fine Arts and Fashion	Dallas Public Library subject departments
7	Philosophy, Psychology, and Religion The Social Sciences The Natural Sciences Fine Arts Literature History and Biography Geography	Shove, Moen, Wezeman and Russell 1963
7	Business, Science, and Industry Education, Philosophy, and Religion Social Science and History Literature Music Art Fiction	Free Library of Philadelphia subject departments

Appendix II

Number of Categories	Category	Source
7	Social Science Business and Technology Literature History, Travel, and Biography Education, Philosophy, and Religion Art and Music Local History	Kansas City Public Library subject departments
8	Applied Science and Technology Education Social Science and Business History and Travel Humanities Natural Science and Useful Arts Music Art	Chicago Public Library subject departments
8	Biography and Travel Literature Philosophy and Psychology History Applied Science Social Science Fine Arts Pure Science	Dick and Berelson 1948
10	Generalities Philosophy, Metaphysics, Psychology, Logic, and Ethics and Morals Religion and Theology Social Sciences, Economics, Law, Government, and Education Philology, Linguistics, and Languages Mathematics and Natural Sciences Applied Sciences, Medicine, and Technology The Arts, Recreation, Sport, and so forth Literature and Belles Lettres Geography, Biography, and History	Universal Decimal Classification
13	Reference Philosophy, Ethics, and Religion Social Studies Languages Pure and Applied Sciences The Arts Sports and Recreation Literature—General Literature—Traditional and Folk	Hodges 1969

Number of Categories	Category	Source
	Biography and History Stories for Intermediate and Upper Grades Picture Books and Stories for Primary Grades	
15	Fiction—Picture Books Fiction—Younger Readers Fiction—Older Readers Encyclopedias Religion and Mythology Sociology Language Science Technology The Arts Literature History Geography of the Ancient World Geography of the Modern World Biography	Colwell, Green, and Parrott 1968
16	Encyclopedias Philosophy and Religion Psychology Business and Economics Social Sciences Education Science and Technology Art Music Theater and Dance Games and Sport Language Literature Geography, Travel, and Archaeology History Biography, Geneology, and Names	*Reference Books for Small and Medium Sized Public Libraries* (American Library Association, Chicago, 1969)
19	Agriculture Art Biography Business Children's Economics Education History Law Literature—Fiction Literature—General Literature—Poetry	Council of National Library Associations, *Bowker Annual 1969* (p. 49)

Number of Categories	Category	Source
	Literature—Drama Medicine Music Religion Science Sports Technology	
20	General Works—Polygraphy (A) Philosophy—Religion (B) History—Auxiliary Sciences (C) History and Topography (D) America (E-F) Geography—Anthropology (G) Social Sciences, Economics, and Sociology (H) Political Science (J) Law (K) Education (L) Music (M) Fine Arts (N) Language and Literature (P) Science (Q) Medicine (R) Agriculture—Plant and Animal Industry (S) Technology (T) Military Science (U) Naval Science (V) Bibliography and Library Science (Z)	Library of Congress classification
21	Reference Art Language and Literature Music Philosophy Religion Speech, Theater, and Dance Astronautics and Astronomy Biology Chemistry Earth Science Engineering Health and Physical Education Mathematics Physics Economics and Business Education History, Geography, and Travel Political Science Psychology Sociology and Anthropology	American Library Association, *Choice: Opening Days Collection* 1967

Number of Categories	Category	Source
23	Agriculture (Dewey 630–639; 712–719) Art (700–711; 720–770) Biography (920–929) Business (650–659) Education (370–379) Fiction General Works (000–99) History (900–909; 930–999) Home Economics (640–649) Juveniles Language (400–499) Law (340–349) Literature (800–810; 813–820; 823–899) Medicine (610–619) Music (780–789) Philosophy and Psychology (100–199) Poetry and Drama (811–812; 821–822) Religion (200–299) Science and Mathematics (500–599) Sociology and Economics (300–339; 350–369; 380–399) Sports and Recreation (790–799) Technology (600–609; 620–629; 660–699) Travel (910–919)	United States of America Standards Institute, *Bowker Annual 1969* (p. 36)
24	Agriculture Business and Economics Chemistry and Physics Children's Education Engineering Fine and Applied Arts General Interest Publications History Home Economics Industrial Arts Journalism and Communication Labor and Industrial Relations Law Library Science Literature and Language Mathematics, Botany, Geology, and General Science Medicine Philosophy and Religion Physical Education and Recreation Political Science Psychology Sociology and Anthropology Zoology	Council of National Library Associations, *Bowker Annual 1969* (p. 47) (from the *Library Journal*)

Number of Categories	Category	Source
24	Reference Art Biography and Personal Narrative Business and Economics Communications Education Geography History Home Economics Humor Journalism Labor Language Arts Literature Music Philosophy and Religion Poetry Political Science and International Affairs Psychology and Psychiatry Science and Technology Social Science Sport and Pastimes Theater Fiction	R. R. Bowker 1969
31	History Business and Economics Sociology and Anthropology Politics Education Psychology Travel Public Administration Law Social Science Engineering Medicine Agriculture General Science Home Economics Biology Mathematics and Statistics Zoology Chemistry Earth Science Physics Architecture and Buildings Botany Physical Science and Astronomy Literature	Bundy 1968

Number of Categories	Category	Source
	Art	
	Entertainment and Recreation	
	Music	
	Religion	
	Language	
	Philosophy	
51	Subject Categories of Appendix I	
58	General Works (A)	Voight and Treyz 1967
	Philosophy and Psychology (B-BJ)	
	Religion (BL-BX)	
	History of Civilization (C)	
	General History (D)	
	History	
	Great Britain (DA)	
	Austria, Hungary, and Czechoslovakia (DB)	
	France (DC)	
	Germany (DD)	
	Greece, Italy, and Netherlands (DE-DJ)	
	Russia, Poland, and Finland (DK)	
	Scandinavia (DL)	
	Spain and Portugal (DP)	
	Switzerland, Turkey, and Balkan States (DQ-DR)	
	Asia (DS)	
	Africa (DT)	
	Australia and Oceania (DU)	
	General America (E 1-143)	
	United States (E 151-F 970)	
	Canada (F 1001-1140)	
	Mexico (F 1201-1392)	
	Latin America (F 1401-3794)	
	Geography and Anthropology (G)	
	General Social Sciences and Statistics (H-HA)	
	Economics (HB-HJ)	
	Sociology (HM-HX)	
	Political Science (J)	
	Law (K)	
	Education (L)	
	Music (M)	
	Fine Arts (N)	
	General Language and Literature (P)	
	Classical Language and Literature (PA)	
	Modern European Language (PB-PH)	
	Oriental Language and Literature (PJ-PL)	

Number of Categories	Category	Source
	General Literature (PN)	
	French Literature (PQ1-3999)	
	Italian Literature (PQ4001-5999)	
	Spanish and Portuguese Literature (PQ6001-9999)	
	English Literature (PR)	
	American Literature (PS)	
	German Literature (PT1-4899)	
	Dutch and Scandinavian Literature (PT5001-9999)	
	General Science (Q)	
	Mathematics (QA)	
	Astronomy (QB)	
	Physics (QC)	
	Chemistry (QD)	
	Geology (QE)	
	Natural History and Biology (QH)	
	Botany (QK)	
	Zoology (QL)	
	Anatomy, Physiology, and Bacteriology (QM-QR)	
	Medicine (R)	
	Agriculture (S)	
	Technology and Engineering (T)	
	Military and Naval Service (U-V)	
	Bibliography and Library Science (Z)	
99	Divisions of the Dewey Decimal Classification system	
99	Divisions of the Universal Decimal Classification system	
202	Subclasses of the Library of Congress Classification system	
219	Subject Areas of Appendix I	
922	Sections of the Dewey Decimal Classification system	

APPENDIX III
PUBLIC LIBRARY PROGRAM STRUCTURE

Appendix III

Program Group	Program	Subprogram	Element	Component	Task	Subelement	Subcomponent

1. Programs to provide physical facilities
  1.1 To provide physical facilities in (first geographical area)
    1.1.1 To provide physical facilities for (first physically separate library unit in geographical area)
      1.1.1.1 To provide building area
        1.1.1.1.1 User Area
          1.1.1.1.1.1 Document exposure area
            1.1.1.1.1.1.1 Physical area
            1.1.1.1.1.1.2 Environment
          1.1.1.1.1.2 User service area (rest rooms, snack room, telephones, and so on)
        1.1.1.1.2 Document storage area
          1.1.1.1.2.1 Physical area
          1.1.1.1.2.2 Environment
        1.1.1.1.3 Staff area
          1.1.1.1.3.1 Physical area
          1.1.1.1.3.2 Environment
      1.1.1.2 To provide user furnishings
        1.1.1.2.1 Seating
          1.1.1.2.1.1 Carrels
          1.1.1.2.1.2 Table-chair combinations
          1.1.1.2.1.3 Lounge chairs
        1.1.1.2.2 Other furnishings
      1.1.1.3 To maintain facilities
        1.1.1.3.1 Janitorial service
        1.1.1.3.2 Repair and replacement
    1.1.2 To provide physical facilities for (second physically separate library unit in geographical area)
    ⋮
    (A subprogram for each physically separate library unit in the geographical area, whether existing or proposed)

Public Library Program Structure

1.2 To provide physical facilities in (second geographical area)
⋮
(A program for each geographical area)
2. Programs to promote library use and to provide access to documents within the library
  2.1 To promote library use and select documents for the general adult and young adult population
    2.1.1 To promote library use for the general adult and young adult population
      2.1.1.1 To provide publications, advertisements, and exhibits
        2.1.1.1.1 Publications
          2.1.1.1.1.1 User guides
            2.1.1.1.1.1.1 Whole library
            2.1.1.1.1.1.2 (First Library unit)
            ⋮
            (A subelement for each library unit)
          2.1.1.1.1.2 Selected bibliographies
            2.1.1.1.1.2.1 Whole library
            2.1.1.1.1.2.2 (First library unit)
            ⋮
            (A subelement for each library unit)
        2.1.1.1.2 Advertisements
        2.1.1.1.3 Exhibits
          2.1.1.1.3.1 (First library unit)
          ⋮
          (A task for each library unit)
      2.1.1.2 To communicate personally with the general adult and young adult population
        2.1.1.2.1 Library initiative
          2.1.1.2.1.1 (First geographical area)

Program Group	Program	Subprogram	Element	Component	Task	Subelement	Subcomponent
							2.1.1.2.1.1.1 Communication outside the library with schools, businesses, community organizations, and individuals
						2.1.1.2.1.1.2 (First library unit in geographical area)	
							2.1.1.2.1.1.2.1 Lectures, classes, and events
							2.1.1.2.1.1.2.2 Tours and instruction on library use
						2.1.1.2.1.1.3 (Second library unit in geographical area)	
						⋮	
						(A subelement for each library unit in geographical area)	
					2.1.1.2.1.2 (Second geographical area)		
						(Subelements and subcomponents are the same as for the first geographical area)	
					(A task, and corresponding subelements and subcomponents, for each geographical area)		

Public Library Program Structure

2.1.1.2.2 Assistance for document identification and location, and for information
    2.1.1.2.2.1 (First library unit)
        2.1.1.2.2.1.1 In-person service
            2.1.1.2.2.1.1.1 General Service
            2.1.1.2.2.1.1.2 (First subject matter category)
            ⋮
            (A subcomponent for each subject matter category)
        2.1.1.2.2.1.2 Telephone service

2.1.2 To select documents and indexes for the general adult and young adult population
    2.1.2.1 To organize the selection procedure
    2.1.2.2 To carry out the selection procedure
        2.1.2.2.1 (First library unit)
            2.1.2.2.1.1 (First document subset, defined by form, subject matter, reading or educational level, language, or publication date)
                2.1.2.2.1.1.1 Documents
                2.1.2.2.1.1.2 Indexes

232   Appendix III

Program Group	Program	Subprogram	Element	Component	Task	Subelement	Subcomponent

2.1.2.2.1.2 (Second document subset)
   (Subelements are the same as for the first document subset)
   ⋮
      (A task, and corresponding subelements, for each document subset)
2.1.2.2.2 (Second library unit)
   (Tasks and subelements are the same as for the first library unit)
   ⋮
      (A component, and corresponding tasks and subelements, for each library unit)

2.2 To promote library use and select documents for the general children population
(There are identical subprograms, elements, components, tasks, subelements, and subcomponents as for program 2.1)

2.3 To promote library use and select documents for special population subsets (for example, the blind; the disadvantaged; persons of different languages, national origins, or races; the physically handicapped; persons in hospitals and institutions; and so on)
   2.3.1 (First special population subset)
   ⋮
      (A subprogram for each special population subset)

2.4 To perform necessary document access activities that are typically undifferentiated by population subset
   2.4.1 To acquire documents
      2.4.1.1 To order documents
      2.4.1.2 To receive documents
   2.4.2 To aid document search within the library by classifying, cataloging and placarding
      2.4.2.1 To classify documents
      2.4.2.2 To catalog documents
         2.4.2.2.1 Individual catalog entries

Public Library Program Structure

```
2.4.2.2.2 Catalog processing
          2.4.2.2.2.1 Catalog preparation
          2.4.2.2.2.2 Catalog dissemination
          2.4.2.2.2.3 Catalog maintenance
2.4.2.3 To provide directional and explanatory placards
    2.4.2.3.1 (First library unit)
        ⋮
        (A component for each library unit)
2.4.3 To process documents
    2.4.3.1 To bind documents
    2.4.3.2 To mark, label, and paste documents
2.4.4 To control location and use of documents
    2.4.4.1 (First library unit)
        2.4.4.1.1 Storage
        2.4.4.1.2 Circulation
            2.4.4.1.2.1 Granting user privileges
            2.4.4.1.2.2 Charging documents to users
            2.4.4.1.2.3 Loans to other libraries
        2.4.4.1.3 Security
    2.4.4.2 (Second library unit)
        ⋮
        (Components and tasks are the same as for the first library unit)
        (An element, and corresponding components and tasks, for each library unit)
2.4.5 To facilitate document use
    2.4.5.1 (First library unit)
        2.4.5.1.1 Accessory equipment
            2.4.5.1.1.1 Microform readers
            2.4.5.1.1.2 Audiovisual equipment
        2.4.5.1.2 Copy Service
        2.4.5.1.3 Other facilitation services
```

| Program Group | Program | Subprogram | Element | Component | Task | Subelement | Subcomponent |

2.4.5.2 (Second library unit)
(Components and tasks are the same as for the first library unit)

2.4.6 To maintain and weed documents
(An element, and corresponding components and tasks, for each library unit)
    2.4.6.1 To determine documents with which to take special action
        2.4.6.1.1 (First library unit)
        ⋮
        (A component for each library unit)
    2.4.6.2 To act upon specific documents
        2.4.6.2.1 Rebinding and repairs
        2.4.6.2.2 Relocating
        2.4.6.2.3 Discarding
        2.4.6.2.4 Tracing

3. Programs to provide access to documents in other libraries
   3.1 To form interlibrary catalogs of holdings
      3.1.1 To assist in the compilation of interlibrary catalogs
      3.1.2 To arrange for use of interlibrary catalogs by users of the library
   3.2 To coordinate and administer interlibrary access agreements
   3.3 To assist users in obtaining documents from other libraries
      3.3.1 To request documents
      3.3.2 To receive documents
      3.3.3 To control documents
      3.3.4 To return documents

4. Programs to provide general planning, administrative, and support activities
   4.1 To plan and administer library service
      4.1.1 To prepare programs, projects, and budgets
      4.1.2 To perform financial administration

Public Library Program Structure

    4.1.2.1 To handle payments and receipts
    4.1.2.2 To perform accounting procedures
  4.1.3 To prepare reports
  4.1.4 To administer personnel activities
    4.1.4.1 Specification of staff positions
    4.1.4.2 Recruitment and selection of personnel
    4.1.4.3 Salary and fringe benefits
    4.1.4.4 Promotion
    4.1.4.5 Training
  4.1.5 To perform other administrative services, as required
4.2 To provide support service
  4.2.1 To provide office supplies
    4.2.1.1 To purchase supplies
    4.2.1.2 To distribute supplies
  4.2.2 To provide printing and duplication service
  4.2.3 To provide internal communications
    4.2.3.1 Telephone
    4.2.3.2 Mail

APPENDIX IV
UNIVERSITY LIBRARY PROGRAM STRUCTURE

Program	Subprogram	Element	Component	Task
I. To provide user area and furnishings				
	A. To provide user area (library unit)			
		1. To provide study area		
			a. Physical area	(1) Private study area
				(2) General study area
			b. Environment	(1) Heating—air conditioning
				(2) Lighting
			c. Maintenance and Repair	(1) Janitorial Service
				(2) Repair
		2. To provide user service area to include rest rooms, snack room, telephone, and so on		
	B. To provide user furnishings (library unit)			
		1. To provide seating	a. Desk-chairs (Carrels)	
			b. Table chair combinations	
			c. Lounge chairs	
		2. To provide other furnishings		
II. To provide access to documents within the library				
	A. To manage document collections (subject category)			
		1. To select documents	a. Selection mechanism	
			b. Documents	

University Library Program Structure

2. To acquire documents
   a. Ordering
   b. Receiving
      (1) Books (subject area)
      (2) Periodicals-serials
      (3) Other

3. To process documents
   a. Binding
   b. Numbering and pasting

4. To weed and maintain collection
   a. Rebinding and repairs
   b. Relocating
   c. Discarding

5. To store documents
   a. Shelving
   b. Physical area
   c. Environment
   d. Maintenance

B. To control use and location of documents (library unit)
   1. Circulation
   2. Loans to other libraries
   3. Periodical control
   4. Reserve service
   5. Reshelving
   6. Security

C. To facilitate document use (library unit)

Program	Subprogram	Element	Component	Task

                                              1. To provide accessory equipment

                                                                                          a. Microform readers
                                                                                          b. Audio equipment
                                                                                          c. Visual equipment

                                              2. To provide copy service

III. To provide access to documents in other libraries

            A. To provide interlibrary document loan (library)

                        1. To assist users in requesting documents from other libraries
                        2. To request, receive, control, and return documents borrowed
                           from other libraries

            B. To coordinate and administer interlibrary access agreements (library)

IV. To provide aids in identifying and locating documents and to provide information

            A. To provide aids to locate documents within the library (library unit)

                        1. To classify documents and to provide catalogs

                                                   a. Document classification
                                                   b. Determining catalog entries
                                                 c. Maintaining catalog

                        2. To prepare and post directional signs and explanatory placards

            B. To provide aids to identify existing documents and to locate documents in other libraries (library unit)

                        1. To manage index collection

                                                   a. Selection
                                                   b. Acquisition
                                                   c. Classification and cataloging
                                                   d. Processing
                                                   e. Weeding and Maintenance
                                                   f. Storage

University Library Program Structure

        2. To control use and location of indexes
        3. To facilitate index use
        4. To assist in compiling cooperative interlibrary catalogs of holdings (library)
    C. To provide personal assistance for document identification and location and to provide information (library unit)
        1. To assist users in performing literature research and in identifying or verifying a specific citation
        2. To provide reference information

V. To promote use of the library
    A. To provide publications, advertisements, and exhibits (library unit)
        1. To provide publications
            a. User guides
            b. Selected bibliographies
        2. To advertise
        3. To construct exhibits
    B. To provide personal communication with members of population being served (library unit)
        1. To perform liaison visits with faculty
        2. To conduct library tours and classes regarding use of the library

VI. To provide general administrative and support services
    A. To provide administrative service (library)
        1. To administer personnel activities
        2. To handle payments, receipts, and accounting requirements
        3. To prepare programs, projects, and budgets
        4. To administer reports
        5. To perform other administrative services as required
    B. To provide support services (library)

Program	Subprogram	Element	Component	Task
		1. To provide office supplies		
		2. To provide copy and duplication service		
		3. To provide internal mail service		
	C. To provide staff area			
		1. To provide physical area		
		2. To provide environment		
		3. To provide maintenance		

SELECTED BIBLIOGRAPHY[1]

Ackerman, Jerome, "Statistical Measures Required for Library Management Decision-Making Under a Planning-Programming-Budgeting System (PPBS)," M.B.A. thesis, University of Pennsylvania, Philadelphia, 1969.

Ackoff, Russell, "The Role of Recorded Information in the Decision Making Process—Operations Research Approach," in Shera, J. H., A. Kent, and J. W. Perry (eds.), *Documentation in Action*, Rheinhold Publishing Corp., New York pp. 253–256 (1956).

Ackoff, Russell L., "Towards a System of Systems Concepts," *Management Science*, 17:661–671 (July 1971).

ACRL Board of Directors, statement approved at the Midwinter 1966 Meeting, "Statement of Service to Library Users," *ACRL News*, No. 2, April 1966.

Adler, Lee, "Systems Approach to Marketing," *Harvard Business Review*, 45:105–118 (May/June 1967).

American Council of Learned Societies, "On Research Libraries," prepared for National Advisory Commission on Libraries, Committee on Research Libraries, American Council of Learned Societies, November 1967, incorporated into Knight, Douglas M., and E. Shepley Nourse (eds.), *Libraries at Large: Tradition, Innovation and the National Interest*, pp. 122–142, 229–236, 265–273, 394–398, R. R. Bowker, New York, 1969.

American Council on Education, *American Universities and Colleges*, Washington, D.C., 10th edition, 1968.

American Library Association, Association of College and Research Libraries Committee on Standards, "Standards for College Libraries," *College and Research Libraries*, 20:274–280 (1959).

American Library Association, *Student Use of Libraries; an Inquiry into the Needs of Students, Libraries, and the Educational Process*, Chicago, 1964.

———, *Library Statistics: A Handbook of Concepts, Definitions, and Terminology*, Williams, Joel (ed.), Chicago, 1966.

———, *Choice: Opening Day Collection*, Chicago, 1967.

———, *Minimum Standards for Public Library Systems, 1966*, Chicago, 1967.

———, *American Library Laws*, Third Edition, 4 Supplements, Chicago, 1964. 2nd Supplement (1965–66), 1967.

———, Library Administration Division, *Library Statistics of Colleges and Universities, 1965–66, Institutional Data*, Chicago, 1967.

———, *Personnel Organization and Procedure: A Manual Suggested for Use in Public Libraries*, Chicago, 1968.

———, *Reference Books for Small and Medium Sized Public Libraries*, Chicago, 1969.

———, *Standards for Library Functions at the State Level: Revision of the 1963 Edition*, Chicago, 1969.

Andrews, Theodora A., "Role of Departmental Libraries in Operations Research Studies in a University Library: Selection for Storage Problems," *Special Libraries*, 59:519–524 (1968).

1. The cutoff date for inclusion in this bibliography is January 1972.

Selected Bibliography

Argyris, Chris, "Management Information Systems: the Challenge to Rationality and Emotionality," *Management Science*, 17:B275–B292 (February 1971).

Arora, S. R., and P. Rameshwar, "Acquisition of Library Materials—A Quantitative Approach," in North, Jeanne B. (ed.), *Cooperating Information Societies, Proceedings of the American Society for Information Sciences*, Vol. 6, Greenwood Publishing Corp., Westport, Conn., 1969.

Association of Research Libraries, *Academic Library Statistics-1967/68*, Washington, D.C.

Axford, H. William, "An Approach to Performance Budgeting at the Florida Atlantic University Library," *College and Research Libraries*, 32:87–104 (March 1971).

Ayres, H. T., R. C. Norris, and R. S. Robinson, "An Investigation of Missing Books in the M.I.T. Science Library," Term Report, M.I.T. Libraries, Cambridge, Mass., 1962.

Bailey, Stephen K., and Edith K. Mosher, *ESEA: The Office of Education Administers a Law*, Syracuse University Press, Syracuse, N.Y., 1968.

Baker, Norman R., "A Descriptive Model of Library/User/Funder Behavior in a University Environment", *Drexel Library Bulletin*, 4:16–30 (1968).

———, and Richard E. Nance, "The Use of Simulation in Studying Information Storage and Retrieval Systems," *American Documentation*, 19:363–370 (1968).

———, and Richard E. Nance, "Organizational Analyses and Simulation Studies of University Libraries: a Methodological Overview," *Information Storage & Retrieval*, 5:153–168 (1970).

Baldwin, Emma V., *Cost Accounting in Public Libraries*, Committee for the Study of Cost Accounting in Public Libraries, Montclair, N.J., 1939.

———, and W. E. Marcus, *Library Costs and Budgets: A Study of Cost Accounting in Public Libraries*, R. R. Bowker Co., New York, 1941.

Baumol, William J., "On the Appropriate Discount Rate for Evaluation of Public Projects," in Hinrichs, Harley H., and Graeme M. Taylor, *Program Budgeting and Benefit-Cost Analysis*, Goodyear Publishing, Pacific Palisades, Calif., 1969, pp. 202–212.

Beasley, Kenneth E., *A Study and Recommendations of Library Districts for Pennsylvania*, Institute of Public Administration, Pennsylvania State Univeristy, University Park, Pa. 1962.

———, *A Statistical Reporting System for Local Public Libraries*, Pennsylvania State University, University Park, Pa. 1964.

———, "A Theoretical Framework for Public Library Measurement," in Goldhor, Herbert (ed.), *Research Methods in Librarianship: Measurement and Evaluation*, pp. 2–14, University of Illinois Graduate School of Library Science, Evanston, Ill., 1968.

Beck, R. E., "Investigation of a Centralized Book Labeling System for the Divisional Libraries," in Burkhalter, Barton R. (ed.), *Case Studies in Systems Analysis in a University Library*, pp. 103–113, Scarecrow Press, Metuchen, N.J., 1968.

———, H. L. Benford, and E. W. Deardorff, "Analysis and Improvement of the Accounting System of the Photoduplication Service," in Burkhalter, Barton R. (ed.), *Case Studies in Systems Analysis in a University Library*, pp. 128–136, Scarecrow Press, Metuchen, N.J., 1968.

Selected Bibliography

———, and M. C. Drott, "A Photo Copier Accounting System for the Library Photoduplication Department," in Burkhalter, Barton R. (ed.), *Case Studies in Systems Analysis in a University Library*, pp. 137–141, Scarecrow Press, Metuchen, N.J., 1968.

Becker, Joseph, "Trends in Library Technology," *Special Libraries*, 62:429–34 (October 1971).

Beer, S., and R. L. Ackoff, "In Conclusion: Some Beginnings," in *Progress in Operations Research*, Volume III, Aronofsky, Julius S. (ed.), *Relationship Between Operations Research and the Computer*, pp. 525–549, John Wiley & Sons., New York, 1969.

Benford, H. L., B. R. Burkhalter, G. C. Ehrnstrum, and L. L. Hoag, "Analysis of Book Reshelving," in Burkhalter, Barton R. (ed.), *Case Studies in Systems Analysis in a University Library*, pp. 76–89, Scarecrow Press, Metuchen, N.J., 1968.

Benford, John Q., "The Philadelphia Project," *Library Journal*, 96: 2041–2047 (June 15, 1971).

Berelson, Bernard, *The Library's Public: a Report of the Public Library Inquiry*, Columbia University Press, New York, 1949.

Bernal, J. D., "The Transmission of Scientific Information: a User's Analysis," in *Proceedings of the International Conference on Scientific Information*, Vol. 1, pp. 77–95, National Academy of Sciences—National Research Council, Washington, D.C., 1959.

Black, Guy, *The Application of Systems Analysis to Government Operations*, Praeger, New York, 1968.

Blasingame, Ralph, *Feasibility of Cooperation for Exchange of Resources Among Academic and Special Libraries in Pennsylvania*, Institute of Public Administration, the Pennsylvania State University, University Park, Pa., 1967.

———, "A Critical Analysis of State-Aid Formulas", *Library Trends*, 19:250–259 (1970).

———, and Ernest R. DeProspo, Jr., "Effectiveness in Cooperation and Consolidation in Public Libraries," in Voigt, Melvin J., *Advances in Librarianship*, Vol. I, Academic Press, New York, 1970.

———, and L. Grundt, *Research in Library Service in Metropolitan Areas*, Rutgers—The State University, New Brunswick, N.J., 1967

Boaz, Ruth L., "Dilemma of Statistics for Public Libraries," *ALA Bulletin*, 63:1572–1575 (1969).

———, "Library Networks and Systems Overview," in Palmer, David C. (ed.), *A National Plan for Library Statistics: Guidelines for Implementation*, Statistics Coordinating Committee of the ALA, Chicago, 1970.

———, *Statistics of Public Libraries Serving Areas with at Least 25,000 Inhabitants, 1968*, National Center for Education Statistics, U.S. Department of Health, Education, and Welfare, Washington, D.C., 1970.

Bommer, Michael, *The Development of a Management System for Effective Decision Making and Planning in a University Library*, Ph.D. dissertation, University of Pennsylvania, Philadelphia, 1971, available from ERIC Clearinghouse on Library Information Sciences, Washington, D.C., ERIC No. ED-071-727.

Booth, A. D., "On the Geometry of Libraries," *J. of Documentation*, 25:28–42 (1969).

Bourne, Charles P., "Some User Requirements Stated Quantitatively in Terms of the 90 Percent Library," in Kent, Allen, and Orrin E. Taulbee (eds.), *Electronic Information Handling*, pp. 93–110, Spartan Books, Washington, D.C., 1965.

Bowen, Alice, "Nonrecorded Use of Books and Browsing in the Stacks of a Research Library," M.A. thesis, The University of Chicago Graduate Library School, Chicago, 1961.

Bowker (R. R.) Co., *The Library Journal Book Review 1968*, New York, 1969.

Bowler, Roberta (ed.), *Local Public Library Administration*, International City Managers Association, Chicago, 1964.

Bradford, S. C., "Sources of Information on Specific Subjects," *Engineering*, 137:85–86 (1934).

———, *Documentation*, Crosby Lockwood, London, 1948.

Brahm, Walter, "Legislation Relating to State Library Agencies," *Library Trends*, 19:260–268 (1970).

Bromberg, Erik, "Simplified PPBS for the Librarian," paper presented at the American Library Association Convention in Dallas, June 1971.

Brookes, B. C., "The Derivation and Application of the Bradford-Zipf Distribution," *J. of Documentation*, 24:247–265 (1968).

———, "Bradford's Law and the Bibliography of Science," *Nature*, 224:953–956 (1969).

———, "Statistical Distributions in Documentation and Library Planning," in Mackenzie, A. Graham, and Ian M. Stuart (eds.), *Planning Library Services*, University of Lancaster, Lancaster, England, 1969.

———, "The Design of Cost-Effective Hierarchical Information Systems," *Information Storage and Retrieval*, 6:127–136 (1970).

———, "The Growth, Utility, and Obsolescence of Scientific Periodical Literature," *J. of Documentation*, 26:283–294 (1970).

———, "Obsolescence of Special Library Periodicals: Sampling Errors and Utility Contours," *ASIS, J. of the American Society for Information Science*, 21:320–329 (1970).

———, "Photocopies vs. Periodicals: Cost-Effectiveness in the Special Library," *J. of Documentation*, 26:22–29 (1970).

———, "The Viability of Branch Libraries," *J. of Librarianship*, 2:14–21 (1970).

———, "Optimum $P\%$ Library of Scientific Periodicals," *Nature*, 232:458–461 (1971).

Brotchie, J. F., A. R. Toakley, and R. Sharpe, "A Model for National Development," *Management Science*, 18:B14–B18 (October 1971).

Bruno, James E., "An Alternative to Uniform Expenditure Reductions in Multiple Resource State Finance Programs," *Management Science*, 17:386–398 (February 1971).

Brutcher, C., G. Gessford, and E. Renford, "Cost Accounting for the Library," *Library Resources and Technical Services*, 8:413-431 (1964).

Bryk, Oliver, "Application of PPB on State and Local Levels," Paper presented at the Institute on Program Planning and Budgeting Systems for Libraries, Wayne State University, Department of Library Science, Detroit, Mich., Spring 1968.

Buckland, Michael K., "The Quantitative Evaluation of Regional Union Catalogs," *J. of Documentation*, 23:20-27 (1967).

———, "An Operations Research Study of a Variable Loan and Duplication Policy at the University of Lancaster," *Library Quarterly*, 42:97-106 (January 1972), reproduced in Swanson, Don R., and Abraham Bookstein (eds.), *Operations Research: Implications for Libraries*, pp. 97-106, University of Chicago Press, Chicago, 1972.

———, and A. Hindle, "Library Zipf," *J. of Documentation*, 25:52-57 (1969).

———, A. Hindle, A. G. Mackenzie, and I. Woodburn, *Systems Analysis of a University Library*, University of Lancaster Library, Lancaster, England, 1970.

———, and I. Woodburn, *Some Implications for Library Management of Scattering and Obsolescence*, University of Lancaster Library Occasional Papers, No. 1, Lancaster, England, May 1968.

———, and I. Woodburn, *An Analytical Approach to Duplication and Availability*, University of Lancaster Library Occasional Papers, No. 2, Lancaster, England, June 1968.

Bundy, Mary Lee, "Metropolitan Public Library Use," *Wilson Library Bulletin*, 41:950-961 (May 1967).

———, "Factors Influencing Public Library Use," *Wilson Library Bulletin*, 42:371-382 (December 1967).

———, *Metropolitan Public Library Users: a Report of a Survey of Adult Library Use in the Maryland Baltimore-Washington Metropolitan Area*, University of Maryland School of Library and Information Services, College Park, Md., 1968.

Bureau of Urban Library Research, Graduate School of Library and Information Sciences, University of Pittsburgh, *Pennsylvania Public Library Statistics 1966*, Pittsburgh, 1966.

Burkhalter, Barton R. (ed.), *Case Studies in Systems Analysis in a University Library*, Scarecrow Press, Metuchen, N.J., 1968.

———, and P. A. Race, "An Analysis of Renewals, Overdues and Other Factors Influencing the Optimal Charge-Out Period," in Burkhalter, Barton R. (ed.), *Case Studies in Systems Analysis in a University Library*, pp. 11-33, Scarecrow Press, Metuchen, N.J., 1968.

Burton, Robert E., and R. W. Kebler, "Half-Life of Some Scientific and Technical Literatures," *American Documentation*, 11:18-22 (1960).

Bush, G. C., H. P. Galliher, and P. M. Morse, "Attendance and Use of the Science Library at MIT," *American Documentation*, 7:87-109 (1956).

Byam, Milton S., "Brooklyn Public Library's District Library Scheme," *Wilson Library Bulletin*, 35:365-367 (1961).

Byrne, R. F., A. Charnes, W. W. Cooper, O. A. Davis, and Dorothy Gilford (eds.), *Studies in Budgeting*, Vol. 11 of *Studies in Mathematical and Managerial Economics*, edited by Henri Theil, American Elsevier Publishing Co., New York, 1971.

Campbell, H. C., *Metropolitan Public Library Planning Throughout the World*, Pergamon Press, Oxford, England, 1967.

Carl, Herbert (ed.), *Statewide Long-Range Planning for Libraries*, Report of Conference, September 19-22, 1965, Chicago, U.S. Department of Health, Education, and Welfare, Office of Education, Washington, D.C., 1966.

Carnovsky, Leon (ed.), *The Public Library in the Urban Setting*, University of Chicago Press, Chicago, 1968.

Cassidy, R. G., M. J. L. Kirby, and W. M. Raike, "Efficient Distribution of Resources Through Three Levels of Government," *Management Science*, 17:B462-B473 (1971).

Chapman, Edward A., Paul L. St. Pierre, and John Lubans, Jr., *Library Systems Analysis Guidelines*, John Wiley & Sons, New York, 1970.

Childers, Thomas, "Community and Library: Some Possible Futures," *Library Journal*, 96:2727-2730 (September 15, 1971).

———, "Managing the Quality of Information Service," unpublished paper, Philadelphia, April 1971.

Churchman, C. West, *The Systems Approach*, Delacorte Press, New York, 1968.

Clapp, Verner W., *The Future of the Research Library*, Urbana, Ill., University of Illinois Press, 1964.

———, and Robert Jordan, "Quantitative Criteria for Adequacy of Academic Library Collections," *College and Research Libraries*, 26:371-380 (1965).

Cohen, Michael E., and Robert A. Carlston, "Analysis of Management Decision Making in Information System Design," paper presented at meeting of The Institute of Management Sciences, March 21-24, 1971, Consad Research Corp., Pittsburgh, Pa.

Cole, P. F., "Analysis of Reference Question Records as a Guide to the Information Requirements of Scientists," *J. of Documentation*, 14:197-207 (1958).

———, "A New Look at Reference Scattering," *J. of Documentation*, 18:58-64 (1962).

———, "Journal Usage Versus Age of Journal," *J. of Documentation*, 19:1-12 (1963).

Colman, William G., "Federal and State Financial Interest in the Performance and Promise of Library Networks," *The Library Quarterly*, 39:99-108 (1969).

Colwell, Eileen, L. Esme Green, and F. Phyllis Parrott, *First Choice: A Basic Book List for Children*, Library Association, London, England, 1968.

Committee on National Library Information Systems, "A National Library Agency," *American Library Association Bulletin*, 62:255-265 (1968).

Conant, Ralph (ed.), *The Public Library and the City*, MIT Press, Cambridge, Mass., 1966.

Consad Research Corporation, "Interim Technical Report 9/30/68: Some Parameters of Metropolitan Library Usage," unpublished paper, Pittsburgh, Pa., 1968.

―――, "A Behaviorial Model for Use in Library Planning: Results of the Short Range Work Program," unpublished paper, Pittsburgh, Pa., June 1969.

Cook, J. J., "Increased Seating in the Undergraduate Library: A Study in Effective Space Utilization," in Burkhalter, Barton R. (ed.), *Case Studies in Systems Analysis in a University Library*, pp. 142–170, Scarecrow Press, Metuchen, N.J., 1968.

Cooper, Marianne, "Criteria for Weeding of Collections," *Library Resources and Technical Services*, 12:339–351 (1968).

Cooper, William S., "On Deriving Design Equations for Information Retrieval Systems," *ASIS, J. of the American Society for Information Science*, 21:385–395 (November-December 1970).

Coughlin, Robert E., Françoise Taieb, and Benjamin H. Stevens, *Urban Analysis for Branch Library System Planning*, Greenwood Publishing Corp., Westport, Conn. (1972).

Council of National Library Associations, *The Bowker Annual of Library and Book Trade Information*, R. R. Bowker Company, New York, 1968, 1969, 1970, 1971.

Cox, Donald, and Robert Good, "How to Build a Marketing Information System," *Harvard Business Review*, 45:145–154 (May–June 1967).

Cox, Julius Grady, *Optimum Storage of Library Material*, Purdue University Libraries, Lafayette, Ind., 1964.

Cox, N. S. M., J. D. Dews, and J. L. Dolby, *The Computer and the Library*, Northumberland Press, Gateshead, England, 1966.

Cox, N. S. M., and M. W. Grose, *Organization and Handling of Bibliographic Records by Computer*, Archon Books, Hamden, Conn., 1967.

Crowley, Terence, and Thomas Childers, *Information Service in Public Libraries: Two Studies*, Scarecrow Press, Metuchen, N.J., 1971.

Cuadra, Carlos A. (ed.), *Annual Review of Information Science and Technology*, Volume 6, Encyclopedia Britannica, Chicago, 1971.

Davis, Marie, "Serving the Disadvantaged from the Administrative Viewpoint," *Library Trends*, 20:382–391 (October 1971).

Davis, Richard, and Catherine Bailey, *A Bibliography of Use Studies*, Drexel Institute of Technology, Graduate School of Library Science, Philadelphia, 1964, available from Clearinghouse for Scientific and Technical Information, Springfield, Va., document number AD-435-962.

Dawson, C., E. E. Aldrin, and E. P. Gould, "Increasing the Effectiveness of the M.I.T. Science Library by the Use of Circulation Statistics," Term Report, M.I.T. Libraries, Cambridge, Mass., 1962.

Densmore, G., and C. Bourne, *A Cost Analysis and Utilization Study of the Stanford University Library System*, Stanford University Libraries, Stanford, Calif., 1965.

Dick, Elizabeth, and Bernard Berelson, "What Happens to Library-Circulated Books?," *Library Quarterly*, 18:100–107 (1948).

Doerschuk, Ernest E., Jr., *Essential Elements of the Pennsylvania Public Library Development Plan*, Pennsylvania State Library, Harrisburg, Pa., 1966.

Downs, Robert B., *A Survey of the Libraries of the University of Utah*, University of Utah Libraries, Salt Lake City, Utah, 1965.

———, *University Library Statistics*, Association of Research Libraries, Washington, D.C., 1969.

———, and J. W. Heussman, *University Library Statistics*, American Library Association, Chicago, 1970.

Drennan, Henry T., "New Directions in Library Legislation," *Library Trends*, 19:182–191 (October 1970).

———, and Doris Holladay, *Statistics of Public Libraries-1962: Part I-Selected Statistics of Public Libraries Serving Populations of 35,000 and Above: Institutional Data*, U.S. Department of Health, Education, and Welfare, Washington, D.C., 1965.

Drexel Institute of Technology, *Problems of Library Services in Metropolitan Areas*, Drexel Press, Philadelphia, 1966.

Drott, M. C., and L. L. Hoag, "Feasibility Study of a Single Point Exterior Book Return System," in Burkhalter, Barton R. (ed.), *Case Studies in Systems Analysis in a University Library*, pp. 90–102, Scarecrow Press, Metuchen, N.J., 1968.

Duggan, Maryann, "Library Network Analysis and Planning," *Special Libraries*, 2:157–175 (1969).

Dunn, O. C., W. Seibert, and J. Schueneman, *The Past and Likely Future of 58 Research Libraries 1951–80: a Statistical Study of Growth and Change*, Purdue University, Lafayette, Ind. 1967.

Ebersole, J. F., "Operating Model of a National Information System," *American Documentation*, 17:33–40 (1966).

Eckstein, Otto, "A Survey of the Theory of Public Expenditure Criteria" in National Bureau of Economic Research, *Public Finances: Needs, Sources, and Utilization*, Princeton University Press, Princeton, N.J., 1961.

Eisener, Joseph, "Public Libraries on the Skids?," *Library Journal*, 96:3094–3095 (October 1, 1971).

Elston, Carolyn R., "Survey of In-Library Use of the M.I.T. Science Library," Term Report, M.I.T. Libraries, Cambridge, Mass., 1966.

Emery, James C., "Management Information Systems," in Aronofsky, Julius S. (ed.), *Progress in Operations Research*, Volume III, *Relationship Between Operations Research and the Computer*, John Wiley & Sons, New York, 1969.

———, *Organizational Planning and Control Systems: Theory and Technology*, Macmillan, New York, 1969.

———, "Cost/Benefit Analysis of Information Systems," SMIS Workshop Report No. 1, Chicago, 1971.

Ennis, Philip H., "The Library Consumer: Patterns and Trends," *Library Quarterly*, 34:163–78 (1964).

Erickson, E. Halfred, *College and University Library Surveys 1938–1952*, American Library Association, Chicago, 1961.

Ernst, Martin L., "Evaluation of Performance of Large Information Retrieval Systems," in *Second Congress on the Information System Science*, pp. 239–249, Mitre Corporation, Bedford, Mass., 1966.

Ernst and Ernst, *Study of Library Services Program*, unpublished report prepared for Pennsylvania State Library, 1969.

Evans, G. Edward, "Book Selection and Book Collection Usage in Academic Libraries," *Library Quarterly*, 40:297–308 (July 1970).

Fairthorne, Robert A., "Algebraic Representation of Storage and Retrieval Languages," in *Proceedings of the International Conference on Scientific Information*, Volume 2, 1958, pp. 1313–1326, National Academy of Sciences—National Research Council, Washington, D.C., 1959, reprinted in Fairthorne, R. A., *Towards Information Retrieval*, pp. 151–169, Butterworths, London, 1961.

———, "Empirical Hyperbolic Distributions (Bradford-Zipf-Mandelbrot) for Bibliometric Description and Prediction," *J. of Documentation*, 25:319–343 (1969).

Fels Institute for Local and State Government, Government Studies Center, *Educational Planning Programming Budgeting System*, Philadelphia, 1969.

Flood, Merrill, "The Systems Approach to Library Planning," *Library Quarterly*, 34:326–337 (1964).

Freiser, Leonard H., "The Civilized Network," *Library Journal*, 92:3001–3003 (1967).

Fry, Ray M., "The United States Office of Education as an Initiator of Library Legislation," *Library Trends*, 19:222–234 (October 1970).

Fussler, H. H., and C. T. Payne, *Development of an Integrated, Computer-Based Bibliographical Data System for a Large University Library*, University of Chicago Library, Chicago, 1968, available from Clearinghouse for Federal Scientific and Technical Information, Springfield, Va., document number PB-79-426.

———, and J. Simon, *Patterns in the Use of Books in Large Research Libraries*, University of Chicago Press, Chicago, 2nd ed., 1969.

Gardiner, G. L., "The Empirical Study of Reference," *College and Research Libraries*, 30:130–135 (1969).

Ginzberg, Eli, and Carol Brown, "Manpower for Library Services," A Report for the National Advisory Commission on Libraries, Conservation of Human Resources Project, Columbia University, New York, 1967.

Glover, Fred, and Darwin Klingman, "Mathematical Programming Models and Methods for the Journal Selection Problem," *Library Quarterly*, 42:43–58 (January 1972), reproduced in Swanson, Don R., and Abraham Bookstein (eds.), *Operations Research: Implications for Libraries*, pp. 43–58, University of Chicago Press, Chicago, 1972.

Goddard, Haynes C., "An Economic Analysis of Library Benefits," *Library Quarterly*, 41:244–255 (1971).

Goffman, William, and Thomas G. Morris, "Bradford's Law and Library Acquisitions," *Nature*, 226:922–923 (1970).

——, and Kenneth S. Warren, "Dispersion of Papers Among Journals Based on a Mathematical Analysis of Two Diverse Medical Literatures," *Nature*, 221:1205–1207 (1969).

Goldhor, Herbert (ed.), *Research Methods in Librarianship: Measurement and Evaluation*, University of Illinois Graduate School of Library Science, Urbana, Ill., 1968.

Goldman, Thomas (ed.), *Cost-Effectiveness Analysis*, Praeger, New York, 1967.

Goyal, S. K., "Application of Operational Research to Problem of Determining Appropriate Loan period for Periodicals," *Libri*, 20:94–100 (1970).

Grant, Robert S., "Predicting the Need for Multiple Copies of Books," *J. of Library Automation*, 4:64–71 (1971).

Greenaway, Emerson, "The Social Responsibility of Libraries," *Pennsylvania Library Association Bulletin*, 25:12–19 (1970).

Groos, Ole V., "Bradford's Law and the Keenan-Atherton Data," *American Documentation*, 18:46 (1967).

Gross, Elizabeth H., *Public Library Service to Children*, Oceana Publications, Dobbs Ferry, N.Y., 1967.

Grundt, Leonard, *An Investigation to Determine the Most Efficient Patterns for Providing Adequate Public Library Service to All Residents of a Typical Large City*, Ph.D. thesis, Rutgers University, New Brunswick, N.J., 1964.

Haas, Warren J., "Columbia University Libraries: A Description of a Project To Study the Research Library as an Economic System," in *Minutes of the 63rd Meeting of the Association of Research Libraries*, pp. 40–45, January 26, 1964.

——, "Research Library Management," in *Minutes of the 72nd Meeting of the Association of Research Libaries*, pp. 19–29, June 22, 1968.

Hajda, Jan, *An American Paradox: People and Books in a Metropolis*, Ph.D. thesis, University of Chicago, Chicago, 1963.

Hamburg, Morris, *Statistical Analysis for Decision Making*, Harcourt, Brace, & World, New York., 1970.

——, Richard C. Clelland, Michael R. W. Bommer, Leonard E. Ramist, and Jerome Ackerman, "A Systems Analysis of the Library and Information Science Statistical Data System: the Preliminary Study," Interim Report, July 1969, University of Pennsylvania, phia, available from ERIC Document Reproduction Service, Bethesda, Md., document number LI 001 825.

———, Richard C. Clelland, Michael R. W. Bommer, Leonard E. Ramist, and Ronald M. Whitfield, "A Systems Analysis of the Library and Information Science Statistical Data System: the Research Investigation," unpublished report to the Office of Education, University of Pennsylvania, Philadelphia, 1970.

———, Leonard E. Ramist, and Michael R. W. Bommer, "Library Objectives and Performance Measures and Their Use in Decision Making," *Library Quarterly*, 42:107–128 (January 1972), reproduced in Swanson, Don R., and Abraham Brookstein (eds.), *Operations Research: Implications for Libraries*, pp. 107–128, University of Chicago Press, Chicago, 1972.

Hartley, H., *Educational Planning, Programming, Budgeting: A Systems Approach*, Prentice-Hall, Englewood Cliffs, N.J., 1968.

Hatry, Harry P., *Criteria for Evaluation in Planning State and Local Programs*, A Study submitted by the Subcommittee on Intergovernmental Relations, U.S. Government Printing Office, Washington, D.C., 1967.

———, and John Cotton, *Program Planning for State, County, City, State-Local Finances Project*, George Washington University, Washington, D.C., 1967.

Haveman, Robert H., and Julius Margolis (eds.), *Public Expenditures and Policy Analysis*, Markham Publishing Co., Chicago, 1970.

Hayes, Robert M., and Joseph Becker, *Handbook of Data Processing for Libraries*, John Wiley & Sons, New York, 1970.

———, and K. D. Reilly, "The Effect of Response Time Upon Utilization of an Information Retrieval System: a Simulation," paper presented to ORSA Annual Meeting, June 1967.

Heinritz, Fred J., "Optimum Allocation of Technical Services Personnel," *Library Resources and Technical Services*, 13:99–101 (1969).

Herner, Saul, "Operations Research and the Technical Information Program," in Singer, T. E. R. (ed.), *Information and Communication Practice in Industry*, pp. 79–91, Rheinhold Publishing Corp., New York, 1958.

———, "A Pilot Study of the Use of the Stacks of the Library of Congress," unpublished, Herner and Co., Washington, D.C., 1960.

Hiatt, Peter, *Public Library Branch Services for Adults of Low Education*, unpublished doctoral thesis, Rutgers—The State University, New Brunswick, N.J., 1962.

Hinrichs, Harley H., and Graeme M. Taylor, *Program Budgeting and Benefit-Cost Analysis*, Goodyear Publishing Co., Pacific Palisades, Calif., 1969.

Hitch, Charles J., *Decision-Making for Defense*, University of California Press, Berkeley, 1965.

Hodges, Elizabeth D., *Books for Elementary School Libraries; an Initial Collection*, American Library Association, Chicago, 1969.

Hodgson, James, *The Literature of Library Standards*, Third Military Librarians Workshop, U.S.

Navy Postgraduate School, Monterey, Calif., 1959, Clearinghouse for Scientific and cal Information, Springfield, Va., document number AD-479-447.

Hoos, Ida R., "Information Systems and Public Planning," *Management Science*, 17:B658–671 (1971).

Houser, Lloyd J., *Effectiveness of Public Library Services: Development of Indices of Effectiveness and Their Relationship to Financial Support*, Ph.D. thesis, Rutgers University, New Brunswick, N.J., 1967, available from ERIC Document Reproduction Service, Bethesda, Md., document number ED-024-405.

Howard, Edward N., "Toward PPBS in the Public Library," *American Libraries*, 2:386–393 (1971).

Humphry, John A., *Library Cooperation*, Brown University Press, Providence, R.I., 1963.

———, and Eleanor A. Ferguson, "The State Library: Institution in Transition," *American Libraries*, 1:949–952 (1970).

Institute for the Advancement of Medical Communication, "Checklist of Library Policies on Services to Other Libraries," Philadelphia, 1968.

———, "Instructions for Administering the Document Delivery Test and Recording Primary Test Data," Philadelphia, 1968.

———, "Interview Guide for Inventory of Library Policies on Services to Individual Users," Philadelphia, 1968.

Institute of Urban Life, *Natural Library Service Zones*, Institute of Urban Life, Chicago, 1969.

International Federation of Library Associations, *International Standardization of Library Statistics: A Progress Report*, London, 1968.

Jain, Aridaman Kumar, *A Statistical Study of Book Use*, Ph.D. thesis, Purdue University, Lafayette, Ind., 1968.

———, "Sampling and Data Collection Methods for a Book-Use Study," *Library Quarterly*, 39:245–252 (1969).

———, F. F. Leimkuhler, and V. L. Anderson, "A Statistical Model of Book Use and Its Application to the Book Storage Problem," *Journal of the American Statistical Association*, 64:1211–1224 (1969).

Jardine, A. K. S., *Operational Research in Maintenance*, Manchester University Press, Manchester, England, 1970.

Jenkins, Harold R., "The ABC's of PPB," *Library Journal*, 96:3089–3093 (October 1, 1971).

Jennings, Michael A., "Optimizating Library Automation with a Central Dynamic Store," *College and Research Libraries*, 30:397–404 (1969).

Jestes, Edward C., "An Example of Systems Analysis: Locating a Book in a Reference Room," *Special Libraries*, 59:722–728 (1968).

Johns Hopkins University, *Operations Research and Systems Engineering Study of a University Library Progress Report*, by R. H. Roy (and others), Baltimore, Md., 1965, available from Clearinghouse for Federal Scientific and Technical Information, Springfield, Va., document number PB-163-087.

———, *Operations Research and Systems Engineering Study of a University Library. Progress Report*, by R. H. Roy (and others), Baltimore, Md., 1965, available from Clearinghouse for Federal Scientific and Technical Information, Springfield, Va., document number PB-168-187.

Joint Economic Committee, *The Analysis and Evaluation of Public Expenditures: the PPB System*, A compendium of papers submitted to the Subcommittee on Economy in Government of the Joint Economic Committee, Congress of the United States, 1969.

Jones, Arthur, "Criteria for the Evaluation of Public Library Services," *J. of Librarianship*, 2:228–245 (1970).

Jordan, R., "Library Characteristics of Colleges Ranking High in Academic Excellence," *College and Research Libraries*, 24:369–376 (1963).

Jordan, R. T., J. M. Goudeau, and L. Shores, *Impact of the Academic Library on the Eduational Program*, U.S. Department of Health, Education, and Welfare, Washington, D.C., 1967.

Keller, John E. "Program Budgeting and Cost Benefit Analysis in Libraries," *College and Research Libraries*, 30:156–160 (1969).

Kendall, M. G., "The Bibliography of Operational Research," *Operational Research Quarterly*, 11:31–36 (1960).

———, "Natural Law in the Social Sciences," *J. of the Royal Statistical Society, Series A.*, 124:1–16 (1961).

Kimber, Richard T., *Automation in Libraries*, Pergamon Press, New York, 1968.

Knight, Douglas M., and E. Shepley Nourse (eds.), *Libraries at Large: Tradition, Innovation and the National Interest*, R. R. Bowker, New York, 1969.

Kochen, Manfred, "Switching Centers for Inquiry Referral," in Becker, Joseph, *Interlibrary Communications and Information Networks*, pp. 132–139, American Library Association, Chicago, 1971.

———, "Directory Design for Networks of Information and Referral Centers," *Library Quarterly*, 42:59–83 (January 1972), reproduced in Swanson, Don R., and Abraham Bookstein (eds.), *Operations Research: Implications for Libraries*, pp. 59–83, University of Chicago Press, Chicago, 1972.

———, and Karl W. Deutsch, "Toward a Rational Theory of Decentralization: Some Implications of a Mathematical Approach," *American Political Science Review*, 63:34–49 (1969).

———, and A. Bertrand Segur, "Effects of Cataloging Volume at the Library of Congress on the Total Cataloging Costs of American Research Libraries," *ASIS: J. of the American Society for Information Science*, 21:133–139 (1970).

Koenig, Michael E. D., Alexander C. Finley, Joann G. Cushman, and James M. Detmer, "Scope: a Cost Analysis of an Automated Serials Record System," *J. of Library Automation*, 4:129–40 (September 1917).

Korfhage, Robert R., U. Narayan Bhat, and Richard E. Nance, "Graph Models for Library Information Networks," *Library Quarterly*, 42:31–42 (January 1972), reproduced in Swanson, Don R., and Abraham Bookstein (eds.), *Operations Research: Implications for Libraries*, pp. 31–42, University of Chicago Press, Chicago, 1972.

Kraft, Donald H., "A Comment on the Morse-Elston Model of Probabilistic Obsolescence," *Operations Research*, 18:1228–1233 (1970).

———, and T. W. Hill, Jr., "The Journal Selection Problem in a University Library System," unpublished paper, School of Library and Information Services, University of Maryland, 1970.

Krauze, Taudeusz, and Claude Hillinger, "Citations, References and the Growth of Scientific Literature: a Model of Dynamic Interaction," *ASIS, J. of the American Society for Information Science*, 22:333–336 (September–October 1971).

Kurmey, William J., "Management Implications of Mechanization," in *Automation in Libraries*, papers presented at the C.A.C.U.L. Workshop on Library Automation, at the University of British Columbia, Vancouver, April 10–12, 1967.

Lacy, D., and V. Matthews, "Social Change and the Library," prepared for the National Advisory Commission on Libraries, National Book Committee, New York, 1967, incorporated into Knight, Douglas M., and E. Shepley Nourse (eds.), *Libraries at Large: Tradition, Innovation, and the National Interest*, pp. 3–41, R. R. Bowker, New York, 1969.

Leach, Richard H., "The Federal Government and Libraries," prepared for the National Advisory Commission on Libraries, Duke University, 1967, incorporated into Knight, Douglas M., and E. Shepley Nourse (eds.), *Libraries at Large: Tradition, Innovation and the National Interest*, pp. 346–393, 411–428, 559–574, R. R. Bowker, New York, 1969.

Lehman, James O., "Cooperation Among Small Academic Libraries," *College and Research Libraries*, 30:491–497 (1969).

Leigh, Robert D., *The Public Library in the United States; the General Report of the Public Library Inquiry*, Columbia University Press, New York, 1950.

Leimkuhler, Ferdinand F., "Systems Analysis in University Libraries," *College and Research Libraries*, 27:13–18 (1966).

———, "The Bradford Distribution," *J. of Documentation*, 23:197–207 (1967).

———, "A Literature Search and File Organization Model," *American Documentation*, 19:131–136 (April 1968).

———, "Mathematical Models for Library Systems Analysis," *Drexel Library Quarterly*, 4:185–196 (July 1968).

———, "Storage Policies for Information Systems," in Mackenzie, A. Graham, and Ian M. Stuart (eds.), *Planning Library Services*, University of Lancaster, Lancaster, England, 1969.

———, "Library Operations Research: a Process of Discovery and Justification," *Library Quarterly*, 42:84–96 (January 1972), reproduced in Swanson, Don R., and Abraham Bookstein (eds.), *Operations Research: Implications for Libraries*, pp. 84–96, University of Chicago Press, Chicago, 1972.

―――, and Michael D. Cooper, "Cost Accounting and Analysis for University Libraries," *College and Research Libraries*, 32:449–464 (November 1971).

―――, and J. Grady Cox, "Compact Book Storage in Libraries," *Operations Research*, 12:419–427 (1964).

Licklider, J. C. R., *Libraries of the Future*, MIT Press, Cambridge, Mass., 1965.

Line, Maurice B., *The College Student and the Library: Report of a Survey in May 1964 of the Use of Libraries and Books by Students in Five Teacher Training Colleges*, University of Southhampton Institute of Education, Southhampton, England, 1965.

―――, *Library Surveys: An Introduction to Their Use, Planning, Procedure and Presentation*, Archon Books, Hampden, Conn., 1967.

―――, "The 'Half-Life' of Periodical Literature: Apparent and Real Obsolescence," *J. of Documentation*, 26:46–54 (1970).

Lipetz, Ben-Ami, "Catalog Use in a Large Research Library," *Library Quarterly*, 42:129–139 (January 1972), reproduced in Swanson, Don R., and Abraham Bookstein (eds.), *Operations Research: Implications for Libraries*, pp. 129–139, University of Chicago Press, Chicago, 1972.

Lister, Winston Charles, *Least Cost Decision Rules for the Selection of Library Materials for Compact Storage*, Ph.D. thesis, Purdue University, Lafayette, Ind., 1967, available from Clearinghouse for Federal Scientific and Technical Information, Springfield, Va., document number PB-174-441.

Little (Arthur D.) Inc., "Library Planning Study," Report to the Bureau of Library Extension, Department of Education, Commonwealth of Massachusetts, 1967, available from ERIC Document Reproduction Service, Bethesda, Md., document number ED-022-491.

Little, John D. C., and Leonard M. Lodish, "A Media Planning Calculus," *Operations Research*, 17:1–35 (1969).

Lubans, John, Jr., "Systems Analysis, Machineable Circulation Data and Library Users and Non-Users," paper presented at American Society for Engineering Education Meeting, June 1971.

Lyle, G., *The Administration of the College Library*, H. W. Wilson Company, New York, 1961.

Lyon, David W., "A Cost Analysis of the Oakland, California Branch Library System," unpublished paper, University of California, Berkeley, Calif., 1968.

Lyon, John K., *An Introduction to Data Base Design*, Wiley-Interscience, New York, 1971.

McClarren, Robert R., "State Legislation Relating to Library Systems," *Library Trends*, 19:235–249 (1970).

McGrath, William E., "Correlating the Subjects of Books Taken Out of and Books Used Within an Open-Stack Library," *College and Research Libraries*, 32:280–285 (1971).

―――, and Norma Durand, "Classifying Courses in the University Catalog," *College and Research Libraries*, 30:533–539 (1969).

——, R. Huntsinger, and G. Barber, "An Allocation Formula Derived from Factor Analysis of Academic Departments," *College and Research Libraries*, 30:51–62 (1969).

McKean, Roland N., "Evaluating Alternative Expenditure Programs" in National Bureau of Economic Research, *Public Finances: Needs, Sources and Utilization*, Princeton University Press, Princeton, N.J., 1961.

Mackenzie, A. Graham, "Library Research at the U. of Lancaster," *Library Association Record*, 73:90–92 (1971).

——, and Ian M. Stuart (eds.), *Planning Library Services*, University of Lancaster Library Occasional Papers, No. 3, Lancaster, England, 1969.

MacRae, Duncan, Jr., "Growth and Decay Curves in Scientific Citations," *American Sociological Review*, 34:631–635 (1969).

Maidment, William R., "Progress in Documentation: Management Information from Housekeeping Routines," *J. of Documentation*, 27:37–42 (1971).

Mandel, B. J., "Work Sampling in Financial Management—Cost Determination in Post Office Department," *Management Science*, 17:B324–338 (1971).

Mandelbrot, Benoit, "An Informational Theory of the Statistical Structure of Language," in Jackson, Willis (ed.), *Communication Theory*, pp. 486–502, Academic Press, New York, 1953.

——, "A Note on a Class of Skew Distribution Functions: Analysis and Critique of a Paper by H. A. Simon," *Information and Control*, 2:90–99 (1959).

——, "Information Theory and Psycholinguistics: a Theory of Word Frequencies," in Lazarsfeld, Paul F., and Neil W. Henry (eds.), *Readings in Mathematical Social Science*, pp. 350–368, Science Research Associates, Chicago, 1966.

Marchant, Maurice Peterson, "The Effects of the Decision Making Process and Related Organizational Factors on Alternative Measures of Performance in University Libraries," Ph.D. dissertation, University of Michigan, Ann Arbor, 1970.

Martin, Lowell A., *Library Service in Pennsylvania, Present and Proposed*, Pennsylvania State Library, Harrisburg, Pa., 1958.

——, *Students and the Pratt Library: Challenge and Opportunity*, Enoch Pratt Free Library, Baltimore, Md., 1963 (Deiches Fund Studies for Public Library Service, No. 1).

——, "Principles of Statewide Library Planning," in Herbert, Carl (ed.), *Statewide Long-Range Planning for Libraries*, U.S. Department of Health, Education, and Welfare, Office of Education, Washington, D.C., 1966.

——, *Baltimore Reaches Out: Library Service to the Disadvantaged*, Enoch Pratt Free Library, Baltimore, 1967 (Deiches Fund Studies for Public Library Service, No. 3).

——, *Progress and Problems of Pennsylvania Libriaries: a Re-Survey*, Pennsylvania State Library Monograph No. 6, Harrisburg, Pa., 1967.

——, *Library Response to Urban Change: a Study of the Chicago Public Library*, American Library Association, Chicago, 1969.

Mason, Charles, "Bibliography of Library Automation," *ALA Bulletin* 63:1117-1134 (1969).

Mathematica, *On Library Statistics*, Princeton, 1967.

———, "On The Economics of Library Operation," prepared for National Advisory mission on Libraries, Princetion, 1967, incorporated into Knight, Douglas M., and E. Shepley Nourse (eds.), *Libraries at Large: Tradition, Innovation and the National Interest*, pp.168-227, 590-596, R. R. Bowker, New York, 1969.

Mayo-Wells, Wilfrid J., *Organization of a National Scientific and Technical Information Center*, Defense Documentation Center for Scientific and Technical Information, Alexandria, Va., 1964, available from Clearinghouse for Scientific and Technical Information, Springfield, Va., document number AD-455-078.

Meier, R. L., "Efficiency Criteria for the Operation of Large Libraries," *Library Quarterly*, 31:215-234 (1961).

Mendelsohn, H., and K. Wingerd, "The Use of Libraries and the Conditions that Promote Their Use," A Report to the National Advisory Commission on Libraries, ERIC No. ED 022 489, Academy for Educational Development, New York, 1967, incorporated into Knight, Douglas M., and E. Shepley Nourse (eds.), *Libraries at Large: Tradition, Innovation and the National Interest*, pp. 41-88, R. R. Bowker, New York, 1969.

Mercel, J., M. H. Friedman, E. H. Holmes, J. F. Knudson, and E. R. Streich, *Overview of Library Services and Construction Act—Title I: Final Report*, Systems Development Corp., Santa Monica, Calif., 1969.

Metcalf, Keys D., *Planning Academic and Research Library Buildings*, (McGraw-Hill, New York, 1965.

Mintzberg, Henry, "Managerial Work: Analysis from Observation," *Management Science*, 18:B97-110 (October 1971).

Molina, Edward, "Application of the Theory of Probability to Trunking Problems," *The Bell System Technical Journal*, 6:461-494 (1927).

Molz, Kathleen, "The Public Library: the People's University?" *American Scholar*, 34:95-102 (1964-1965).

Monat, William R., *The Public Library and Its Community: A Study of the Impact of Library Services in Five Pennsylvania Cities*, The Institute of Public Administration, Pennsylvania, 1967, available from ERIC Document Reproduction Service, Bethesda, Md., document number ED-021-580.

Monypenny, Phillip, *The Library Functions of the States*, American Library Association, Chicago, 1966.

Mood, Alexander M., "Macro-Analysis of the American Educational System," *Operations Research*, 17:770-783 (1969).

Morelock, M., and F. F. Leimkuhler, "Library Operations Research and Systems Engineering Studies," *College and Research Libraries*, 25:501-503 (1964).

Moriarty, John H., "Measurement and Evaluation in College and University Library

Studies: Library Research at Purdue University," in Goldhor, Herbert (ed.), *Research Methods in Librarianship: Measurement and Evaluation*, University of Illinois, Urbana, Ill., 1968.

Morse, Philip M.,"Probabilistic Models for Library Operations with Some Comments on Library Automation," presented at Annual Meeting of Association of Research Libraries, January 1964.

———, "On the Prediction of Library Use," in Planning Conference on Information Transfer Experiments, *Intrex*, Appendix N, pp. 225–234, 1965.

———, *Library Effectiveness: a Systems Approach*, MIT Press, Cambridge, Mass., 1968.

———, "Search Theory and Browsing," *Library Quarterly*, 40:391–408 (1970).

———, "Measures of Library Effectiveness," *Library Quarterly*, 42:15–30 (January 1972), reproduced in Swanson, Don R., and Abraham Bookstein (eds.), *Operations Research: Implications for Libraries*, pp. 15–30, University of Chicago Press, Chicago, 1972.

———, and Caroline Elston, "A Probabilistic Model for Obsolescence," *Operations Research*, 17:36–47 (1969).

Mullick, Satinder K., "Optimal Design of a Stochastic System with Dominating Fixed Costs," *Journal of Financial and Quarterly Analysis*, 1:55–74 (1966).

Mushkin, S., and M. Willcox, *An Operative PPB System: a Collaborative Undertaking in the States*, State-Local Finances Project, George Washington University, Washington, D.C., 1968.

Myatt, D., and D. Barclay, "Position Paper on Extra-Library Information Services," prepared for National Advisory Commission on Libraries, Science Communications, Inc., Washington, D.C., 1967.

Nance, Richard E., "An Analytical Model of a Library Network," *ASIS, J. of the American Society for Information Science*, 21:58–66 (1970).

Naranan, S., "Bradford's Law of Bibliography of Science: an Interpretation," *Nature*, 227:631–632 (1970).

———, "Power Law Relations in Science Bibliography—a Self-Consistent Interpretation," *J. of Documentation*, 27:83–97 (1971).

National Academy of Sciences and National Academy of Engineering, *Scientific and Technical Communication: a Pressing National Problem and Recommendations for Its Solution*, National Academy of Sciences, Washington, D.C., 1969.

National Advisory Commission on Libraries, "Library Services for the Nation's Needs toward Fulfillment of a National Policy," Washington, D.C., 1968, reproduced in Knight, Douglas M., and E. Shepley Nourse (eds.), *Libraries at Large: Tradition, Innovation and the National Interest*, pp. 495–521, R. R. Bowker, New York, 1969.

National Center for Higher Education Management Systems at WICHE, "RRPM-1 Model Gives Hard Answers to 'What-If?,' " *Higher Education Management*, 1:1–4 (September 1971).

National Conference on Library Statistics, a conference cosponsored by the Library Administration Division/American Library Association and the National Center for Educational Statistics, U.S. Office of Education, American Library Association, Chicago, 1967.

Nelson Associates, Inc., *Strengthening and Coordinating Reference and Research Library Resources in NYS*, prepared for New York State Education Department, New York, 1963.

———, *American State Libraries and State Library Agencies: An Overview with Recommendations*, a report prepared for the National Advisory Commission on Libraries, New York, 1967.

———, *Methods and Procedures for Measuring Patron Use and Cost of Patron Services for the Detroit Metropolitan Library Project*, New York, 1967, available from ERIC Document Reproduction Service, Bethesda, Md., document number ED-032-084.

———, *Public Libraries in the United States: Trends, Problems, and Recommendations*, report prepared for the National Advisory Commission on Libraries, New York, 1967.

———, *An Evaluation of the New York State Library's NYSILL Pilot Program*, New York, 1968.

———, *The New York State Library's Pilot Program in the Facsimile Transmission of Library Materials*, New York, 1968.

———, *Public Library Systems in the United States: a Survey of Multijurisdictional Systems*, American Library Association, Chicago, 1969.

Nelson, Charles A., and Anne H. Nelson, "Systems and Networks: the State Library Role," *American Libraries*, 2:883–887 (1971).

New Jersey Library Association, Library Development Committee, *Libraries for the People of New Jersey: or Knowledge for All*, by Lowell Martin and Mary Gaver, New Brunswick, N.J., 1964.

New York (State), Division of Evaluation, *Emerging Library Systems: the 1963–66 Evaluation of the New York State Public Library Systems*, The University of the State of New York, State Education Department, Division of Evaluation, Albany, 1967.

———, Executive Chamber, *Proceedings of the First Governor's Library Conference*, State Capitol, Albany, 1965.

New York (State), The State Education Department, *Report of the Commissioner of Education's Committee on Library Development*, University of the State of New York, The State Education Department, Albany, 1970.

Nitechi, André, "Cost Accounting Forms Designed by the Cost Accounting Study Committee of the Library Administration and Technical Services Section," *Michigan Librarian*, 29:19–21 (1963).

Novick, David (ed.), *Program Budgeting: Program Analysis and the Federal Budget*, Harvard University Press, Cambridge, Mass., 1965.

Oliver, Merrill R., "The Effect of Growth on the Obsolescence of Semiconductor Physics Literature," *J. of Documentation*, 27:11–17 (1971).

Olson, Edwin E., "Method for Characterizing User Populations," speech delivered at the 31st annual meeting of the American Society for Information Science, 1968.

———, "Quantitative Approaches to Assessment of Library Science Functions," unpublished paper, Institute for the Advancement of Medical Communication, Philadelphia, 1968.

———, "Libraries Serving Medical School Populations: Science Policies and Utilization Patterns," unpublished paper, Institute for the Advancement of Medical Communication, Philadelphia, 1969.

Orr, R. H., V. M. Pings, I. H. Pizer, and E. E. Olson, "Development of Methodologic Tools for Planning and Managing Library Services: I. Project Goals and Approach," *Bulletin of the Medical Library Association*, 56:235–240 (1968).

———, V. M. Pings, I. H. Pizer, E. E. Olson, and C. C. Spencer, "Development of Methodologic Tools for Planning and Managing Library Service: II. Measuring a Library's Capability for Providing Documents," *Bulletin of the Medical Library Association*, 56:241–267 (1968).

———, V. M. Pings, E. E. Olson, and I. H. Pizer, "Development of Methodologic Tools for Planning and Managing Library Services: III. Standardized Inventories of Library Services," *Bulletin of the Medical Library Association*, 56:380–403 (1968).

Osborn, E., "The Location of Public Libraries in Urban Areas," *J. of Librarianship*, 3:237–244 (October 1971).

Overhage, Carl F. J., and R. Joyce Harman, *Intrex: Report of a Planning Conference on Information Transfer Experiments*, MIT Press, Cambridge, Mass., 1965.

Palmer, David C., *A National Plan for Library Statistics: Guidelines for Implementation*, Statistics Coordinating Committee of the American Library Association, Chicago, 1970.

Palmour, Vernon E., and Robert Wiederkehr, "A Decision Model for Library Policies on Serial Publications," paper presented at XVII International Conference of The Institute of Management Sciences, London, July 1970.

Parker, E. B., and W. J. Paisley, "Predicting Library Circulation from Community Characteristics," *Public Opinion Quarterly*, 29:39–53 (1965).

Peston, Maurice, "The Theory of Spillovers and Its Connection with Education," *Public Finance*, 21:184–199 (1966).

Peterson, Stephen L, "Patterns of Use of Periodical Literature," *College and Research Libraries*, 30:422–430 (1969).

Phelps, Rose, and Janet Philips (eds.), *The Library as a Community Information Center*, Allerton Park Institute, Champaign, Ill., distributed by Illini Union Book Store, Champaign, Ill., 1959.

Pings, V. M., E. E. Olson, and R. H. Orr, "Summary Report of Analysis of Academic Medical Library Statistics," unpublished paper, Institute for the Advancement of Medical Communication, Philadelphia, 1968.

Pizer, Irwin, and Alexander Cain, "Objective Tests of Library Perfromance," *Special Libraries*, 59:704–711 (1968).

Plain, E., "Costs of Public Library Service 1968," *ALA Public Library Association*, Vol. 7, No. 3, October 1968.

"Planning-Programming-Budgeting System: a Symposium," *Public Administration Review*, 26:243–310 (1966) and 27:67–79 (1967).

Pratt (Enoch) Free Library, *Reference Books: A Brief Guide for Students and Other Users of the Library*, Baltimore, 1966.

Prentiss, S. Gilbert, "The Evolution of the Library System (New York)," *Library Quarterly*, 39:78–89 (1969).

———, "Library Leadership and the State Library Agency," *American Libraries*, 2:186–191 (1971).

Price, Bronson, *Library Statistics of Colleges and Universities, Data for Individual Institutions*, National Center for Educational Statistics, Washington, D.C., 1967.

Price, Derek J. de Solla, "Networks of Scientific Papers," *Science*, 149:510–515 (1965).

Quatman, Gerald, *The Costs of Providing Library Service to Groups in the Purdue University Community—1961*, Purdue University Libraries, Lafayette, Ind., 1962.

Raffel, Jeffrey A., and Robert Shishko, *Systematic Analysis of University Libraries: An Application of Cost-Benefit Analysis to the M.I.T. Libraries*, M.I.T. Press, Cambridge, Mass., 1969.

Rapaport, Anatol, "Comment: the Stochastic and the 'Teleological' Rationales of Certain Distributions and the So-Called Principle of Least Effort," *Behavioral Science*, 2:147–161 (1957).

Resnikoff, H. L., and J. L. Dolby, *Access: a Study of Information Storage and Retrieval with Emphasis on Library Information Systems*, U.S. Office of Education, Washington, D.C., 1971 available from ERIC Document Reproduction Service, Bethesda, Md., document number ED-050-773.

ReVelle, Charles S., David Marks, and Jon C. Liebman, "An Analysis of Private and Public Sector Location Models," *Management Science*, 16:692–707 (1970).

———, and Ralph W. Swain, "Central Facilities Location," *Geographical Analysis*, 2:30–42 (1970).

Reynolds, Maryan, David W. Taylor, Robert C. Meier, Roger L. Miller, Jonathan Stanfield, and William H. Scholz, *A Study of Library Network Alternatives for the State of Washington*, Washington State Library, Olympia, Wash., 1971.

Roberts, R. G., "Reilly's Law: the Law of Retail Gravitation," *Library Association Record*, 68:390–391 (1966).

Rogers, Rutherford D., and David C. Weber, *University Library Administration*, H. W. Wilson, New York, 1971.

Rohlf, Robert H., "Analysis of Nelson System Study," in *PLA Newsletter*, 10:2–3 (March 1971).

Rosenberg, Victor, "A Study of Statistical Measures for Predicting Terms Used to Index Documents," *ASIS, J. of the American Society for Information Science*, 22:41–50 (1971).

Rothenberg, Leslie Beth, Judith Lucianovic, David A. Kronick, and Alan M. Rees, "A Job-Task Index for Evaluating Professional Utilization in Libraries," *Library Quarterly*, 41:320–328 (October 1971).

Rothkopf, Michael, "The Future Circulation Rate of a Book, and an Application of Queuing Theory to Library Problems," Course Term Report, M.I.T. Libraries, Cambridge, Mass., 1962.

———, "Two Phases of an Operations Research Study of M.I.T.'s Science Library," unpublished paper, M.I.T., Cambridge, Mass., 1962.

Ruefli, Timothy W., "PPBS—An Analytical Approach," in Byrne, R. F., A. Charnes, W. W. Cooper, O. A. Davis, and Dorothy Gilford, *Studies in Budgeting*, Vol. 11 of *Studies in Mathematical and Managerial Economics*, edited by Henri Theil, American Elsevier Publishing Co., New York, 1971.

Rzasa, Philip V., and Norman R. Baker, "Measures of Effectiveness for a University Library," paper presented at the meeting of the Operations Research Society of America, Dallas, Tex., May 1971.

St. Angelo, Douglas, A. M. Hartsfield, and H. Goldstein, *State Library Policy: Its Legislative and Environmental Contexts*, American Library Association, Chicago, 1971.

Salamone, Peter, "Survey of Methods for Determining Information Requirements," MIS Research Center, University of Minnesota, paper delivered at meeting of The Institute of Management Sciences, October 1, 1971, Detroit, Mich.

Salverson, Carol A., "The Relevance of Statistics to Library Evaluation," *College and Research Libraries*, 30:352–361 (1969).

Sandison, A., "The Use of Older Literature and Its Obsolescence," *J. of Documentation*, 27:184–199 (1971).

Schick, Frank L., "Approach Toward a National Statistics Program," *American Library Association Bulletin*, 57:71–74 (1963).

———, "Library Statistics: a Century Plus," *American Libraries*, 2:727–731 (July–August 1971).

——— (ed.), *The Future of Library Service: Demographic Aspects and Implications*, Graduate School of Library Science, University of Illinois, Urbana, Ill., 1962.

Schiller, Anita R., *Characteristics of Professional Personnel in College and University Libraries*, Illinois State Library, Springfield, Ill., 1969.

Schultz, Claire K., "Cost-Effectiveness as a Guide in Developing Indexing Rules," *Information Storage and Retrieval*, 6:335–340 (1970).

Schwartz, Eugene S., and Henry I. Saxe, *A Bibliographic Bank for Resource Sharing in Library Systems: a Feasibility Study*, IIT Research Institute, Chicago, 1969.

Scott, K. P., P. Sonnenblick, and P. T. Uller, "An Analysis of the In-Room Use of the M.I.T. Science Library," Term Report, M.I.T. Libraries, Cambridge, Mass., 1962.

Shaughnessy, Thomas W., *Progress and Problems of Pennsylvania Libraries: A Re-Survey, Appendix: A Study of Distance and Time as Factors Influencing the Use of District Center Libraries*, Pennsylvania State Library, Harrisburg, Pa., 1967.

Shove, R. H., B. E. Moen, F. Wezeman, and H. G. Russell, *The Use of Books and Libraries*, University of Minnesota Press, Minneapolis, Minn., 10th ed., 1963.

Silver, Edward A., "Quantitative Appraisal of the M.I.T. Science Library Mezzanine Books, with an Application to the Problem of Limited Shelf Space," Term Report, M.I.T. Libraries, Cambridge, Mass., 1962.

Simon, Herbert A., "On a Class of Skew Distribution Functions," *Biometrika*, 42:425–440 (1955), reprinted in Simon, Herbert A., *Models of Man: Social and Rational*, pp. 145–164, John Wiley & Sons, New York, 1957.

Simon, Kenneth A., and W. Vance Grant, *Digest of Educational Statistics*, U.S. Dept. of Health, Education, and Welfare, Washington, D.C., 1967.

Sinha, Bani K., *Operations Research in Controlled Acquisition and Weeding of Library Collections*, Ph.D. dissertation in Operations Research, University of Pennsylvania, Philadelphia, 1971.

Smith, C. E., *Aspects of Public Library Administration*, Council of the City of Newcastle, New South Wales, Australia, 1969.

Smith, Hannis S., "General Legislation Dealing with the Organization, Management and Financial Support of Public Libraries," *Library Trends*, 19:269–281 (1970).

Spencer, Carol C., "Random Time Sampling with Self-Observation for Library Cost Studies: Unit Costs of Interlibrary Loans and Photocopies at a Regional Medical Library," *ASIS, J. of the American Society for Information Science*, 22:153–160 (1971).

Statistics of Virginia Public Libraries, 1967–1968, compiled by The Extension Division, Virginia State Library, Richmond, 1969.

Sternberger, H., J. Renz, and G. Tasolina, "Planning-Programming-Budgeting-System (PPBS) in Nassau County, N.Y.," in U.S. Congress, Joint Economics Committee, Subcommittee on Economy in Government, *Innovations in Planning, Programming, and Budgeting in State and Local Governments*, Washington, D.C., 1969, pp. 105–189.

Stitleman, Leonard, "Cost Utility Analysis Applied to Library Budgeting," paper presented at an Institute on Program Planning and Budgeting Systems for Libraries, Wayne State University, Department of Library Science, Detroit, Mich., Spring 1968.

Stockfish, Jacob A., "The Interest Rate Applicable to Government Investment Projects," in Hinricks, Harley H., and Graeme M. Taylor, *Program Budgeting and Benefit-Cost Analysis*, Goodyear Publishing, Pacific Palisades, Calif., 1969, pp. 187–201.

Strain, Paula M., "A Study of the Usage and Retention of Technical Periodicals," *Library Resources and Technical Services*, 10:295–304 (1966).

Summers, F. William, "State Library Standards, Revised: a Critique," *Library Journal*, 96:1191–1192 (April 1971).

———, "A Change in Budgeting Thinking," *American Libraries*, 2:1174–1180 (December 1971).

Swanson, Don R., and Abraham Bookstein, *Operations Research: Implications for Libraries*, University of Chicago Press, Chicago, Ill., 1972.

System Development Corporation, Information Systems Technology Staff, "Technology and Libraries," Santa Monica, California, November 1967, prepared for National Advisory Commission on Libraries, incorporated into Knight, Douglas M., and E. Shepley Nourse (eds.), *Libraries at Large: Tradition, Innovation and the National Interest*, pp. 282-341, R. R. Bowker, New York, 1969.

Tauber, M. F., C. D. Cook, and R. H. Logsdon, *The Columbia University Libraries: a Report on Present and Future Needs*, Columbia University Press, New York, 1957.

Tauber, M. F., and I. Stephens, *Library Surveys*, Columbia University Press, New York, 1967.

Taylor, Robert S., "Measuring the Immeasurable: or Can We Get There from Here?," paper presented at Conference on Approaches to Measuring Library Effectiveness, Syracuse University, School of Library Science, July 1971.

———, and C. E. Hieber, *Library Systems Analysis: Manual for the Analysis of Library Systems*, Report No. 3, Lehigh University, Center for the Information Services, Bethlehem, Pa., 1965.

Trueswell, Richard W., "Two Characteristics of Circulation—and Their Effect on the Implementation of Mechanized Circulation Control Systems," *College and Research Libraries*, 25:285-291 (1964).

———, "A Quantitative Measure of User Circulation Requirements and Its Possible Effect on Stack Thinning and Multiple Copy Determination," *American Documentation*, 16:20-25 (1965).

———, "Determining the Optimal Number of Volumes for a Library's Core Collection," *Libri*, 16:49-60 (1966).

———, "Some Behavioral Patterns of Library Users: the 80/20 Rule," *Wilson Library Bulletin*, 43:458-461 (1969).

———, "Article Use and Its Relationship to Individual User Satisfaction," *College and Research Libraries*, 31:239-245 (1970).

U.S. Advisory Commission on Intergovernmental Relations, *Measures of State and Local Fiscal Capacity and Tax Effort*, Government Printing Office, Washington, D.C., 1962.

———, *State Aid to Local Government*, Government Printing Office, Washington, D.C., 1969.

———, *Measuring the Fiscal Capacity and Effort of State and Local Areas*, Government Printing Office, Washington, D.C., 1971.

U.S. Congress, House of Representatives, *Congressional Record*, April 6, 1971, p. 2471.

U.S. Department of Health, Education, and Welfare, Office of Education, *National Inventory of Library Needs*, American Library Association, Chicago, 1965.

———, *Library Statistics of Colleges and Universities 1963-64: Institutional Data* by Theodore Samore and D. Holladay, U.S. Government Printing Office, Washington, D.C., 1966.

———, *Statewide Long-range Planning for Libraries*, Report of Conference, Chicago, edited by H. Carl, U.S. Government Printing Office, Washington, D.C., 1966.

——, *Library Statistics, 1966–67, Preliminary Report on Academic Libraries*, National Center for Educational Statistics, Division of Statistical Operations, U.S. Government Printing Office, Washington, D.C., 1967.

——, *Library Statistics of Colleges and Universities, 1963–64: Analytic Report*, by Theodore Samore, U.S. Government Printing Office, Washington, D.C., 1968.

United States of America Standards Institute, *Bowker Annual 1969* (from *Publishers Weekly*), New York, 1969.

——, *USA Standard for Compiling Book Publishing Statistics*, New York, 1969.

——, *USA Standard for Library Statistics*, New York, 1969.

University of Durham, *Project for Evaluating the Benefits from University Libraries*, Durham, England, 1969.

University of Illinois, Graduate School of Library Science, *Changing Environment for Library Services in Metropolitan Areas*, Urbana, Ill., 1965.

——, *1962 Statistics of Public Libraries Serving Populations of Less than 35,000*, Urbana, Ill., 1966.

University of the State of New York, The State Education Department, Division of Evaluation, *Emerging Library Systems: the 1963–66 Evaluation of the New York State Public Library System*, Albany, N.Y., 1967.

——, Division of Library Development, *Public and Association Libraries: Statistics 1965*, Albany, N.Y., 1965.

——, Division of Library Development, *Commentary on Emerging Library Systems: the 1963–66 Evaluation of the New York State Public Library Systems*, Albany, N.Y., 1967.

——, Division of Library Development, *Public and Association Libraries: Statistics 1966*, Albany, N.Y., 1967.

——, the New York State Library, Library Extension Division, *Improving Reference and Research Library Resources in New York State*, The State Library, Albany, N.Y., 1965.

Unruh, Jesse M., "The Politics of Education, or How I Learned to Stop Worrying and Vote Increased School Subvention," address to the National Committee for Support of the Public Schools, December 5, 1966.

Vickery, B. C., "Bradford's Law of Scattering," *J. of Documentation*, 4:198–203 (1948).

——, "Methodology in Research," *ASLIB Proceedings*, 22:597–606 (1970).

Voigt, Melvin J., and Joseph H. Treyz, *Books for College Libraries,* American Library Association, Chicago, 1967.

Wall, Eugene, "Further Implications of the Distribution of Index Term Usage," in *Proceedings of the American Documentation Institute*, Volume I, *Parameters of Information Science*, pp. 457–466, Philadelphia, 1964.

Wallace, Sarah L., "Many Shall Run to and fro, and Knowledge will be Increased," *Wilson Library Bulletin*, 41:908–909 (1967).

Warncke, Ruth, "Library Objectives and Community Needs," *Library Trends*, 17:6–13 (1968).

Wasserman, Paul, and Mary Lee Bundy, "Manpower Blueprint," *Library Journal*, 92:197–200 (1967).

———, and Mary Lee Bundy, *Reader in Library Administration*, National Cash Register Co., Dayton, Ohio, 1968.

Wessel, C. J., "Criteria for Evaluating Technical Library Effectiveness," *ASLIB Proceedings*, 20:453–481 (1968).

———, and B. A. Cohrsson, *Criteria for Evaluating the Effectiveness of Library Operations and Services, Phase I: Literature Search and State of the Art*, John I. Thompson and Company, Washington, D.C., 1967, available from Federal Clearinghouse for Scientific and Technical Information, Springfield, Va., document number AD-649-468.

———, and B. A. Cohrsson, *Criteria for Evaluating the Effectiveness of Library Operations and Services, Phase II: Data Gathering and Evaluation*, John I. Thompson and Company, Washington, D.C., 1968.

Westly, Barbara Marietta (ed.), *Sears List of Subject Headings*, 9th ed., H. W. Wilson Co., New York, 1965.

Wheeler, J., and H. Goldhor, *Practical Administration of Public Libraries*, Harper & Row, New York, 1962.

White, Carl M., *A Survey of the University of Delhi Library*, University of Delhi, Planning Unit, Delhi, India, 1965.

Williams, Gordon, Edward C. Bryant, Robert R. V. Wiederkehr, Vernon E. Palmour, and Cynthia J. Siehler, *Library Cost Models: Owning Versus Borrowing Serial Publications*, U.S. Office of Education, Washington, D.C., 1968, available from ERIC Document Reproduction Service, Bethesda, Md., document number ED-026-106.

Williams, Harry, *Planning for Effective Resource Allocation in Universities*, American Council of Education, Washington, D.C., 1966.

Williams, Joel, *Library Statistics of College and Universities, Data for Individual Institutions*, National Center for Educational Statistics, Washington, D.C., 1968.

Wilson, Louis, and M. Tauber (eds.), *The University Library*, Columbia University Press, New York, 1956.

Wilson Library Bulletin, "A Kaleidoscopic View of Library Research," *Wilson Library Bulletin*, 41:896–949 (May 1967).

Wood, D. N., "User Studies: a Review of the Literature from 1966 to 1970," *ASLIB Proceedings*, 23:11–23 (1971).

———, and C. A. Bower, "The Use of Social Science Periodical Literature," *J. of Documentation*, 25:108–122 (1969).

Zipf, George Kingsley, *Human Behavior and the Principle of Least Effort: an Introduction to Human Ecology*, Addison-Wesley, Cambridge, Mass., 1949.

INDEX

Access
　to documents within the library, 229–234
　to other libraries, facilitation of, 134–136, 234
Accounting, 25
　cost, 189–191
　general, 187
　systems, 1
Acquisition of documents, 62, 107–108
ACRL Board of Directors, 11
Administration, 139–150, 234–235
Advertisements, 138, 149
Allocation of funds, 6
American Library Association, 37, 58, 197, 203, 205, 219, 221, 222
Arora, S. R., 91

Baker, Norman R., 139–140
Baldwin, Emma V., 190
Barber, G., 90
Baumol, W., 33
Beck, R. E., 124, 125
Becker, Joseph, 141–142, 156–158
Benefits, 9, 14, 17, 27
　and cost difference, 26, 73
　monetary value of, 33, 36
　ratio of to cost, 26, 73
Benefit-cost analysis, 93
Benefit-cost criteria, 8
Benford, H. L., 123, 124
Bernal, J. D., 126
Bhat, U. N., 135
Bibliographic aids, 133–134
Binding of serials, 108–109
Boaz, Ruth, 35, 206
Bommer, Michael, 89, 91–93
Book. See also Document
　copies, 90–94
　relabeling of, 125
　subject matter and year, 85–90
　use models, 86–89, 116
　weeding, 113–119, 125–126
Booth, A. D., 119–120, 120–121
Bourne, Charles P., 128–129
Bower, C. A., 134
Bradford, S. C., 94, 95, 96
Bradford-Zipf law of scattering, 78, 79, 89, 94–102, 104–105, 111, 120, 124, 128, 134
Bradford-cut method, 104
Branch library, 54
　base-level use rate, 82
　commercial access index, 83
　effective service radius, 83
　location, 81–84
　market area, 82
　overlap, 83
　retail gravitation, 83–84
　school access index, 8
　viability of, 77–79
Brookes, B. C., 78–79, 98–100, 104–105, 124, 129, 130–131, 132, 134
Browsing. See Document exposure
Brutcher, C., 26
Bryant, Edward C., 103–104
Buckland, Michael K., 19, 20, 80, 93–94, 102–103, 104, 108–109, 121–122, 134–135
Budgeting, 47
Building area, 77–84
Bundy, M. L., 51, 52, 54, 219, 224
Burkhalter, Barton R., 122–123
Burton, Robert E., 126–127

Cataloging
　at Library of Congress, 112–113
　original, 111–112
　temporary, 111–112
Catalog use, 113
Centralization of libraries, 77–81
Childers, Thomas, 24, 136–137
Circulation. See Document exposure
　demand regression model, 91–92
　use, 144–145
Classification, 63, 109–113
Cole, P. F., 96–97, 101, 127–128
Colwell, E., 221
Communication, library initiative, 138–139, 149
Compact storage, 113–119
Computers, 150
　applications to libraries, 209–210
Computer technology, 7
Conditional probability, 109
Congress. See U.S. Congress
Conrad Research Corporation, 90
Constraints, 46
Contour-cut method, 104–105
Cook, J. J., 84
Cooper, Marianne, 125
Cooper, William S., 109–110
Copies of books, number of, 90–94
Correlation, 112, 112 n, 122, 136, 139, 141
Costs, 24, 27, 30, 71
Coughlin, Robert E., 82–83
Council of National Library Associations 51, 52, 221, 223
Cox, Julius Grady, 118–119

Cross-cut method, 104
Crowley, Terence, 136
Current-awareness service, 138–139

Data processing, 141
Deardorff, E. W., 124
Decentralization of libraries, 77–81
Decision making, 3, 8, 9, 11, 43
Decision models, 6, 7, 8
Demand
  probability distribution of, 91–92
  proportion satisfied, 19
  unsatisfied, 87–88, 91
Depreciation, 26, 189
Design equation, 109
Deutsch, Karl W., 80
Dewey Decimal Classification System, 56, 112, 122, 226
Dick, E., 220
Dimensions, 47
Document(s), 16, 57, 68
  acquisition, 62, 107–108
  cataloging, 63, 109–113
  classification, 63, 109–113
  control, 63, 113–124
  facilitation of use of, 124–125
  form, 57
  location in other libraries, aids for, 133–134
  maintenance, 125
  processing, 62, 85–107
  resources, 148
  retrieval time, 19
  selection, 62, 85–107
  subject matter, 57, 219
  subsets, 47, 57
  weeding, 64, 125–133
Document exposure, 4, 5, 16, 22, 28, 73, 89, 144–146
  circulation, 164, 166, 167, 169, 170–171, 172–173, 175–176, 178–179
  and costs, 24, 26, 36, 71
  counts, 4, 20
  imputed value of, 33, 36, 72
  indirect library use, 164, 171, 172, 174, 177–178
  in-library use, 164, 167, 168–169, 171, 172, 173–174, 177
  interlibrary loan, 164, 172, 174–175, 176–177, 210
  measuring, 20
  number of exposures. See Performance measures

photocopy use, 164
time. See Performance measures
Document retrieval time. See Performance measures
Dolby, J. L., 110–111
Downs, R., 38
Drott, M. C., 123, 124
Duggan, Maryann, 135
Durand, Norma, 172

Education, 146–147
Effectiveness, library. See also Performance measures, evaluation of, 1
Ehrnstrum, G. C., 123
Elementary and Secondary Education Act, 201
Elston, Carolyn R., 89
Emery, James C., 152, 165
Empirical findings, library, 76–150
Enoch Pratt Free Library, 219
Evans, G. Edward, 107
Exception principle, 153–154
Exhibits, 138, 149
Exposure. See Document exposure

Facilities, physical, 148, 228–229
  maintenance of, 61
  provision of, 61, 67
Factor analysis, 90, 139
"Fair-share" formulas, 206–208
Financial Plan, 47
Free Library of Philadelphia (The), 3, 17, 27, 82–83, 143–150, 219
Functions of library activity, 6, 7, 47, 59–61
Fussler, H. H., 113–114, 117, 173

Glover, Fred, 106–107, 126
Goffman, William, 101
Goldstein, H., 139
Goyal, S. K., 122
Grant, Robert S., 91
Groos, O. V., 97
Guttman scaling, 139

Half-life of journals, 126–130
Hamburg, Morris, 80 n
Hartley, H., 44
Hartsfield, Annie Mary, 139
Hayes, Robert M., 141–42, 156–158
Heinritz, Fred J., 108
Higher Education Act, 201
Hill, T. W., Jr., 105–107
Hillinger, Claude, 131–133

Index

Hindle, A., 80, 93–94, 102–103, 108, 121–122, 134–135
Hinrichs, H., 44
Hoag, L. L., 123
Hodges, E., 220
Home exposure to books, 146–147
Hours, library, 84
Huntsinger, R., 90

Indexes, 62
Indexing, 109–111
 imbalance, 109–110
Indicators, 46
Indirect exposure. *See* Document exposure
Information directory, 137–138
Information retrieval time, 154
Information service, 136–138
Information system
 benefits and costs of, 165–167, 168
 design of, 152, 153, 156–162, 165, 167–170, 191
 Hayes-Becker design, 157–162
 need for, 151
 quality of, 153
Information system characteristics
 accuracy, 154–155
 flexibility, 155–156
 generality, 155
 reliability, 155
 selectivity, 153–154
 specific content, 152–153, 162
 time lags, 154
In-library use, 122, 144–145. *See* Document exposure
Institute for the Advancement of Medical Communication, 20
Interest potential, 116–117
Interlibrary loan, 65, 134–135. *See* Document exposure
Inventory of library services, 20
Item-use-days. *See* Performance measures

Jain, A. K., 116, 117, 133
Jardine, A. K. S., 85
Jestes, Edward C., 138
Journal
 obsolescence, 126–133
 photocopying, 104
 selection, 94–107
 use over time, 101–102
 weeding (discarding), 126–133

Kansas City Public Library, 220
Kebler, R. W., 126–127

Kendall, M. G., 96, 100
Klingman, Darwin, 106–107, 126
Knight, Douglas M., 200
Kochen, Manfred, 80–81, 112–113, 137–138
Korfhage, Robert R., 135
Kraft, Donald H., 89, 105–107
Krauze, Taudeusz, 131–133

Lacy, Dan, 191
Leach, Richard H., 199
Legislation, library, 139
Leimkuhler, Ferdinand F., 97, 114, 116, 117, 118, 120, 121, 125–126, 133
Library of Congress
 cataloging, 112–113
 classification system, 56, 112, 122, 222
 MARC Project, 209
 Shared Cataloging Program, 209
Library Services and Construction Act, 200, 201
Library systems, 198–199
 development of, 206
Library use. *See* Document exposure
Library/User/Funder Analysis, 139–140
Licklider, J. C. R., 210
Likert, Rensis, 140
Line, Maurice B., 130
Linear function, 81 n, 87, 125
Linear programming. *See* Models, library
Lipetz, Ben-Ami, 113
Lister, Winston Charles, 114–115, 117
Loan period, 85–88, 121–122
Logarithm, 94 n, 97 n, 110
 common, 94 n, 110
 natural, 97 n

McGrath, William E., 56, 90, 122, 172
Mackenzie, A. G., 80, 93–94, 102–103, 108, 121–122, 134–135
MacRae, Duncan, Jr., 129–130
Maintenance, 84–85
Management analysis, 2
Management information, 2
Management information system, 1, 2, 6, 7, 8
Management problems
 of large public libraries, 2
 of university libraries, 2
Management science, 3, 4, 9, 41
Management system, 2, 6
MARC Project. *See* Library of Congress
Marchant, M. P., 140–141
Marcus, W. E., 190

Markov book-use model. *See* Models, library
Martin, L., 50, 51, 52, 145–147, 149
Mathematica, 142
Meier, Robert C., 21, 112, 135–136
Mendelsohn, H., 51, 147, 149
Metcalf, Keyes D., 119, 120
Microfiche, 124
Miller, Roger L., 112, 135–136
Model construction, 3
Models, library, 76–150
analytical, 93
dynamic programming, 105–106
growth, 114, 117, 141–142
industrial dynamics, 139–140
linear programming, 81, 81 n, 82 n, 84, 105–106, 142–143
macroeconomic, 78
Markov book use, 86–88, 89, 105, 114, 116
mathematical programming, 144, 149–150
nonlinear programming, 107–108
queuing, 85–88, 90–91, 92, 93, 105, 121, 122
regression, 91–92, 137
sensitivity analysis of, 115
simulation, 79, 84, 93–94, 108, 119, 121–122, 139–140
static, 105
stochastic process, 96
Monograph. *See* Book
Morris, Thomas G., 101
Morse, Philip M., 19, 20, 79–80, 84, 85–89, 90–91, 93, 105, 114, 116–118, 121, 122, 133, 150
Mullick, S. K., 107–108
Multiyear plan, 5

Nance, Richard E., 135, 139–140
National Agricultural Library, 199–200
National Center for Educational Statistics, 202
National Center for Higher Education Management System at WICHE, 142
National Library of Medicine, 199–200
Nelson Associates, 198, 207
Networks, 135–136
Nourse, E. Shepley, 200

Objective functions. *See* Performance measures
Objectives, 3, 4, 8
in decision making, 9, 11, 17, 18, 44, 46

interdependence of, 9, 12
public library, 10, 14, 24
societal, 14
university, 10
university library, 10, 11
Obsolescence
of journals, 126–133
Markov model of, 86–88, 89, 105
negative exponential law of, 89, 101–102, 104–105
Office of Education. *See* U.S. Office of Education
Oliver, Merrill R., 131
Organization, 47, 66
Orr, R., 19
Osborn, E., 82
Overdues, 123

Palmour, V. E., 103–104
Participative decision making, 140–141
Performance measures, 1, 3, 4, 5, 8, 9, 11, 13, 17, 23, 24, 36, 39, 44, 46, 76, 109
alternative, 18
computation of, 26
document exposure time, 4, 22, 28, 170, 172, 179–181
document retrieval time, 4, 170, 181–182
general, 164, 188–189, 212
item-use-days, 4, 21, 170, 172, 178–179
library, 170–182
number of document exposures, 170, 172–178
program indicators, 182–185
satisfaction rate, 170, 181–182
Periodical. *See* Journal
Personal assistance, 136–138, 149
Photocopy use. *See* Document exposure
Photoduplication, 124
Planning, 3, 8, 9, 11, 43, 65, 139–150, 234–235
Planning–Programming–Budgeting-System (PPBS) 5, 43, 44
criticism of, 44
elements of, 44
Population, 43, 47, 49, 65
public library, 10, 49
subsets, 49, 50, 52, 53, 54, 55
university library, 10, 55
Prepayments, 25
Probability distribution, 79 n, 80 n, 86 n
exponential (negative), 84, 86, 89, 91, 92, 101, 104, 107, 127, 129, 130
geometric, 79–80, 88, 104, 130
lognormal, 110–111

Probability distribution (*continued*)
  normal, 110
  parameters of, 86 n
  Poisson, 84, 86, 87, 93, 107, 116
Processing, 108–109
  work flow, 108
Program
  activities, 47
  budgets, 189, 190
  categories, 48
  evaluation, 71
  feasible package of, 47, 73
  indicators, 8
  multiyear, 47
  structure, 5, 46, 47, 67, 70, 228–235, 237
Projecting library growth, 141–142
Promotion, 65, 68, 229–234
Publications, 138, 149

Queuing models. *See* Models, library

Race, P. A., 123
Raffel, Jeffrey A., 44, 84, 107, 111–112, 119, 120, 124–125, 133–134, 135, 190
Rameshwar, P., 91
Random variable, 79 n, 110 n
Readers, 145–146
Reference room, 138
Reference service, 136–138, 149
Reilly's law, 83–84
Renewals, 123
Reserve room copies, 92–93
Reshelving, 123
Resnikoff, H. L., 110–111
Resource allocation
  for public libraries, 143–150
  for university libraries, 142–143
Retrieval systems, 135
Return of circulated library materials, 122–123
ReVelle, Charles S., 81–82
Revenue sharing, 202
Reynolds, Maryan, 112, 135–136
Roberts, R. G., 83–84
Rosenberg, Victor, 109

St. Angelo, Douglas, 139
Sandison, A., 131
Satisfaction rate. *See* Performance measures
Scattering. *See* Bradford-Zipf law of scattering
Scholz, William H., 112, 135–136
Schultz, Claire K., 110

Search
  expected length, 109–110
  theory of, 116–117, 120
Seating and space utilization, 84
Security guards, 122
Segur, A. Bertrand, 112–113
Selection effort, 107
Selection of documents, 85–107
  book subject matter and year, 85–90
  for compact storage, 113–118
  number of copies, 90–94
Semilog paper, 128 n
Service effort, 148–149
Shaughnessy, T., 51, 52
Shishko, Robert, 84, 107, 111–112, 119, 120, 124–125, 133–134, 135, 190
Shove, R. H., 219
Siehler, Cynthia J., 103–104
Simon, Herbert A., 96, 100, 117
Simon, J., 113, 173
Simulation models. *See* Models, library
Sinha, Bani K., 90, 91, 126
Slope, 128 n
Social institutions, 1
Social participation, 146–147
Stacks, library, 118–120
Standard deviation, 110 n
Standards, 4, 5, 37
Stanfield, Jonathan, 112, 135–136
State library agency, 203–205
Statewide library development, 203–208
Statistical information system, 1, 3, 7, 8
Statistical sampling, 155, 166, 168–169, 172, 173, 174, 175–177, 180–181, 184–185, 208
Stevens, Benjamin H., 82–83
Stockfish, S., 38
Storage of library materials, 118–121
Subject areas, 55, 213
Subject categories, 55, 213
Swain, Ralph W., 81–82

Taieb, Françoise, 82–83
Taylor, David W., 112, 135–136
Telephone use, 144–145
Trueswell, Richard W., 113–114

United States of America Standards Institute, 57, 223
Universal decimal classification, 220
University of Durham, 138–139, 142–143
University of Pennsylvania, 2, 56
University of Pennsylvania Libraries, 3
User furnishings, 61, 67

User satisfaction, 4
U.S. Census of Population—1970, 52, 53, 54
U.S. Congress, 199, 200
U.S. Office of Education, 199
  role of, 200–203

Vickery, B. C., 96
Voight, Melvin J., 225

Wallace, Sarah L., 144
Weeding, 64, 113–119, 125–133
Westly, Barbara M., 59
Wharton School (The), 2
Wheeler, J., 50, 52
Wiederkehr, Robert R. V., 103–104
Williams, Gordon, 103–104
Wingerd, K., 147, 149
Wood, D. N., 134
Woodburn, I., 80, 93–94, 102–103, 104, 108–109, 121–122, 134–135

Zipf, George Kingsley, 96
Zipf power law principle of least effort, 111